# Women and Space

# Cross-Cultural Perspectives on Women

*General Editors*: Shirley Ardener and Jackie Waldren,
for The Centre for Cross-Cultural Research on Women, University of Oxford

CROSS-CULTURAL PERSPECTIVES ON WOMEN | VOL. 5

# Women and Space

## *Ground Rules and Social Maps*

Edited by

*Shirley Ardener*

BERG

*Oxford / Providence*

Revised edition published in 1993 by

**Berg Publishers Limited**

Editorial offices:
221 Waterman Street, Providence, RI 02906, USA
150 Cowley Road, Oxford, OX4 1JJ, UK

© Shirley Ardener 1993

**Library of Congress Cataloging-in-Publication Data applied for.**

**British Library Cataloguing in Publication Data**
Women and Space : Ground Rules and Social Maps. – 2 Rev. ed. – (Cross-
cultural Perspectives on Women Series)
    I. Ardener, Shirley  II. Series
    305.42
    ISBN 0 85496 728 1

Printed in the United States by E. B. Edwards Brothers, Lillington, N.C.

# Contents

# Preface to New Reprint

This new reprint under the Berg imprint has been made in response to requests, since the first edition has been out of print for over a decade. It has not been totally rewritten, since text is inevitably stamped with the date of its creation and the discourse of that time. We have been assured that most of it can stand the light thrown on it today. All the authors here feel, of course, that they might write different papers today, although bravely none have repudiated their chapters. Some paragraphs cut from the original introduction to shorten it have been restored. It was also felt to be useful in certain cases for authors to make reference to some new writings of relevance to their papers that have appeared since the original edition. Brief updates have been included at the end of some chapters. As a result the bibliography has additional entries, although it makes no claim to include all or even the most critical recent works.

The papers were originally presented for the Oxford University Women's Study Committee by members of the Anthropology Seminar on Women at Queen Elizabeth House which is still convened under the auspices of the Centre for Cross-Cultural Research on Women. We hope that the book proves as useful today as we understand many felt it to be when it was first issued in 1981. Since *Women and Space* was first published, the Centre has sponsored further books with Berg Publishers which are listed at the front of the book, and some with other publishers of which a selection is listed at the end of the book. The Centre thanks the contributors who have waived part of their royalties in order that the Centre's programme may continue. Dr Jackie Waldren has given editorial help with this reprint.

# 1

# Ground Rules and Social Maps for Women: An Introduction

*Shirley Ardener*

## The Partition of Space

A restricted area like a club, a theatre or a nation-state has a set of rules to determine how its boundary shall be crossed and who shall occupy that space. Those who enter it will share certain defining features: they will perhaps have met specific criteria of club membership, bought a ticket or passed a citizenship test. In some way they must be recognised, say by a gate-keeper, such as a hall porter, an usherette or an Immigration Officer, or by the other members of the category. So, too, other systems of classification will be decided by taxonomic rules of some kind, which will define 'X' in contrast to 'non-X'. Thus, in studying the way people pattern their perceptions, attention has been especially drawn to the significance of the perimeters of the categories that we make in order to codify and confront the worlds we create, in which we then live, and how we cope with some of the problems that arise from the existence of these boundaries (see, for example, Douglas 1966; S. Ardener 1978).

These few words have already found us deeply involved with the point on which the chapters in this volume depend: space. For in discussing ways in which humans perceive and pattern their social worlds a notion (the boundary) has been seized and applied to the meaning of concepts, and to classification into groups, whose label is taken from the register of terms which is used primarily for the three-dimensional 'real' world. The extended use of such spatial terms is firmly embedded in the language in which this is written. Obvious cases would be 'high society', 'wide application', 'spheres of interest', 'narrow-mindedness', 'political circles', 'deep divides of opinion', and so forth. Such practices merely remind us that much of social life is given shape, and that when dimension or location are introduced we assert a correspondence between the so-called 'real' physical world and its 'social reality' (cf. Durkheim and Mauss 1903).[1] There is, of course, an interaction such that appreciation of the *physical* world is in turn dependent on *social* perceptions of it. Measurements, and what is measured, for instance, are neither totally imperative nor just random; choice enters 'reality'. Societies have generated their own rules, culturally determined, for making boundaries on the ground, and have divided the social into spheres, levels and territories with invisible fences and platforms to be scaled by abstract ladders and crossed by intangible bridges with as much trepidation or exultation as on a plank over a raging torrent.

This brief preamble is by way of indicating why this book on 'women and space' links 'ground rules' with 'social maps' and why such ambiguous pairs of terms were selected for the sub-title. As a preliminary to introducing the chapters and to giving special consideration to women, a few more general points may quickly be raised, in condensed form. It will become apparent that, while divisions of space and social formations are intimately associated, no simple one-way 'cause and effect' pertains, and their cumulative interdependence suggests that we should think rather in terms of 'simultaneities' (see E. Ardener 1971, 1977, 1978, 1989), and this should be remembered when considering the following section.

Communication systems are primarily associated in our minds with words. Nevertheless, it is by now well recognised, of course, that society has also devised many other symbolic codes. Of one, Edwin Ardener has written: 'We might visualise a semiotic system that depended, in the absence of the power of speech, upon the apperception by the human participants of contextually defined logical relations among themselves in space. Let us say: the relevant position of each participant to another in a gathering, and to items in a fixed environment' (1971: xliii–xliv). Thus people may 'jockey for position' knowing that their fellows may 'read' from this their social importance. Thus, as Hall puts it, *space speaks*.

Goffmann suggests that 'the division and hierarchies of social structure are depicted microecologically, that is, through the use of small-scale spatial metaphors' (1979: 1). This suggests that *space reflects social organisation*, but of course, once space has been bounded and shaped it is no longer merely a neutral background: it exerts its own influence. A dozen people in a small room 'is not the same thing' as a dozen people in a great hall; seating-space shaped by a round, rather than square, table, may influence the nature of social interaction among those seated. The 'theatre of action' to some extent determines the action. The environment imposes certain restraints on our mobility, and, in turn, our perceptions of space are shaped by our own capacity to move about, whether by foot or by mechanical or other transport. So: *behaviour and space are mutually dependent*.

As Judy Matthews in her study of community action has noted, social identity is partly determined by 'the physical and spatial constituents of the groups' environment' (1980: 4); that is to say: *space defines the people in it.* At the same time, however (again reflexively), the presence of individuals in space in turn determines its nature. For example, the entry of a stranger may change a private area into a public one (see S. Ardener 1978: 32; 1993 ed.: 18 and Rodgers, below); similarly, 'the Court is where the king is'. Thus: *people define space.*

Not only people, but, as Goffmann has said, 'Objects are thought to structure the environment immediately around themselves; they cast a shadow, heat up the surround, strew indications, leave an imprint, they impress a part of themselves, a portrait that is unintended and not dependent on being attended, yet, of course, informing nonetheless to whomsoever is properly placed, trained and inclined' (1979:1). Further, as anyone who has played chess will know, *objects are affected by the place in space of other objects*; not only their presence, and their position, but even their absence, or 'negative presence', may be important.[2]

Structural relationships, such as in hierarchies or other ranking patterns, and systems of relationships like those of kinship, are treated in this volume as 'social maps', which are frequently, but not necessarily, realised on 'the ground' by the placing of individuals in space. In many situations we find (real or metaphysical) 'spaces within spaces', or 'overlapping universes'. To understand them we may be required to 'pull them apart' in order first to identify each simple map (of, say 'X' and 'non-X'), before reconsidering the way these correspond or are interrelated. It is as if we provide one map showing only where the roads are (or are not), and another setting out the water courses, and so on, before we compile a complex map of all the features of the terrain. Correspondingly, ideally we may 'map', say, the relationships between a wife and her husband (where they draw the various limits) before 'mapping' the same woman's relationships to her children, in order to compile a complete picture of her family life.

Individuals (and things) belong, then, to many pairs, groups or sets, each of which may be thought of as occupying its own 'space', or as sharing a particular 'universe'. Members of one group may be 'dominant' relative to members of another group in one 'universe', while in turn being 'muted' in relation to members of a third group sharing with them a universe differently defined.[3] A woman may be 'muted' relative to her husband and 'dominant' in relation to her children; gypsy men are 'dominant' in their own culture and structurally 'muted' *vis-à-vis* the English (Okely 1978). In a society where, say, (a) men take precedence over women and (b) the religious is dominant in relation to the secular, the following ordering is possible: *monks* ← *lay-men* ← *nuns* ← *lay-women* (where *gender* is the predominant critical distinction). Alternatively (as in some Buddhist processions), where the space is primarily *religious* (but gender counts), we may find a redistribution of space between the poles: *monks ← nuns ← lay-men ← lay-women*. The second ordering is interesting because the (religious) precedence of *nuns* over *lay-women* may tend to obscure the priority of males between the sexes. This might be particularly so if, at any time or place, no *monks* or *lay-women* are present (that is, the sequence is incomplete). This may account for the inability of some to distinguish assymetries, that even bear upon them disadvantageously. In other 'real' or 'social' spaces femaleness may be the dominant determinant, but in others yet again, gender may be irrelevant, or insignificant. Age, class and many other features, may add further complexities in situations of multiple dimensions (see S. Ardener 1992). If relationships (say between *monks*, *nuns* and *lay-persons*) are expressed by the distribution of people on the ground, then the application of the term 'map' is probably unambiguous to most readers of this book. If, however, the relationships cannot be actually 'seen' in physical arrangements, but only detected in other ways (such as by who speaks first, or in what manner, or by who bows to whom) then possibly the use of the term 'map' may be challenged. Even when an ordering is 'jumbled up' to the eye, or intangible, it may, however, still be *convenient* to our understanding to think of that ordering as a 'map' on which the 'jumble' has been simplified by a logical rearrangement of the information. No map corresponds to what can be seen: the London underground system is not accurately and completely portrayed on the map provided to the public.

Thus, in this volume the term 'social map' has been used broadly, and sometimes in different ways. The concept is applied to 'historical time' (in which 'yesterday' may seem 'closer' than the 'distant' past; just as some kin, living or dead, may seem 'close' relative to other kin). The notion of 'private' as opposed to 'public' is seen as a criterion for 'mapping' metaphysical space, as 'inner' does in opposition to 'outer', *regardless* of the fact that some 'private places' can really be walked into. No emphasis has been given to the distinction between 'place' and 'space', as used by geographers. The term 'social map', as used in this book, may be taken, perhaps, as a temporary and handy 'folk' term, rather than as having the status of a definitive scientific label.

Space, then, is not a simple concept. In certain societies it is coloured. Thus, among the Zuni of America, north is thought of as blue, south as red, and east as white (Durkheim and Mauss [1903] 1963: 44; Needham 1973: 33). Among the Atoni of Indonesia, south is again red (it is also associated with rulers), east is again white (and is connected with warriors, west is black (and is associated with village headman) and the north is – not blue (Zuni) – but yellow. The Irish have coloured space (Ardener 1975). Here, however, south is black (and the sphere of music, slaves, witches and the dead).

If space is an ordering principle, so, of course, is gender. These principles are often also linked, though not always in the same way. For the Irish, south is associated with women. In contrast, the Chinese see the south as male and the north as female.

In 1909 Robert Hertz wrote a classic text 'The Pre-eminence of the Right Hand'. It is available in Needham's 1973 translation from French into English. Thus over 80 years ago Hertz wrote:

> Society and the whole universe have a side which is sacred, noble and precious, and another which is profane and common; a male side, strong and active, and another, female, weak and passive; or, in two words, a right side and a left side . . . . (Needham: 10)

He also equated the right with 'rectitude', 'dexterity', 'the juridical norm' (p.11), 'life' (p.12), the 'inside' (p.13), the 'sacred' (p.12), 'good', and 'beauty' (p.12).

He associated the left with the 'profane' (p.12), the 'ugly' (p.12); with 'bad' (p.12), 'death' (p.12), the 'outside, the infinite, hostile and the perpetual menace of evil' (p.13).

Hertz (drawing on Wilson's report of 1891) noted that among North American Indians 'The right hand stands for me, the left for not-me, others'. Drawing on Mallery (1881) Hertz noted that 'The raised right hand signifies bravery, power, and virility, while on the contrary the same hand, carried to the left and placed below the left hand, signifies, according to context, the ideas of death, destruction, and burial'.

After discussing Australian beliefs (of the Wulwanga), Hertz concludes it is not chance that God took one of Adam's left ribs to create Eve, 'for one and the same essence characterises woman and the left side of the body – two parts of a weak and defenceless being, somewhat ambiguous and disquieting, destined by nature to a passive and receptive role and to a subordinate condition'.

Since Hertz, social anthropologists have travelled the world collecting world-views from different cultures. Many have described systems of dual classification, and a selection of studies can be found in Needham (1973). These schemes of perception which elsewhere Bourdieu (1977: 15) speaks of finding, include those 'which divide the world up in accordance with the oppositions between male and female, east and west, future and past, top and bottom, right and left. . . . ' To which we may add public/private and inside/outside (a particular concern of modern Greeks, as shown by Hirschon below). Thus Faron (Needham: 196) provides two lists from Chile demonstrating the 'Mapuche inferior-superior, left-right hand associations' adding that 'There are many indications of male superiority and association with the right as well as with good and the sacred'. There is also 'an unmistakable and literal connection between left and evil, right and good'. Again, van der Kroef (ibid.: 180) correlates pairs of oppositions among the people of Amboyna in Indonesia. Other sets of dual classification for the Gogo of Tanzania (Peter Rigby: 279), for the Kaguru of Tanzania (Beidelman: 151), for the Meru of Kenya (Bernardi: 116), and for the Fulani of West Africa (Stenning: 122), document this approach. Reference to the association of women and the left arise in the discussions below (see, for example, Sciama) and the disempowered (Rodgers).

Now it would be a diversion to go into further details on dual classification here; it is a field requiring delicate handling – especially of the relationship between concepts placed in vertical lists. There is, indeed, no attempt here at a comprehensive analysis of all the characteristics of space; the literature is in any case already extensive. McDowell, for example, has provided a useful review of material on the gender division of urban space. For some Marxist analyses of place and space see the work of David Harvey. The few simple, but fundamental points raised above are merely reminders of the general context in which the following discussions are to be viewed. The chapters below provide illustrations of them, and give some examples of their special relevance to women. Although there is no pretence to comprehensiveness, one more aspect must, nevertheless, be mentioned: the relationship of time and space. When we speak of 'the world getting smaller' through the advent of air travel, or of a distance being 'five minutes' walk away', we clearly acknowledge that time and space are 'mutually affecting spheres of reality', where 'reality' is understood to depend upon human apperceptions. Paine quotes a resident of Israel who felt that by settling in Israel he had taken a leap back in time which made him closer to David and Uzziah than to the contemporary *shtetl* in Poland. One could say that by a change of place time had been collapsed, or elided. This reminds us of Harvey's comment that 'nearness does not consist of shortness of distance' (1990) and Edwin Ardener's study of 'remoteness' (1987). 'Time-systems occupy spaces which are generated by and with the physical and social space' (E. Ardener 1975b: 11).[4]

## Time and Place

Time, then, is particularly closely associated with space. Indeed, for some, space and time are homologous. Drid Williams, for example, in her description of the daily routine of the Carmelite nuns shows how her situation in space can always be told by her situation in time (and vice versa). Thus 'a nun who spends sixty years in a Carmelite enclosure... is in the same place at the same time exactly 42,800 times during those years'. But further subtleties emerge which take us into a more abstract realm. Williams writes, 'It is as if the Carmelite has two "maps": one which locates her in ordinary space-time, and another consisting of an "interior territory" of a spiritual and psychological nature in which she is located at the same time.' As Williams writes, 'this represents a rather different notion of space and time from that which a "secular" person might have' (1975: 113).

Sarah Skar provides us below with a fascinating example of a whole popular culture in which no clear boundary is placed between abstract time and space. Among the Matapuquio of Peru one term (*pacha*) is employed to embrace both concepts. This is not, of course, simply a substitution of one word where English would use two, since the term reflects a very different view of the nature of the world and human existence. In the practical, daily world of the Matapuquio, the intertwining of space and time is exemplified by the difference between the tops of the mountain where crops take a long time to mature, and the lower slopes where the maturation of plants is quicker. The passage of time and the place of space are thus intimately linked.[5] Each day the women move from the village midway on the slope to the high ground where they tend cattle, while the men can be seen moving down towards the plantation in the valley. In the evening the village again becomes their meeting place. We find that the association of women with the higher ground is replicated and formalised in the dual organisation of the village: the upper section is symbolically female, while the lower moiety is regarded as male.[6]

In a more recent study Henrietta Moore (1986) records the complex perceptions of the Endo of Kenya. There are many ways of synthesising Endo experiences of space/time but, Moore notes, the perspective which the Endo themselves stress is the pivotal relationship between men and women. Like those in Peru, described by Skar, the villages of the Endo are built on a mountain slope, and daily movement from the residential area or village to the fields on the valley floor is a constant process of moving up and down. Relative location on the slope, the very axis of daily life, is always specified. The principal orientation up/down is further complicated by the use the Endo make of the term *tai,* meaning 'right' or 'right-sided' (it also means 'in front' or 'ahead') and, in contrast, *let* which means 'left' (or 'behind').

For the Endo, *tai* and *let* are essentially terms of direction and orientation, and contain, as a result, aspects of both space and time. *Tai* and *let* are also associated with the movement of the sun which itself is most explicitly linked with men. Women, by contrast, are associated with the moon. The permanence of the sun and of men is contrasted to the impermanence of the moon and of women. The moon is said to be on the left of the sun, behind it, just as the woman is on the left of the man. This complex of ideas is reflected in the orientation of huts within each family compound and its rubbish heaps. To cut a long story short, Moore shows how male and female huts face each other such that the door opening of the man's sleeping hut looks to the north along the escarpment (the reliable sun rising on his reliable right hand), while the woman's cooking hut facing his looks to the south. According to Moore, the concept of male permanence versus female impermanence is one of the major ways in which the Endo 'genderise' space and time.

## Political Arenas

The Matapuquio women Skar describes are free to participate in political discussions, which are held in public. But not all societies exhibit such egalitarian practices. Elsewhere in the world, Iatmul males in New Guinea, for example, control the main political forum – the Men's House – and rigidly exclude women from entry. Silvia Rodgers takes this fact as one of her starting points for comparison with the British House of Commons, access to which is, in principle, open to both women and men, yet in practice, as is well known, the space is very far from being shared equally. Like Skar for Peru, Rodgers seeks for some explanations of attitudes in the House among wider world views within society: about nature and culture, and men and women in relation to them. The absence of women in political arenas in many societies has for long been a matter of comment (e.g. Tiger 1969). *Defining Females* (Ardener 1978), gave examples of the way in which women in public life have tended to be those who are not yet, or have ceased to be, childbearing, thus lacking the defining criterion which 'specifies' them as women – they become 'generic' and are subsumed into the category for men (Hastrup 1978: 49ff; Berg reprint 1993: 34–50; and also Callaway, below). Rodgers presents a parallel argument when she suggests that one of the modes which the dominant (male) group in the House of Commons has generated (with the compliance of some women) is the reclassification of women as men. This enables those women who do become Members of Parliament to be absorbed into the political body, while preserving its masculinity.

It is interesting that women who have been associated with male politicians who have died with, as it were, their work uncompleted, have sometimes been among the few women privileged to have stepped onto the political stage. These women, as Hilary Callan (verbal communication) remarked, are not exactly redefined as men; however, they may be seen to 'stand for' the men who might have kept their places had they lived longer. On the British scene we can include Lady Phillips and Lady Airey Neave with those politically elevated (in their case to the House of Lords) after the untimely deaths of their husbands, for whom they were (initially) metaphors. International figures could include Mrs Corey Aquino of the Philippines. We can, perhaps, sum up all these cases by saying that in certain circumstances women have become 'fictive men'. The political picture may, however, be changing.

Political expression in England takes place, of course, in many theatres of action other than the Palace of Westminster. In her new and original analysis of the stage, and in particular of the actress who treads it, Juliet Blair argues here that, although actors and actresses do not usually have direct political power themselves, they hope to influence the audience, who will perhaps take action elsewhere. The actress is seen as a social analyst of sorts, for her professional training requires her to study the emotions, ideas and circumstances of women in order to portray them. She is far from being a passive vehicle for the playwright's thoughts, but can, through her art and the independence and the power this brings, express her own ideas, and experiment with new modes of living, in fact and fiction. Sometimes her art may even have assisted the actress in gaining overt political power (e.g. Madame Mao, Eva Peron, Glenda Jackson).

In other cultures, too, women who are not formally represented in the political arena as recognised in the dominant ideology may, in fact, still exert political influence and be necessary to its processes. In the traditions of the Mamasani district of Iran, for example, women are not encouraged to speak in public on political matters. Yet, as Wright shows below in her subtle analysis of this Moslem community, they do participate in political processes, moving about gathering information and testing reactions in ways hardly recognised in the culture – they operate what may be called a 'muted structure', sometimes coded into talk about chickens. It is interesting that these women do pass on their information, by commenting to their husbands when they meet in the evening, when the house is supposedly reserved for their private domestic concerns. It appears, however, that the husband is likely to disdain to ask direct questions, and gives little sign of attention or encouragement, thus maintaining the fiction that the wife does not participate in politics; she is structurally 'muted' although she speaks.

## Women as Mediators of Space

The fact that women do not control physical or social space directly does not necessarily preclude them from being determinants of, or mediators in, the allocation of space, even the occupation of political space. Callaway, for instance, notes that Yoruba women, as custodians of the royal regalia, have the power in principle to deny political room to a successor to kingship. And we find, in East Africa, that among the matrilineal Luguru of Tanzania 'the women choose the leader (male) of the basic, autonomous political and landholding group, the subclan. . . . Not only do the women choose the leader, they may also depose him should they be dissatisfied with him' (Brain 1976: 266). In some democratic societies where women electors outnumber male electors they, too, have the power, in principle, to determine who enters political arenas and who wields political authority, which they do not themselves directly exercise (see Rodgers, below).

In considering physical space it may be noted that among the polygynous Ibo of Nigeria women do not 'own' land; they do, however, have important entrenched rights of use. Further, the allocation of land to men here is determined by women, according to the tradition that (apart from a small extra allocation to the first son) the land inherited by brothers and half-brothers is divided according to the farm plots worked by their mothers (E. Ardener 1959).

Women may also be significant in determining what, on a social map, we may call 'genealogical space'. For instance, an Ibo woman's fertility determines the success and continuation of her husband's patrilineage (not her own); her children will belong to it providing the bridewealth given to her patrilineage has not been refunded – even if the husband is not the biological father of her children. It may also be noted that it is the Jewish mother who confers Jewish identity on children.

## Hidden Virtues

Lidia Sciama, in her discussion of private space in two different communities and in Oxford and Cambridge colleges, warns us not to be ethnocentric in our evaluations if we are to understand other cultures (see also Ardener and Sciama in Callan and Ardener 1984). Communities often regard the space closest to that occupied by the family as a relatively secure and predictable inner world in contrast to the potentially hostile and untrustworthy space outside. Yet the placing of the boundary which divides these spaces may vary widely between cultures and between different contexts in the same culture. 'Privacy', as Sciama shows below, is thus seen to be relative to its contextual universe.

In the Peruvian Andes both men and women feel relatively safe in the village and on the slopes around. It is at the periphery, on the mountain tops, in the valley bottom and outside the valley, where gods and strangers may be encountered, that the world becomes fraught with danger, and where movement, particularly of women, is inhibited. In England also, the world outside the home has generally been felt to be safe and congenial, but even here precautions have long been taken - for instance in the streets at night. When considering segregation in other societies the English, for example, should note that in their own communities women feel increasingly at risk, and are sometimes warned that they are,[7] and that the elderly, in particular, in certain districts enter *de facto* seclusion after dusk.

Sciama, then, shows below that, in cultures where there is little expectation of trust beyond the family circle, the domestic environment represents a sanctuary from the perils outside. Taken in conjunction with the material presented on Iran by Khatib-Chahidi and Wright below, we can understand more fully attitudes towards privacy and seclusion, even the veil, in other cultures. It is timely to be reminded of this, perhaps, since much attention has been focused on the restrictions encountered by women in the Moslem world, and on deprivations and even violence found within households based upon the nuclear family in Western cultures; these have been contrasted with desirable freedoms to be found outside the home. Indeed, one may be tempted to argue that when the line between hostile and favourable environments is drawn close to the front door, the importance of the home and the status of the woman inside, as its symbol and guardian, become correspondingly greater. The strong position of the mother in the Jewish household, which has often had to survive in hostile communities, comes to mind.[8] Rosemary Ridd's material below from the non-white community in the system of apartheid of South Africa, where women had to dominate the home, may be relevant here. However, it should be noted that a woman who is 'domineering' in the sense of forcing others to conform to behaviour which she advocates, may still be 'muted' in so far as the pattern she enforces has not been generated by her; it may not even be in her interests. The South African picture is complicated because the domestic model adopted by women in District Six described by Ridd, appears to be largely modelled on one they believe to have existed in the truly dominant European culture. A further caution when generalising is necessary since, as Smock notes in her discussion of Bengal, where men make most of the household decisions, 'it does not seem that women's confinement to the home and its designation as a female sphere mean that women exercise control over domestic affairs' (Smock 1977: 99). We may note also that although Luguru women, according to Brain, have the power to choose their clan leader and are unusually outspoken for Tanzanian women, they are nevertheless, 'in no sense dominant' (Brain 1976).

The 'dangers' of 'the outside' arise from encounters which impinge on all social life, and which may be a threat to prestige and comfort, as represented by a range of social resources. Among these is that important social capital: information. Exclusive knowledge – the secret – whether positive or negative, needs to be safeguarded. Rodgers shows below how women MPs have been effectively excluded from sharing the most secret official material. Lidia Sciama discusses another aspect of secrecy when she considers data on lying as a mode of hiding the truth, in the context of her own discussion of privacy. Juliet Blair, in contrast, gives us an analysis of a forum (the stage) where political, economic and sexual secrets are brought before the public, albeit again in the form of fiction, when she discusses here the actress, who is shown to specialise in revealing the private, domestic, life of women and men.

Aida Hawile once tellingly remarked that the boundary between the 'private' and 'public' may, in some contexts and under some conditions, be measured primarily by earshot. We see from this remark that a map of significant spaces identified by gaze might not coincide with a map of significant sound zones. Rodgers draws our attention below to how such a distinction may be applied to the political arena. But here the priority is reversed, for, strangely perhaps, in Men's Houses (including the House of Commons) women have sometimes been permitted – indeed expected – to listen while being forbidden to see. And Sue Wright offers us material from Iran, which shows that there too, while women are compelled to withdraw from space occupied by male company assembled round the hearth, it is expected that they will listen to the debates from outside the doorway. University wives, Jewesses and nuns in church provide us with similar cases.[9]

## Crossing the Line

When rules of separation pertain, many difficulties arise at critical points and various devices are then introduced to cope with them while maintaining the underlying principles of classification. Mechanisms for entering private or exclusive space may be needed. Under apartheid, for instance, passes were issued to enable certain 'blacks' to enter service in 'white' space; this controlled the breach. The House of Commons turns women into 'fictive men'. Among the strict Shiite Moslems, described by Khatib-Chahidi, there is a sharp division between the space occupied by the domestic unit, where the sexes mingle comparatively freely, and the sphere outside where they do not. Those privileged to share the domestic freedoms are: those already married one to the other, and those between whom marriage is forbidden because of kinship, between whom sexual congress is unthinkable. Persons eligible for marriage must be avoided. The range of forbidden kin is quite wide, but even so the restrictions become irksome at times, and to circumvent them various forms of 'fictive marriage' are entered into. These are legal unions, but temporary and unconsummated. Indeed the partners may not be mature, and may not even meet; yet their contract may permit the mingling of others who have thereby become kin in law and unable to marry. The adoption of the veil and the practice of eye-avoidance are among the other methods for giving greater freedom, through 'fictive invisibility'.

Intrusions may be controlled by confinement to the periphery. In Kenya, for example, the Swahili traders in Lamu needed close contacts with the important foreign trader, but he could not be admitted to sleep in the house without risking the honour of the women, so he was accommodated just outside the front door of the fortress-like family house, where a stone bench and guest room were provided. In this 'liminal area' the necessary but potentially dangerous confrontation with the 'other' could be contained (Donley 1980). The diagrams provided below by Khatib-Chahidi and Tamara Dragadze give us further examples of how contact with strangers is kept to the periphery by the placing of guest rooms and use of verandahs. In the House of Commons also we see that visitors are diverted away, not only from the centre of the horizontal plane, but as far up as possible on the vertical plane from the place of power down on the floor of the Chamber. We may be reminded here of Jewish women in the gallery of their synagogue and some Greek Orthodox women in their church.

It has long been recognised that boundaries, where the difference between 'what it is' and 'what it is not' is put to the test, are frequently marked and reaffirmed by rituals. The incorporation of new elements into a space (which involves a breach of the boundary) may thus be accompanied by ceremonies. New members of the House of Commons come before the Bar of the House (a white line, symbolically the boundary) accompanied by sponsors. Students may be matriculated. Such ritual behaviour concentrates public attention on the change in attribution, and allows readjustment to the situation.

Many contacts between, say, the inner family circle and the outside are, of course, of a transient nature, but we may still detect ritualisation where they occur (cf. Hocart 1969). The activity at the margin of the Greek suburban 'prefab' described here by Hirschon – for example, the orientation of chairs, so seemingly casually arranged to the untutored eye – marks a dangerous point of entry: the doorstep. We may note that in the House of Commons, too, the 'stranger' is identified and closely controlled, thereby indicating that this 'public' forum is in some respects a 'private' zone. The hospitality shown to visitors at the Greek table and the elaborate greeting behaviour which, in some cultures, identifies the visitor, enable defensive guards to be lowered and safe-conduct to be extended to the potentially hostile outsider. Yet the very elaboration (even the fresh fruit in Greek homes is processed before presentation) signifies that this is no ordinary member of the group, and wariness may be required. Ritual may also emphasise social distance (see the behaviour of male MPs towards their female colleagues in Rodgers, below). It is possible to argue that where the contrast between inside and outside the family, home or institution is strongest, the more marked will be the observances when the boundary is breached (cf. Douglas 1970a: 14). On the other hand, absence of ceremonial may itself be a sign of privilege, and the sign of being an insider, as in the case of the friend who may drop in unannounced through the back door.

Of course, the breaching of a boundary is not always regarded as a bad thing. Some social interaction is necessary for both physical and social survival, and is welcomed. Indeed to be ignored can seem like a denial of existence. The entry into a group of a person of high status, or of one who is loved, may well be an occasion for rejoicing, and may be 'marked' as such by entertainment or kissing, or the like. On the other hand, outside, 'public', life is sought or desired because it provides 'prizes' and (perhaps because of the risk of failing to get them) excitement.

## Objects in Context

One of the features noted in Rodgers's paper is the sacred nature of the House of Commons which sets it apart from the secular world outside, and which is also characterised by certain ritualistic behaviour. Renée Hirschon takes us into the interiors of an estate of prefabricated homes in a suburb of Athens and shows us how, even in the most cramped and modest circumstances, environments can be imbued with values of great emotive power. Attention has already been drawn to the capacity of human beings to enrich life by placing great significance on seemingly trivial events (S. Ardener 1978: 16–19; 1993 ed.: 47). The human spirit, it seems, creates its own visions of heaven and its triumphs as well as its own damnations and failures, even in apparently unpromising environments. From Hirschon's account here, too, it appears that the home, far from being an arid arena deprived of rich significance compared to the world outside, may render up spiritual meanings lacking elsewhere. The treatment of bread (collecting of crumbs, as for communion bread) suggests it has a sacramental nature.

Campbell-Jones has described elsewhere how the convent environment was restructured when the Carmelite order was reformed in the 1960s. Changes in the symbols signalled changes in the fabric of religious life and alterations in social relations were reflected in changes in spatial patterns; cubicles were provided in dormitories and individual tables appeared. In some cultures (for example, as noted, the Irish, and the Zuni[10]) spaces have inherent colours. And some communities manipulate hue to mark space. In the traditional convent the 'chapel and religious pictures were light; the ceiling of the chapel was blue, the walls white. The "earthly" secular area of the convent was dark red. All the colours there were sombre and heavy; light and sunshine were excluded, reserved for the brilliant stained glass of the chapel' (Campbell-Jones 1979: 183). It is interesting in this connection to note that the House of Commons is carpeted in green, while the floor of the House of Lords is red.[11]

Goffmann notes that we routinely seek 'information about those of an object's properties that are felt to be perduring, overall, and structurally basic, in short, information about its character or "essential nature"' (Goffmann 1979: 7). He would agree, however, that objects also take on different meanings according to their 'frames' or contexts. We are again confronted with a reciprocal process. As noted at the beginning, items take their value, not only in relation to the value of other objects, and the absence of other objects (scarcity) but also from their place in relation to them. Other factors mentioned earlier will also be relevant, such as the mobility of an item, and its effect as a stationary object in blocking space to others, and the like. Thus from Hirschon's material it would seem that in Greece the doublebed placed in the marital home differs markedly from the same bed in the carpenter's workshed or in the department store, and from single beds; its association with its new environment, its use, and its symbolic value have changed its definition, adding qualities which transform a three-dimensional assembly of wood and metal into a multi-dimensional 'sacred' object with ritualistic taboos. Rodgers has laid stress on the hostile reaction among Members of Parliament to the incursion of features associated with nature, at its most creative, into the political culture of the House of Commons. The double bed might well also be a reminder of the awesome creative power of nature, for it is often the place of generation, from conception to the ultimate fruition of birth. Indeed, in Greece, it is often also the *locus* of the other finite boundary of life: death – when the supernatural might be thought to be closest to fully mature humanity. Hirschon also demonstrates how a wide range of other household objects are 'marked' by symbolic connotations. For those who find rewards within such systems of meanings, the gains of employment or a career may well require some sacrifice or result in some loss, which should not, perhaps, be ignored or be abandoned by inadvertence. It may be instructive to note, however, the compelling importance in some business spheres of the type and quantity of office furniture which is allocated.

Campbell-Jones's case of the convent demonstrates how changes in belief were deliberately paralleled by changes in artifacts and in spatial arrangements. When the nuns' sleeping quarters were refurnished, the statuettes taken down, and the walls redecorated, 'the effect, in very real terms as well as in symbolic ones [was] of blurring boundaries, the boundaries between the convent and the outside world, between the nun and her God, who was now much more accessible'. Some Sisters in small open communities found themselves asking 'Why am I a Nun?' and the answer frequently was to seek a dispensation from their vows (Campbell-Jones 1979: 184). It is as if the 'theatre' and the 'action' were integrated in this 'theatre of action'. Caroline Humphrey (1974) has provided us elsewhere with an interesting example of how a Mongolian tent can be re-equipped with modern items, while many aspects of the symbolic distribution of space (see p.26 below) remain stubbornly constant. Although there have been many recent adaptations 'Mongols still have socially designated places in the tent for people and objects, and give them value'. Tamara Dragadze's paper also gives an interesting example of the continuity of belief within the household in part of the Soviet Union, despite many changes in the economic and political environment, and Khatib-Chahidi notes a similar effect in Tehran, where arrangements in a modern apartment block recreate to some extent the traditional 'stage' on which family life is played out.

## Relative Space

The space in the prefabs of Athens described by Hirschon has been subdivided and extended upwards, sideways and downwards into the earth, as physical conditions have permitted, as a result of the desire of each family to provide living accommodation as part of the marriage dowry of the daughters. This Greek case gives an interesting example of what over time may become a group of matrilineally related women living together, with their husbands and children, while the kinship system, although it recognises descent in both lines, lays particular stress on family continuity through the male line and places the husband at the head of each nuclear family (see Hirschon:1978). Yet the nuclear family which her husband heads is located in space which the wife has determined, and nestles among that occupied by her female matrikin and their husbands and children.

I have noted elsewhere similarities between the material from Christian Greece with that found among some Moslems (S. Ardener 1978: 30–31). The research of Donley (undertaken independently of Hirschon's) usefully substantiates this. The Swahili families in Lamu, Kenya, arranged their sons' weddings to local girls so as to strengthen economic and political relations. Daughters were married to men from overseas, for the same reason. Yet the latter practice could be risky if a daughter was taken far away to a place where she could be harmed or the family be dishonoured. If, however, a stone mansion was built locally for the bride and groom by her father, the foreign trader was firmly tied to her family and the daughter protected. Donley also writes, 'I offer this explanation to account for the surprising fact that houses were being built for daughters in a totally patrilineal and patrilocal Islamic society' (Donley 1980: 12). 'Even when she marries, [a bride] may stay [in her father's house], while her parents move elsewhere, or her father may build a new house on top of this one with interconnecting stairs. Even if a house is built across the street, a bridge will be constructed to allow passage between the houses without going outside' (Donley 1980: 15). We are reminded here not only of Greek practices in Athens, but also of the apartment blocks being built in Tehran to house married daughters and their families, as described by Khatib-Chahidi below.

Donley remarks that a father 'may wish to guard his daughter's purity to the point that she will never go outside until the day she dies' (Donley 1980: 15). Such a restrictive practice with regard to women's access to space would be extreme. Helen Callaway offers us here an interesting contrast. Among the Yoruba of Nigeria there is another sort of difference between the relationship of men and women to their places of residence. Again we are considering a patrilineal system.[12] It is one also commonly called 'patrilocal', which would strictly imply that everyone, at least ideally, lives in their fathers' place of residence. This, of course, is a male-centred interpretation which after marriage would apply only to men, since women then move to live in the compounds of their husband's father. If widowhood and remarriage, and/or divorce and remarriage, are common, we may, however, find the difference between the sexes in a 'patrilocal' system even more marked. For then a man's birthplace remains his home base, with all the psychological and material support this provides, throughout his life, while a woman may pass from place to place, a stranger crossing boundaries into new family structures on new ground, from which she can later withdraw or be ejected (see Callaway, below).

Wright's analysis below of the difference between men's and women's uses of space in a Mamasani village in Iran has something in common with the picture described by Callaway for Nigeria. In both societies the men live patrilocally among their male blood-kin. The adult women of the family are scattered through the village. Wright shows that in Iran there is a network of places occupied by female kin for a woman to visit, besides that of her male kin in her own birth-compound, where news can be gathered and given, and support obtained. The Georgians of the Soviet Union have solved some of the problems of alienation by favouring the intermarriage of cousins (see Dragadze, below).

Rosemary Ridd's material from South Africa connects at many points with data in several other papers presented here. We find, again, groups of female kin living together, with the husband – although ideologically head of the nuclear family – being the 'stranger' among them. Yet as in the cases for Greece and Iran described by Hirschon and Khatib-Chahidi below, and that from Kenya quoted from Donley, and unlike the same-sex residential groups of men (and wives) considered by Callaway and Wright, their matrilocal groups do not seem to be 'part of the programme'; patrilocality (or virilocality – domicile in the husband's place) remains the dominant principle. Perhaps these matrilineally related female groups should be seen as examples of de facto 'muted structures', which can sometimes be detected, as Callaway suggests, when there is an observable discrepancy between theory and practice, or perhaps they are by-products of changing environments (they seem to be associated with urbanism, where the 'other' may begin at the front door). The re-evaluation of matriliny and matrifocality by Wendy James (1978) is very relevant here.

Societies that are admittedly matrilocal do exist, of course, and an unusual case comes from the polygynous Ga, where the 'prevailing residential arrangement in Centra Accra [Ghana] is that women live with their female matrilateral relatives, and men with their male patrilateral relatives, so that the area is a honeycombe of separate male and female compounds' (Robertson 1976). A different residential pattern is found among the matrilineal Luguru of Tanzania where

> it is common for a couple to separate when their son has married; after he has produced an heir for his wife's group, he is allowed to exercise the 'delayed right of bride removal', whereby he takes his wife to live at his maternal uncle's hamlet. At this point his mother, now an honoured grandmother, moves to the same place, so that she and her brother are once more together, as well as her brother's heir – her son. (Brain 1976: 278–79)

The foregoing examples indicate something of the wide variation in patterns of residential space found in different parts of the world and, of course, show that for any given society the life-map for women may differ markedly from that of men in the same society. In all these cases it should be noted that the physical distances between dwellings may not be great, whereas socially they may be very far apart: thus the ground maps may not match the social maps.

## Worlds Apart

Evelyn Waugh tells an amusing anecdote about Sir George Sitwell, who, looking to the distant horizon from the terrace of Renishaw across an English valley teeming with population, said: 'You see, there is no one between us and the Locker-Lampsons' (Sitwell 1949: 341). Sir George's population map was idiosyncratic in the extreme, but it again suggests that we all have social maps in our heads, with some selected populations receiving greater 'marking', and being 'coloured in', while others are overlooked. It can therefore reasonably be assumed that in the community studied by Wright, to take an example, any map generated by a man living among his concentration of male relatives, who become more distantly related to him as they live further from him, would look very different from that of his wife whose significant same-sex kin are widely dispersed, and whose male patrikin are concentrated elsewhere from her. We can also guess that in a family structure which stresses the male line of descent, a woman's experience of historical or genealogical time (like space on the family tree) must be different from that of a man's, especially where the female is not thought to contribute biologically to procreation, except as a carrier of the man's child (see Callaway 1978). His life is diachronically related to his patrilineage (and its lands) while her life is synchronically associated with it.

I have noted elsewhere that a discussion of gendered assymetries does not depend upon simple biological determinism, since 'women experience the world differently from men, regardless of whether or not innate differences are significant' (S. Ardener 1975: xviii). Some people reject the idea that men and women, individually or collectively, live in different worlds. But I would suggest that it is not adequate to say that men and women merely have a different viewpoint, as if they are seeing 'the same thing' or observing the same hard 'reality'. Their social constructions and their experience of the world must often (but not always) differ fundamentally if only as a result of their accumulated experiences and the way these will inevitably affect their perceptions. To take another case, Sarah Skar shows that the Matapuquio world differs fundamentally from our own; they do not merely have a different 'viewpoint'. Similarly, Godfrey Lienhardt notes that 'there appears to be a dimension of the Dinka self into which an outsider cannot really enter, excluded as he is from the intensely felt relationship of clanship. . . .' (1980: 82).

If one were to agree, then, that in any community the constructs of women and of men will often differ, this need not be taken to mean that they will vary in all or even most respects, or in the same way everywhere. And it can be seen that because individuals of both sexes are constituted of multiple personhoods (see S. Ardener 1992) worlds may correspond in certain contexts of relevance and differ in others. On the other hand it can be argued, of course, that even if there are elements in two discrepant constructs which look superficially the same they cannot be, because differences in other elements will cause a 'shadow' effect or exert 'pull'[13] and thus will affect their meanings or values; as noted above, 'objects are affected by the place in space of other objects'.

As the discussion of 'muted groups' elsewhere has suggested, one social group's construction (or map) of the world, or a sub-structure of it, may dominate the constructions generated by others to the point where they fail to be overtly expressed, or even to be substantially recorded, articulated and encoded. Nevertheless, adjustments can be made and worlds can be put into contact one with the other. Enough compatibility must be reached for practical purposes, although there is no guarantee that there will not be misunderstandings or conflict. Sarah Skar could live in the Andes, and translations of the word *pacha* may be attempted. Some idea of what a strange system must be like can be construed. Another's world can almost be comprehended given enough time, and to some extent this is what social anthropologists try to do. But all this does not negate the basic hypothesis that individuals, groups and cultures generate different worlds.

As several of the chapters below suggest, one element in a cosmology can only be fully understood in relation to all the other constituents. With these provisions in mind, juxtapositions might nevertheless be set up to stimulate further examination. For instance, the special relationship between women and space in one community may be compared and contrasted to the relationship of men and space in a second community. Thus, to use our earlier example, the cognitive map of a man in a (patrilocal) village in the Mamasani district of Iran might well more resemble, in certain respects, that generated by a woman of Athens who lives alongside her female matrikin, than would a map generated by his own wife whose same-sex kin are dispersed. And some women may well experience a flash of recognition when they read that among the Bororo Indians of Brazil the 'married man never feels "at home" in his wife's house', and that '"His" house, the one where he was born, and the home he remembers from childhood, lies on the other side of the village' (Lévi-Strauss 1961: 205).

Discussions of differences between the sexes have tended to concentrate attention on the social conventions which have prevented women from entering given spaces. Besides considering such aspects, this book also covers some of the ways women do enter and exploit space. Furthermore, of course, seclusion, exclusion and social separation are not only required of some women. The seclusion huts described by Watson-Franke for the crisis-solving process in a matrilineal, matrilocal society in Northwestern South America may contain men as well as women. There are more men than women in English jails. Indeed, men may be excluded from many areas which women may enter. In Kano, Nigeria, for instance, 'a man would normally not enter the house of a younger married sister. He might, but probably only with the husband's permission, enter the home of an older married sister, but even then once both siblings are fully grown their statuses as male and female take precedence over the kinship relationship, and the man does not normally enter his sister's house' (Schildkrout 1978: 115; cf. S. Ardener 1992: 5). In this case, however, as Schildkrout's material indicates, it is men who decide which 'women's space' other men may enter, and it could be argued, therefore, that this is to be understood as part of men's space also. Perhaps the peripheralisation of men in the home, as described by Ridd here, is a clearer form of exclusion by women.

I noted earlier that mobility is not only, to some degree, determined by the nature of physical space; it also affects the appreciation of space. Magrit Eichler has argued that the notion that men are mobile while women are not has been greatly exaggerated. Working (employed) women (in the West) are probably more 'ambulatory' than men because, she thinks, in addition to their work, they are more likely to do the shopping and 'ferry the children around'. Eichler would bury the inside/outside dichotomy as a description of reality (Eichler 1980: 36). In many cultures, women are very active outside the house, of course, and are far from seen, even ideally, as 'stationary' or 'sedentary' (for example, the Yoruba market women (see Callaway below), the Bakweri farmers (E. Ardener 1972), the Matapuquenians (Skar, below)).

The foregoing notwithstanding, there have been a number of social practices which have probably contributed, whether advisedly or indirectly, to the greater restriction of movement in space of some (possibly minority) groups of women. Foot-binding, tight corsetting, hobble skirts, high heels, all effectively impede women's freedom of movement, and make them dependent on mechanical and other forms of transport. If for any reason the latter are not at their disposal, they are clearly at a disadvantage. For instance, if women are not encouraged to ride bicycles or horses, to paddle canoes or to learn to drive cars, or to own these means of transport, their freedom to enter spaces may be relatively curtailed in comparison to men's. Arrangements for childcare, or responsibility for the aged, may also restrict mobility. Another inhibitor may be an ideology which encourages women to be physically frail, or to think that they are (for a discussion of bicycling and of the effect of women's education on their health and activities, see Delamont and Duffin 1978).[14] Nevertheless, as we consider next, physiological differences exert a real influence on use of space and on the mental maps of women and men.

## Vulnerability

Within the Pincos Valley of Peru, described below, there is something approximating to complementary egalitarianism between the sexes. However, outside the valley women are the more vulnerable to molestation from strange men (women in general do not fear other women). This imposes restraint on their movement and their independent use of space, with consequent unequal access to the benefits (for example, economic ones) which outside contacts can bring. This is likely, in the long run, to change the relationships between Matapuquenians themselves. Signe Howell has also returned from Malaysia with descriptions of social life (among the Chewong) where there is equal respect and freedom of movement in the village for all. Here, too, however, when contact with foreign men occurred, women found themselves more vulnerable because (it was said) they could not run away from danger as easily as men.[15] Consequently they are reluctant to travel to distant markets to obtain cash for their surpluses, but instead rely upon men to trade on their behalf. The importance of human flight for self-preservation may have been underestimated, in favour of strength of arms. It is interesting to note that a BBC television programme on attacks by English youths on elderly people was called 'The old do not run so fast'.

The vulnerability to rape and other deprivations is a basic asymmetry (from which, perhaps, many others may spring or upon which others are built), which has a bearing on how women use space. Indeed, the desire and capacity to rape may possibly be one of those deep-seated 'biological predispositions' which, to use Callan's phrase, 'may or may not be transformed into manifestations through the mediation of culture' (Callan 1978: 214ff; 1993 ed.: 168ff). However, the interdependence of men and women, the various affective predispositions which also undeniably exist and which face-to-face relations seem to encourage, and the overdetermining effects of social structures, together entail that these negative latent potentials normally fail to be transformed into manifestations: rape is still exceptional. In certain circumstances, however, it does occur, sometimes on a large scale (see, for instance, Brownmiller 1975) and in institutionalised form (for example, among the Iatmul), and this possibility is well known to women (see note 7) and must be considered when the question of women's use of space is discussed.

The vulnerability of women is made much of in fiction; indeed, most horror movies rely upon viewers imagining women being violated, while they sometimes also provide for the woman's ultimate rescue from attack, making this more socially acceptable. Such fiction (that involving vampires, for example) may at the same time have a mythic quality and perhaps belongs to that worldwide genre in which social norms are reversed, and in which events most abhorred in real life (such as incest, fratricide, bestiality) are represented. But in our culture, at least, the representations are asymmetrical in so far as women only rarely seem to create images of women violating men, and when the latter are generated by men they are infrequently permitted equivalent public airings. Fiction is particularly interesting because, potentially at least, it provides us with 'mental maps' which are most free from the constraints of 'reality': it is quintessentially human.

## 'The Final Frontier': Outer Space

We now turn to the allocation of space in theatres of action as described by popular writers of space fiction (and not only because of the possible implications of the title!). Prophets, of course, have long claimed the attentions of social anthropologists. The projections into the future, or into realms of fantasy, by writers of fiction (of whatever quality) are of especial interest precisely because they remind us that even in their imaginations people (including prophets) are 'culture-bound' (see E. Ardener 1989), and that when we see in stories history repeating itself despite new guises, we can by no means be certain that this is not an accurate forecast of the future. Indeed, it can be argued, of course, that the writer of fantasy often uses other worlds precisely in order to present our contemporary society more vividly. Nevertheless, as Juliet Blair also shows us below in her consideration of actresses, the creative artist frequently does claim to be an experimenter of new social forms (or others make that claim for them), and some at least of these may be realised in due course. They may in themselves attract emulation and resemble self-fulfilling prophesies. The previously unthinkable is thought; the previously undoable may then be done. For all these reasons the fiction of 'outer space' merits some notice in this volume.

It seems that, with exceptions, and until some recent work by, in particular, female writers, women readers have had little reason to rejoice from the predictions of the allocation of theatres in action in outer space. In her introduction to a collection of stories by women about women, Pamela Sargent states that most science fiction has been written by men (in the 1970s, only about 10 to 15 per cent of writers were women), a readership of 90 per cent male being not unusual (Sargent 1978: 11). In an interesting study Colin Greenland[16] states that science fiction, by an overwhelming majority, 'was written by men for men – or some would say, adolescent boys' (Greenland 1980). More recently, Sarah Lefanu agrees that this literature, 'popularly conceived as male territory', probably was so in the heyday of magazine science fiction in the 1930s and 1940s, but argues that even then there were some women writers behind the pen names (Lefanu 1988: 2).

What social and physical spaces are occupied by women, then, in such fiction? Possibly because female protagonists have been relatively rare (Sargent 1978: 23; Lefanu 1988: 2); until recently the theme of the dominant women 'has never played a very large role in the genre' (Sargent 1978: 3). On the contrary,

> Science fiction provided a world in which a male could experience high adventure and the interplay of scientific ideas and technological gadgets free from the interference of females. Sf became the neighbourhood clubhouse where boys could get together away from the girls . . . who were a nuisance anyway. They got in the way in the clubhouse; they got in the way of the stories, too, unless they stayed in their assigned domain (Sargent 1978: 29–30).

A sample of 25 copies of the science fiction magazine *Astounding*, published between 1959 and 1961, taken by Greenland, yielded 'only one cover picture with a woman in it, and she is far away in the background . . . serving behind a counter' (Greenland 1980). The alternative, and more common image in the sf magazines, however, was that projected by *Amazing Stories* which, from the 1950s, produced covers 'decorated with busty women whenever feasible (and often when not)' (Greenland 1980). Science fiction of this genre produced 'a familiar scene: the bug-eye monster leering over a helpless maiden' (Greenland 1980). The image, conjured up in association with the Mad Monster of Mogo – a woman, 'considerably *deshabillée*, swept aloft in the arms of a winged man, a veritable seraph and (as far as we can see) nude' (Greenland 1980) – has its predecessor in the ever-popular King Kong, and its successor in Jaws.[17]

As for social structure in space fiction, the notion 'that the sexes could live and work together harmoniously, in an equal fashion, was rarely considered and is still being questioned', writes Sargent (1978: 43). Colin Greenland quotes Ash as saying 'People whose work lay in space had no business with marriage and children', and to this Greenland adds, 'and for "people" read "men", of course'.

In the 1950s, however, some stories, often written by women, did feature housewife heroines. 'These characters were usually passive or addle-brained and solved problems inadvertently, through ineptitude or in the course of fulfilling their assigned roles in society.' (Sargent 1978: 19). In 1971 Joanna Russ also complained of the paucity of explorations of '"innate" values and "natural" social arrangements' in a genre, which, as Sargent states, at its best 'can provide a new and different literary experience . . . . Only sf and fantasy literature can show us women in entirely new or strange surroundings' (Sargent 1978: 47, 48). She calls for more truly innovative work. The continuing appeal of Dr Who and Star Trek on television might be instructive in this respect. We find the main female character in the former, often displaying childlike characteristics, has been an assistant to the hero. The two most important women in Star Trek, out on 'the final frontier', are derivatives of the switchboard operator and the nurse.[18] Dr Who has been reincarnated several times as a man, but not yet (1992) as a woman.

Lefanu describes the evolving contribution of women writers in the genre since Mary Shelley, among whom some have recently addressed social issues, noting, however, that 'The feminist intervention in science fiction has not been an easy one: writers have had to struggle not only against the weight of the male bias of the form but also against the weight of a cultural and political male hegemony that underpins the form itself. Nevertheless,' she concludes, 'feminism can engage in a fruitful interplay that explores new relations between ideas of inside and outside, self and the world' (Lefanu 1988: 4).

At the beginning I quoted Bourdieu, who has referred to perceptual or mental dispositions. I see these, following Hertz and others, as providing a widespread capacity to seize upon handy 'natural' dichotomies (such as handedness) which at both the individual and social level are (often unconsciously) applied, elaborated upon, and built into castles of the mind. It was with some amusement and (as a woman) with some chagrin, that I read that brilliant mathematical castle-building by Edwin Abbott which offered one early (1877) fictional alternative to three-dimensional worlds. In *Flatland* it is 'a Law of Nature . . . that a male child shall have one more side than his father . . . , so that each generation shall rise (as a rule) one step in the scale of development and nobility, from the three-sided triangle to the multi-sided (almost round) polygon of the Priestly Order'. There is one class for women, who are all straight lines! (p. 8 in 1962 edition). I was sorry to learn that since women 'have no pretensions to an angle, being inferior in this respect to the very lowest of the Isosceles [soldiers and Lowest Classes of Work-men], they are consequently wholly devoid of brain-power, and have neither reflection, judgement nor forethought, and hardly any memory' (p.14). Women, being needlelike, are nevertheless quite formidable, even dangerous, because of the physical damage, even fatalities, they can cause. It is not surprising to find, therefore, that in some states of Flatland women are, as on earth today (see below), confined to their houses except for religious festivals, and in others they must be chaper-oned by a man in public, or keep up a 'peace cry' to warn men of their presence. A woman in Flatland also has the familiar power of making herself practically invisible at will (see the discussion of 'fictive invisi-bility' above and below) by confronting others point on.

Of particular interest here is Abbott's diagram of a house in Flatland which replicates the symbolic divisions of space found in the Mongo-lian tent described by Humphrey (1974) where, traditionally,

> . . . the floor area . . . was divided into four sections, each of which was val-ued differently. The area from the door, which faced south, to the fireplace in the centre, was the status half, called by the Mongols the 'lower' half. The area at the back of the tent behind the fire was the honorific 'upper' part, named the *xoimor*. The division was intersected by that of the male, or ritual-ly-pure, half, which was to the left of the door as you entered, and the female impure, or dirty section to the right of the door, up to the xoimor . . . . It was considered a sin to move any utensil from its right place into another part of the tent. A woman's object was considered to pollute the men's area and a special ceremony might have to be performed to erase this.

We can now note that in Flatland (Abbott: 80) the arrangement of the domestic unit (see figure 1) suggests that the family structure appears to be patrilocal, the house being occupied by a man, his four sons, his two orphaned grandsons and four male servants – and only two women (his wife and daughter). The rooms are distributed so that the more junior males are near the large entrance to the west; the man and his wife are to the rear. As in Mongolia, the rooms of the wife and daughter are located on the left side (looking to the entrance); so in Flatland are the servants. In the Mongolian tent young wives (unsigned in the plans for Flatland) walk discreetly behind the tent. In Flatland women enter by the rear and the rooms for women are 'constructed with a view to denying them [the] power to turn round and attack so', the fictitious author claims, 'you can say and do what you like' then.

Thus the data suggest that it is possible to divide both the Flatland house and the Mongolian tent horizontally into increasingly inner (superior) and outer (inferior) zones. From the most inner (most superi-or) point one can then divide the house/tent into left (females, children

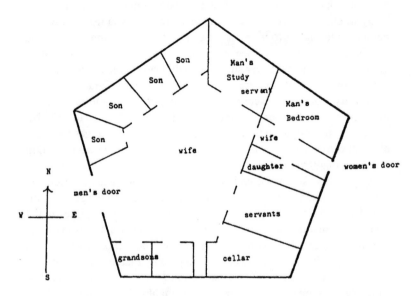

**Figure 1.1:** A house in Flatland; from the drawing by Edwin A. Abbott (1877) in *Flatland*, Oxford Blackwells, 1962.

and servants)/right (adult male) sections. If one may presume that Abbott was ignorant of Mongolian systems, the coincidence of these pervasive patterns raises interesting speculations about human perceptions and manipulations of space. Further examples of hierarchically ordered spatial zones linked to, among other characteristics, gender can be found below in the papers by Rodgers, Khatib-Chahidi and Wright.

Perhaps a digression can be made here, in view of our interest, described in *Perceiving Women* and *Defining Females* (which includes the Mongolian case) in modes of expression and 'muting', to note that in Flatland – as in Mongolia – discourse between the sexes differs from that between men alone. In Flatland, of course, the customs operate differently. Here with women men speak of 'love': among themselves they refer to 'the anticipation of benefits': 'duty', used in talking to women, becomes 'necessity' or 'fitness'; 'other words are correspondingly transmuted. Moreover, before women, language implying the utmost deference for their Sex is used, but behind their backs they are both regarded and spoken of . . . as being little better than 'mindless organisms' (Abbot 1877: 50). Men, the author thinks, have to lead 'a kind of bi-lingual, and I may almost say bi-mental, existence' (ibid.:49). 'Now my humble fear is that this double training, in language as well as in thought, imposes somewhat too heavy a burden upon the young, especially when, at the age of three years old, they are taken from the maternal care and taught to unlearn the old language . . . and to learn the vocabulary and idiom of science . . . . I say nothing of the possible danger if a Woman should ever surreptitiously learn to read and convey to her Sex the result of her perusal of a single popular volume; nor of the possibility that the indiscretion of disobedience of some infant male might reveal to a Mother the secrets of the logical dialect' (ibid.: 50). No doubt with his tongue in his cheek, the purported author urges the highest Authorities to reconsider the regulations of Female education, in order to safeguard men.

Presumably Abbott's own book did fall into the hands of a female, since seven years after it was issued, in an apologia to the second edition, he admits to having changed his views. He 'now inclines to the opinion . . . that the Straight Lines are in many important respects superior to the Circles. But, writing as a Historian, [the author] has identified himself . . . with the views generally adopted by Flatland, and...even by Spaceland, Historians; in whose pages (until very recent times) the destinies of Women and of the masses of mankind have seldom been deemed worthy of mention and never of careful consideration' (ibid.:xiii–xix). Some might say that he could have been writing recently!

For those who seek change in the allocation of domains among the sexes, Outer Space, as depicted, has often looked disappointingly familiar, but it is perhaps because of this reassurance that some readers have found it satisfying. On the other hand, recent science fiction has been increasingly responding to changing attitudes towards women's access to places of decision-making outside the home, and to, for example, their current active roles in the police and military – cyberpunk spacewomen are now equipped with ray-guns and more complex technology. Some writers are experimenting with new literary and societal forms. These and other reflections make such literature an interesting indicator of current social debates and practices, as well as of new maps of possible futures.

## Back to Earth

At the beginning of this introductory essay I drew attention to the proposition that physical space and our perceptions were 'mutually affecting spheres of reality', and to certain definitional relationships between space and persons and objects. I then moved on to consider a few of the many strands in the various chapters presented here which weave a pattern through this volume, and I related them to some other material. The chapters below have a lot more to say than I have indicated, of course. Yet, with such a wide variety of customs, and of thought across the world, the small sample of case studies considered here can still only hint at some of the aspects to be found when studying women and space. Nevertheless, there are many different insights and lessons below for the incautious generaliser, since the volume has aimed for variety of treatment and data rather than conformity.

Already there exists a large literature on space produced by architects, geographers, psychologists, sociologists, as well as social anthropologists, each with their different orientations, which space itself, and the context in which this volume was generated, have precluded us from doing justice to here. It is hoped that our volume will nevertheless add its mite to this work and be found of some use to those who have not before considered women in relation to space.

## Notes

1. Speaking of various indigenous groups in Australia and America, Durkheim and Mauss wrote: 'Cosmic space and tribal space are thus only very imperfectly distinguished and the mind passes from one to the other without difficulty, almost without being aware of doing so' (1903, reprinted 1963, trans. Needham, p. 65). 'Shape' and 'space' are used in this book in the sense of 'topological space', where alterations in the boundaries may still preserve the integrity of the space: thus a Regency chair may occupy the same 'conceptual slot' or 'conceptual space' as a Victorian chair, though their actual forms may differ; we can assume them both to be 'chair-shaped' nevertheless; similarly a tree may grow, and change its appearance in other ways, while remaining a tree.

2. See Saussure [1916] (1964). The study of sign systems ('semiology') was advocated by Saussure in the period around the turn of the century (see his posthumous work: 1916) and has been elaborated by many scholars subsequently.

3. For the original presentation and extensive discussions of the notion of 'mutedness' and who generates social concepts and the words that label them, see E. Ardener, (1972; 1975a, 1975d), and S. Ardener (1975, 1978). The concept has since been taken up and documented in Spender (1980) and applied by other researchers.

4. See section 'Time and Space' in E. Ardener (1975b). For 'simultaneities' see E. Ardener (1975d). The phrase 'mutually affecting spheres of reality' is borrowed from Hastrup (1978).

5. Durkheim and Mauss (and many others) have pointed out the association of time and the seasons with space [1903] 1963, 71).

6. Among the Chinese, north is said to be female and south male (Durkheim and Mauss [1903] 1963, 69); see also note 10.

7. The *Oxford Mail* wrote (on 9 November 1979): 'A shock report yesterday . . . warned women between the ages of 20 and 34 to: "Keep out of town on Sunday nights".' The newspaper also quotes Superintendent Mackie of the Oxford Police Force as saying 'Any woman walking alone after dark *invites* trouble' (my italics). Judge Kenneth Mynett, QC, is quoted: 'The streets of Oxford are unsafe for people to walk on after ten o'clock at night'.

8. The segregation of women in Orthodox synagogues, where they occupy the upper galleries, must be noted, however. Compare the visitors' galleries in the British House of Commons.

9. At St John's College, Oxford, the small side-chamber attached to the chapel is known as the 'hen-pen' (cf. Mrs Thatcher's nickname in Rodgers, below); access can be gained direct from the President's lodgings, and occupants are hidden from the (fomerly celibate) College Fellows and students. In Orthodox Jewish synagogues women have sometimes followed proceedings from behind a curtain or from a separate room (Rabbi Julia Neuberger, paper delivered at Women's Studies seminar, Oxford, November 1980).

10. To the Zuñi, north is blue, south is red, east is white, etc. (Durkheim and Mauss, [1903] 1963, 44). To the Irish the South quarter (Munster) is associated with women (and music, slaves, witches, the dead) and the colour black; see E. Ardener (1975c).

11. S. Rodgers, personal communication.

12. As Callaway notes below, certain other groups of Yoruba reckon descent through both paternal and maternal lines ('cognatically').

13. For 'language shadows', and a discussion of 'world structures', see E. Ardener (1975d).

14. For a view of the effect on mental maps of asymmetrical access to motor transport, see the case of 'Mr and Mrs Stock' (in the United States) in Downs and Stea (1977, pp. 2, 6–8). This interesting book, with an emphasis on urban cognitive mapping in the United States, gives little special attention to sexual differences. It is regretted that it is outside the scope of this introduction to consider the literature by psychologists on perceptions of space in relation to gender. Of great interest also is Drid Williams's work on human movement in relation to space, including her application of ballet notation to religious and other theatres of action, and her general 'semasiological' approach (see also the *Journal for the Anthropological Study of Human Movement*, New York).

15. Verbal communication during a paper on her fieldwork, at the Oxford Women's Social Anthropology Seminar, 1979.

16. Colin Greenland very kindly allowed me to read his chapter 'Love Among the Mannequins' in his thesis concerned with science fiction, which I hope will soon be published.

17. Sometimes an additional salve has been prepared, for the monsters themselves may turn out to have hearts of gold: King Kong, far from intending harm to the heroine, is motivated by love, and the Mad Monster of Mogo turns out to be a Venusian social worker called Green Flash. It is interesting to note here that, in contrast, in a highly regarded book, *Left Hand of Darkness*, by the distinguished writer Ursula Le Guin, rape between males and females is not possible, since all sex must be by mutual consent (Sargent, 1978).

18. In the 1950s, however, some science fiction stories, often written by women, did feature housewife heroines. 'These characters were usually passive or addlebrained' (Sargent 1978: 19).

19. Other planets on which women occupy political space have appeared from time to time in isolated episodes, but their societies have usually been only lightly sketched in, and they are merely tangential to the world of the regular heroes of the series, who have not, therefore, fully had to come to terms with them. Interestingly, the only (barely) significant female in the 1979 box-office success 'Star Wars', was a rather ambiguous princess, not, for instance, a reigning queen, or a pilot, or even crew member. For attitudes to, and symbolism of, virgins, see Hastrup (1978) and S. Ardener (1978).

# Acknowledgement

I would like to thank Sandra Burman, Helen Callaway and Edwin Ardener for their helpful comments on my text.

# 2

# Andean Women and the Concept of Space/Time

*Sarah Lund Skar*

## The Spatial Context: A Point of Departure

The theme of this book suggests a point of departure for addressing a question of general concern to those interested in women's studies, that is: to what extent can we look upon the particular situation of women in space as a reflection of basic cultural ideologies about sexual differentiation and of a more generalised 'world view'? This chapter discusses a particular example taken from one of South American's largest Indian groups. This case is, however, also of wider interest because it tells us about how women's and men's activities in a given physical space are integrated with and become an expression of something all-embracing. The subsystems in the cosmology of the Quechua-speaking Indians from the Peruvian Andes interrelate in a variety of ways, each one giving a deeper and richer meaning to the others, and ultimately merging to create a whole 'world view'.[1] To demonstrate this I shall begin from the Quechua concept of *pacha.*

The data on which this paper is based were collected when I did fieldwork, together with my husband, in 1976–7.[2] We lived in the small village of Matapuquio in the Pincos Valley, in the Department of Apurimac, Peru. Tropical to subtropical valleys rise up to peaks of over 5,000 metres. The vertical slope from the valley bottom to mountain top is extremely steep and nowhere do you find the flat plateaux with human habitation so typical, for example, of the Cuzco region. Instead, villages are spread out on the slopes. The difference in altitude from neighbour to neighbour can be up to one hundred metres, and in the case of Matapuquio the altitude span of the entire village is from 2,800 m to 3,800 m. Such valleys as the Pincos, though relatively close in proximity to small urban centres such as Andahuaylas and Abancay, are in effect extremely isolated.

Both my husband and I carried out research on Peruvian land reform and the effects this particular legislation was having on the indigenous communities (H. Skar 1979). My specific concern was the extent to which the new and drastic transformations in the land tenure sector were

31

changing women's position in Quechua society, and the isolation of factors which were crucial to such a process of change (S. Skar 1978, 1980). I tried to understand how Quechua (or Runa, as they would say themselves) women are viewed within their own culture, to define their status and role within the community, and particularly within the household, and to consider the perimeters of their daily existence. From this initial consideration, I was led through a maze of associations which eventually forced me to confront the problem of *pacha*.

## The Quechua Concept of Space/Time

In the Quechua language, time and space are designated by one and the same concept: *pacha*. Therefore, to define the term involves understanding its use in the context of time and in the context of space. A clear-cut distinction between the two usages, however, is impossible, the universe of time and space somehow merging into a single conceptual unit. At its widest interpretation, *pacha* would seem to express the world view of the Runa in which time is neither past, present, nor future but eternally being, and space is the physical/cultural realm in the state of existence.

According to various Quechua dictionaries, the term is primarily defined as 'circumstances', 'conditions', 'world', 'earth'; and secondly as 'time', 'era' (Parker 1964). In many instances, the term *pacha* is translated with the Spanish word *mundo*, which has the extended meaning of 'a people', 'a realm', or 'a society' (Soto Ruiz 1976). The most lengthy discussion of the term *pacha* is found in Cesar Guardia Mayorga's (1971) short, but detailed, dictionary of the Cuzco dialect. Guardia specifically states that *pacha* refers to 'the animated world as a totality, a universe from beginning to end, boundary to boundary'. *Pacha* as time is not to be understood as being abstract or isolated[3] but as it is unified with the earth (*mundo*). The most common example of the use of *pacha* as time is in reference to a particular epoch, as for example, *naupa pacha* ('former or ancient times'). *Naupa pacha* in no way refers to a limited or specific timespan but rather to a state of the world from the point of view of time. Of all the dictionaries, it is only Guardia's which introduces 'space/time' ('*mundo/tiempo*') as the best translation of the word *pacha*. Though we may feel uncomfortable with this combination, it is important to remind ourselves that to the Runa time and space are not two separate abstractions but are only aspects of one and the same phenomenon. Though the following paragraphs first dissect the concept of space/time into space *and* time, I will later return to the totality of the concept by reinterpreting the interconnection in the light of the specific ethnographic material.

## Women and Men of the Mountain

The world of the Matapuqenians is confined by the boundaries of the valley. These boundaries are not only of a geographical nature but are closely associated with what Andeanists (for example, Murra 1972) have called 'the vertical zonation of the Andean ecology'. The traditional view of *pacha* is contained in the interrelationships of the vertical zones of the valley slopes. As agriculturalists, first and foremost, the people place an emphasis on the agricultural cycle which at once distinguishes and unites all the zones of the valley.

In the Pincos Valley a single family can, and indeed must, have plots of land in the various crop-zones: the lower-lying wheat and barley fields, the most favoured maize fields, and, at the top range, the numerous plots for the cultivation of tubers. Two of the factors which distinguish these vertical zones are altitude and water. A third factor, the angle of the slope, can offset the impact which relative altitude may have on the ecology. As a general rule, however, the higher up the slope the fields are located, the longer the time required for the maturation of the crops. Because the slopes of the Pincos Valley are so steep, it is possible to pass in a single day's climb from the tropical valley bottom where sugar cane and citrus fruits are grown, right up to the *puna* or high pasture areas where the frosty nights make agricultural production an impossibility. Thus Matapuqenians have agricultural experience with close-lying lands in all the strata. Because of this immediate and compact contact with all of the zones of the Andean ecology, the villagers do not need to seek beyond their own valley for the fulfilment of their own subsistence needs. Unlike people in other areas of the Andes, as for example those in Bolivia reported on by Olivia Harris (1976), the Matapuqenians do not specialise in one crop from a single zone and use part of the harvest for barter to obtain produce grown by others elsewhere in another zone. This has contributed to the very bounded, self-contained conceptualisation the Matapuqenians have of their *pacha*. They observe and experience first hand the rhythms of the entire universe within the boundaries of their own valley.

In their universe, physical space is divided into three parts: the valley bottom, the mid-slopes and the high mountains. Both extremes of high and low are associated with evil, with strong spirits, and with disruptive elements which threaten and are an intrusion upon the boundaries of the Runa world. In the valley bottom we find the long-established former *hacienda* or landed estate.[4] Before land reform this was owned and run by a German immigrant who specialised in the production of sugar cane alcohol. The existence of the *hacienda* represents the encroachment of the dominant national culture on the indigenous population. Over generations the *hacienda* has imposed a system of production and land tenure which has greatly complicated the simplified version of Indian agricultural production (as basically the combination of resources from various zones on the slopes). Traditionally villagers did not pursue agricultural production in the valley bottom. Their indigenous crops required the more temperate climate of the slopes. However, with the development of the *hacienda* system in the valley, their land was gradually alienated. In order for the villagers to continue their traditional subsistence agriculture, they were forced to work on the *hacienda* in exchange for usufruct rights to land on the slopes.

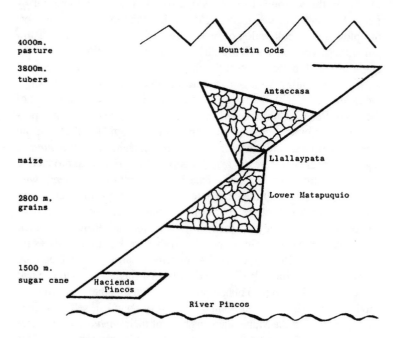

**Figure 2.1:** Representation of Matapuquio Village, Peru

Today, for approximately two weeks of every month, the men of the village descend to the valley to work in the sugar-cane fields where they earn a small daily wage and protect their rights to land. Unlike traditional agriculture, production in the valley is carried out by men alone. The demand for a male labour force partially reflects the attitudes of the dominant Peruvian culture which excludes women from production outside the household. Undoubtedly, however, the absence of women in the valley also reflects a certain protectionist tactic on the part of the Indians. Indian relations with whites and mestizos have for hundreds of years been characterised by exploitation, violence and, where Indian women are concerned, rape. The absence of women in the valley is clearly a means of avoiding these unfortunate influences which contact with the national culture implies.

In contrast to the valley, the upper slopes are the focus of specialised female activity: the herding of sheep, cows, horses and, to a lesser extent, pigs. Every morning the women leave for the heights with their animals. In the evening they return to their homes in the village to prepare the evening meal. Only women are allowed to do the milking of the cows and the goats and it is their responsibility to make the cheese from the milk. Through the management of her animals, a woman has the possibility of acquiring money. Whereas no agricultural products produced in the mid-latitudes on the slopes are ever sold for cash and are rarely even bartered, animals may be sold for money to help maintain a widow or to pay for her necessary contributions for a village *fiesta* or family ritual. In this way, female activity on the upper slopes parallels the male-dominated labour in the valley. Both give access to cash and serve as examples of the exclusive division of labour between these two extremes of the spatial continuum.

The upper slopes are no more considered safe than is the *hacienda*-controlled valley. Only a decade ago they were the scene of bandit raids. Thieves from nearby towns would ride into the mountains to pillage the vulnerable village herds. The heroic actions of many women to ward off the attacks of the robbers often reach myth-like proportions. Today law and order seem to be nearly established but the risk of association with this high boundary of the Runa world is still threatening. On the upper slopes one is close to the fierce and jealous mountain gods, the *apus*. If angered these gods may send down disaster on the women's herds. Animals may die from a fall off a cliff or the entire herd may be destroyed by disease. All misfortunes affecting the animals arise out of the displeasure of the *apus* and the risk involved with such close association is considerable.

At the very heart of the Matapuquio world, located on the benevolent mid-slopes, is the focal point of Runa culture: the village itself. Here the (approximately) 200 households are located, each situated in the midst of its own maize fields. Maize is the only crop the villagers grow which requires irrigation, and the layout of the community is oriented along sources of water. Irrigation ditches from a small river that transverses the slope, and from two separately located springs, have meant that the village itself is extremely dispersed. There is no plaza, no church, no administrative town centre. In fact, there is only one geographical feature which marks the village and that is the deep gorge made by the stream, which becomes a torrential river during the rains. The gorge runs diagonally through the village cutting it into two physical halves which correspond to the dual social structure of the village.

## Dual Organisation and the Articulation of Space

Any discussion of how the Matapuqenians view their social space must take into account the pervasive nature of their dual social organisation. It is precisely in such organisational principles as duality that we can find, spelled out for us, a fundamental ordering of their universe. Ultimately this is based upon the two essential components in creating culture itself: man and woman.

In its most generalised form, the social duality of the village is evident in the division of the village into two halves or moieties. That the most distinctive physical feature of the dispersed village happens to be the natural barrier of the gorge dividing the community is not in itself sufficient to explain the dual organisation, but in spatial terms it serves to separate, and visually emphasise, the difference between the two village halves.

In Matapuquio, the two moieties, one called Antaccasa, which is the upper village, and the other simply retaining the name of Matapuquio, which is the lower village, are two highly endogamous entities. Intermarriage within each half is approximately 75 per cent. Thus, there is a strong tendency for certain families to be associated with one of the two moieties and the competition between the two halves is great. Each moiety maintains its own rudimentary school. The political leaders or *varayoqkuna* organise village activities and maintain peace and order; two come from Antaccasa and two from lower Matapuquio. Village religious celebrations or *fiestas*, which centre around the neutral ritual area of Llallaypata located between the two halves, are fraught with conflict. Fights often break out between families of opposing moieties and often expand to include nearly the entire village. Other ritualised forms of fighting occur between men and women, particularly at *Carnavales* just prior to Lent. Similar fights reported from other areas (Isbell 1973; Gifford and Hoggarth 1976; Hurley, personal communication) have been interpreted as another form for expression of the antagonism between moieties, the women symbolically representing the upper village and the men the lower.

Complementary to their dual social organisation, the Matapuqenians also have a bilateral kinship system which has had far-reaching consequences on the way in which space/time is perceived by the individual.

The bilateral system is *ego*-centred and places equal importance on the families of both *egos'* parents. Both men and women inherit land and animals, and residence after marriage seems to be a question of how best to combine and protect rights over the land which each spouse brings to a union.

The division of labour between the sexes underlines the principles inherent in the bilateral kinship system. Though individual ownership of land and animals is always kept in mind, agricultural work is considered a joint responsibility. Men and women together prepare the fields for planting, irrigate and plough, and finally plant maize, the villagers' most valued crop. Both the male and female principles are seen as essential: the men drive the oxen and steer the plough while the women plant the seed. The symbolic implications need hardly be pointed out. Harvesting is a joint effort as well. However, when all the crops are gathered in and brought to the family courtyard, the women take over the responsibility of carefully sorting and storing the produce. Part of the harvest is set aside as seed for the coming year. Another small portion may be separated for barter. The rest of the produce is sorted as to quality and consumption use. The harvest is then carefully arranged in the *marka* (family storeroom) in which only women are allowed entry. Thus, the woman of the household, with her procreative capacities, has the ultimate say over the use of and consumption from the *marka*.

A 'world view' such as the one expressed in the Quechua concept of *pacha*, is basically an individual's view of how he orders his universe and where he perceives his place in that universe to be. During socialisation, children begin to understand their place in the world through their actions, and the people with whom they most closely associate. Activities and tasks within the village itself are much the same for boys and girls and for men and women. But here the close association ceases. As young boys begin to work in the *hacienda* with their fathers, and young girls take over more and more of the herding responsibilities in the heights, it can be interpreted that each day's actions brings out and emphasises the individual's strong associations and personal perceptions of his particular place in his universe. Whether boy or girl, the early morning hours witness an exodus from the village, the men and boys following the path down the valley and women and girls climbing up the slope in search of pasture. When evening comes families are again reunited in their homes in the village, where the sexes meet on equal footing. This movement to the extremes of high and low underlines the boundaries of *key pacha*, or 'this earth', and the return to the village where social life has its origins marks the centre of focus of the Runa world.

We find this pattern of movement and the articulation of space is repeated in many aspects of village social organisation, all of which are based on the structural dualism. In village *fiestas*, for example, members from the two moieties converge on Llallaypata, the ritual and geographical centre of the village. As the families gather, those from (symbolically female) Antaccasa form a procession which comes down the mountain to join the festivities, while those from the lower (male) village meet at the lowest houses and climb up to Llallaypata. When everyone is congregated the drinking begins, a ritual which is always carried out when two parties reach an agreement or come together in comradeship.

The village work-projects, or *faenas*, reflect the same perceptions of space and ideology of social order. *Faenas* held to clean the irrigation ditches are organised so that all the moiety members from Antaccasa meet together with their *varayoqkuna* at the top of the irrigation system. As might be expected, those from Matapuquio meet at the lowest extension of the irrigation system. The two teams, under the direction of their respective *varayoqkuna*, clean out the ditches, the one working down the slope, the other up the slope. At the end of the day they meet at the village centre where food and maize beer are provided for everyone by the *varayoqkuna*. The very fact that a system of community work-projects such as these *can* function implies the superordination of the whole over its parts, but just as the totality of the universe is experienced and perceived by individuals from a particular vantage point, so too it is only through enacting their spatial separateness that the moieties can give expression to their place in the whole. In this way the movement of groups in the context of *faena* and *fiesta* is similar to the expression of the separateness, yet equality, of men and women in their recurring pattern of exodus to the boundaries and return to the centre of their vertical world.

Thus far, we have gained some indication of the perimeters of the concept of *pacha* as *physical space*; that is (1) the valley world and the close spiritual connections which the Runa feel with this natural setting; (2) *pacha* as individual space through which any *ego* can perceive of his own individuality, his own realm of action, and his own particular domain in relationship to his universe, and finally (3) *pacha* as social space in which the boundaries of social life are distinguished through the articulation of the dual social organisation of the village, and the unity of social life is expressed through the coming together or merging of this duality. Now I will proceed to a discussion of *pacha* as *time*, reminding you again that in fact 'time' in this context is the mere 'being of, or continuity of, the earth'.

## Time as a Process of Regeneration

Actually this reminder places us right at the very heart of the timelessness of time in the concept of *pacha*. Simply to state that time is cyclical is far from sufficient to express the integrative nature the time element has in the concept. The kernel of *pacha* as time is the progression from conception, through gestation, birth, maturation, to death. But it would be wrong to begin with a long discussion of the sequence of agricultural activities from planting to harvest. The agricultural cycle as such should rather be seen as one manifestation of the continuing process of recreating the spatial components.

The several vertical ecological zones on the mountain slope each have their own reproductive time-piece, so to speak, and it is only because of the perfect synchronisation of that time-piece that combined agricultural production is possible. The synchronisation is actually a result of altitude, the higher-lying crops taking a considerably longer time to reach maturation due to the effects of lower temperatures and to some extent less water. Thus, a phenomenon which we are tempted to place on the time side of the concept, *pacha*, actually cannot be separated from the element of space. This is a good concrete example of the implications of space/time. First, potatoes are planted in the heights, then the first maize fields at the very top of the village are ploughed and planted. Slowly the process is repeated down the slope until the entire village is under cultivation. Then the grains are planted, after which it is time to return to the heights to bank the potatoes and then to the village to cultivate the maize. The sequence in time is a sequence in space as well. The agricultural cycle which we might tend to analyse in terms of what is accomplished in the course of each month of the year, is better understood as a progression through space/time. The ultimate goal, or result of the progression, is a recreation or renewal of the universe.

In an unspecified sense, the cyclical processes of human reproduction are viewed in much the same way. A man and a woman together conceive a child. We will recall that symbolically they signify the lower and upper regions of space and their union represents a reconciliation of these two opposite forces; a reconciliation which is the basis of social life, or *pacha* in the sense of 'society'. There is a very strong chance that the pair will both be from the same moiety and, indeed, a careful examination of the genealogical material shows that their union will more than likely follow a pattern of family alliances which is repeated every second generation. Not only will they have married with a family into which their grandparents married, but the alliance will often be duplicated or triplicated between the two sibling groups. From a certain perspective, then, the individual appears on this earth (*kay pacha*) as the culmination of the seed of his forefathers and, through marriage into groups formerly aligned with his family, will recreate similar conditions for his descendants. His personal role is only transitory, but forms an essential link to the perpetuity of the social universe.

As was the case with the agricultural system, the *fiesta* system celebrated throughout the Andes has been referred to as *fiesta* cycle'. Together with the agricultural cycle, which it indeed reflects, it is most often analysed in terms of the Christian church calendar from which it in part originated. That this necessarily implies an inaccuracy is true insofar as it places the emphasis on *the singular event* (that is, a date) or even, in a more perceptive analysis, on *the generalised event* (with which it corresponds in the agricultural cycle). This compartmentalised way of looking at the various *fiestas* in the cycle seems to me to overlook a very important aspect. One *fiesta* really only gains its full meaning when seen in relation to all the others in the official *fiesta* cycle and in relation to other unofficial ritual activities which fall outside of the religious *fiesta* calendar altogether. Two examples of such in Matapuquio would have to include the festivities associated with the cleaning of the irrigation ditches and with the rain rituals which come at the very end of the dry season.

The *fiesta* cycle in Matapuquio is an expression of anxiety over, or belief about, the regenerative process which is the continual or timeless quality of *pacha*. As we found when considering *pacha* as space, the time element of the concept is also dominated by two extreme and opposite climatic conditions, each associated with a sexual principle of male or female and providing a necessary part of the propelling mechanism which regenerates life on the slope. The two opposing and life-giving forces are the rainy season and the dry season (*paray mita*, literally 'rainy half' and *rupay mita* or 'hot half').

In their ritual activities, both within the context of the more orthodox *fiesta* calendar as well as in the ritual activities of household and village, both men and women actively participate in the progression from the rains to the dry season to the rains again. The form this participation takes is in part a consequence of the Runa view about the nature of fertility, an attribute of the earth, personified by the passive diety *Pachamama* ('mother earth'), and of women. However, fertility cannot come to fruition without intervention. A man impregnates a woman. If a child is not conceived it is felt the man is not satisfactorily fulfilling his duty to the woman. Ridicule is often expressed in the idiom of a poor planter. Men will say to the would-be father, 'Let me come and work your "field". Then surely a child will be conceived'. In turn, the fruitfulness of the earth (*pachamama*) is dependent upon both men and women working in the cultivation of the fields as well as fulfilling a progression of ritual acts linked with these agricultural activities. To the Runa, both the ritual act and the agricultural production are seen as an integrated process to ensure the fertility of the earth.

Two rituals particularly link the women with the rains. The one corresponds to the Roman Catholic celebration of the Fiesta of Santa Rosa, which falls on 30 August. Unlike other *fiestas* throughout the year, this celebration is sponsored by women only. Together with her sisters and female affines, the sponsor prepares huge quantities of maize beer for the entire village. From her own money, she buys the necessary barrel of cane alcohol and may hire a small local band to play throughout the week-long festivities. Animals from her herds will be slaughtered to feed the large number of participants. The beginning of September is the time when the first maize fields are being prepared for planting and, as has been indicated earlier, this initial ploughing occurs first in the highest-lying fields of Antaccasa. That women play the central role in the *fiesta* at this time marks the commencement of cultivation on the slopes and the renewing of the fields which have lain fallow since harvest. As guardians of the seed and sole administrators of the storehouses, the women's actual as well as symbolic control over the forces of procreation is complete. Once the seed is planted everyone anxiously awaits the beginning of the rains.

Some time during the month of October, a second ritual is performed in which women again play a central role and which in turn links them specifically with this half of the year. As the tiny maize plants are first sprouting they are in desperate need for water, which during this time of year is in short supply. Irrigation only occurs before planting, so the available water supply is already being claimed by neighbours further down the slopes who are just beginning to plough, when young plants higher up on the slopes are in risk of drying out. This crucial period is a time when the entire village turns its attention to the coming of the rains. Their preoccupation culminates in the performance of rain rituals. Crosses guard all the mountain passes into the village. They are believed to contain potent spirits which are akin to the *apus* or mountain gods. In the heights they stand as sentinels marking the upper boundaries of the Matapuqenian universe. During the rain procession, which most often occurs at night, these crosses are carried from mountain top to mountain top before being brought down to Llallaypata. Leading the procession are the women of the village who wail in archaic Quechua with words which are no longer fully understood but which are the necessary ingredients in the supplication for rain. Just as the rains are needed for the germination of the seed, only the wailing of the women's voices is felt to be powerful in bringing on the rains. With their voices calling in the night to the beating of the drums, the women actively participate with those regenerative forces which are at that time essential to the continuation of *pacha*. The processions may continue sporadically for several weeks until at last the rains do begin.

During the course of the next six months or so the crops on the slopes gradually mature, each in turn according to their place in the spatial continuum of the slope. In May the rains are abating and the harvest begins. Essential for the preservation of the maize, in particular, is the need for sun to dry out the husks and prevent the kernels from rotting. Sun at this time is as crucial as rain at the beginning of the growing season. All the produce, whether maize, grain or potatoes, is exposed in heaps to dry. Only then is it placed in the storeroom. The final harvesting activities which are concentrated on the thrashing and winnowing of the grains are completed near the end of June. Then begin the important *fiestas* of San Juan, on 24 June, and San Pedro, on 29 June. Though again closely associated with the Roman Catholic calendar, in fact their celebration coincides with the winter solstice which in Incan times was the occasion for the elaborate festival of the sun, Inti Raymi. The Inca himself was the human incarnation of the sun and the festival was performed as a form of thanks for the bountiful harvest as well as a supplication for the sun to return to the earth in its full strength. Though much of this content is now absent from the village *fiestas*, the celebrations at this time are dominated by male bravado in the bullring and during the horse races.

The ritual activities described thus far coincide with particularly critical moments in the procreation of the crops and in the transition from one condition of time (when it rains) to the other (when the sun shines). Though women and men each dominate the ritual activities which usher in a new stage in the recreation of the universe, other *fiestas* are marked by a more balanced participation between the sexes. New Year *Ano Nuevo*, Carnaval (*Carnavales*, just prior to Lent), Easter (*Pascua*) and All Saints (*Todos Santos*) are all important celebrations in the village and are bound up, whether implicitly or explicitly, with the process of regeneration and with the continuity of time as existence. Essentially the elements are the same and are thoroughly grounded in the dualism so characteristic of Runa social organisation. Just as the upper and lower moieties are essential to the unity of the village, and man and woman are of equal importance in the creation of a child, so too the rainy season and the dry season together are the absolutely necessary ingredients for agricultural production on the slope and the perpetuity of *pacha*.

## Conclusion

Let us recapitulate how Runa cosmological views of space and time are integrated in the concept of *pacha*. First we were told by Guardia that the term referred to the animated world as a totality, from boundary to boundary. In the case of Matapuquio, this proved to be the world on the slopes of the valley bounded by the River Pincos and mountain peaks above (see Figure 2.1). The existence of this world is expressed through certain social/cyclical processes. One such is the daily movement of women to the high mountain pasturelands and men to the valley bottom with their reunion in the village in the evening. This daily cycle gives expression to the boundaries of their universe and the divisions within the totality, in terms of labour and is associated with each of the sexes. This structuring of space and its expression through the movement of the population, forms the pattern for social organisation on other levels. I am referring here to the dual organisation of the village and the way in which the functioning of this duality expresses the opposition of the parts and their ultimate unity. This is the focus of the social content of the *pacha* concept.

Another social/cyclical process which we found to be very instructive in terms of how time and space are virtually one and the same, was the agricultural cycle. Differences in time between the cycles in each of the ecological zones were found to be related to differences in altitude or space. The incorporation of all the zones into a single agricultural cycle focuses on the renewal and regeneration of life as a totality. In a much more extended sense, human reproduction can be seen in the same way. Choice of marriage partner, and multiple sibling-group marriage exchanges, show a certain generational patterning. The individual's place in this pattern is to pass the pattern on to his descendants, that is, to regenerate the cultural traditions and social groupings which form the basis for society. Finally, taken in isolation, each particular ritual was found to be an occasion for the restatement of the opposition and unity of the two village halves. However, when considered in its entirety, the ritual cycle could be rather seen as another expression for the concern over the continuity and renewal of space/time or *pacha*. The state of being of the universe, its existence, is steeped in the endless business of birth and death and rebirth. Space, which is permeated by this process, at once defines the conditions of the regeneration and is itself the product of that regeneration.

In this paper I have tried to show how women's movement in space is only a small portion of a much more comprehensive cultural map which the Runa use in ordering their world. That map has been analysed in terms of the Quechua concept of *pacha* or space/time. In our discussion, we have found that many elements of the Runa dual world are strongly associated with male or female principles; the mountain heights as opposed to the valley bottom, the rainy season as opposed to the dry. These associations not only indicate basic attitudes held about the nature of men and women, but they also provide us with a kind of blueprint as to how the entire Runa world, social, cosmological, as well as physical, is perceived to be interrelated. The two elements in nature, whether man/woman, mountain/valley, or rainy season/dry season, are seen as being opposite yet inextricably linked and somehow equal on another level. Male and female are opposites in terms of human reproduction, and yet from the point of view of the bilateral kinship system and their nearly identical roles in terms of agricultural production, both are seen as equally important to the maintenance of society. The spatial extremes of high and low, and opposites such as rain and sun, interact in much the same way. The extremes identify boundaries, both spatial and state-of-being, and yet it is at the juncture of these oppositions where the essential components of social life are generated.

The juncture of high and low occurs in the village where social life is perpetuated relatively free from the antagonistic elements on the outer borders of the Runa world. Duality thus ties human categories together in a larger structure which we have here viewed from the concept of *pacha* and in which women and men form only a part.

In closing, it should be kept in mind that the conceptualisation of space/time is an ideal pattern which the Runa apply to a world of real-life happenings which are not always consistent with the conceptualisation. Beyond the boundaries of an ideal *pacha*, many incongruencies emerge. Migration to urban centres, both in the highlands and on the coast, places the native perception of the order of the world under extreme tension. Women's mobility in many instances is extremely limited and the absence of the dual organisational form at the local level in these foreign environments creates a structural vacuum at the very focus of the cosmological view. To a certain extent, new organisational forms have appeared to fill this vacuum.[5] However, even when absent from it, the valley and the village remain the migrants' most important reference point. Many eventually return home, their sojourn in the outer world receding to the realm of a fading adventure. Others travel back to the village yearly to celebrate one of the important *fiestas*. For those who never return, a breakdown in the continuity of the system seems never to be complete. Always there remains a deep-seated loyalty and affinity to the land of one's birth; to the earth itself, whose rhythms and expanses are at the very centre of life's meaning.

# Notes

1. The crystallisation of my ideas along these lines was greatly influenced by the work of Billie Jean Isbell (1976), Vallée (1972), and Barette (1972).

2. Field research was made possible by a generous grant from the Norwegian Council for Research in Science and the Humanities and the Lumholtz Fubd, the University of Oslo.

3. The Quechua word for time in the sense of a particular event is *kuti*, thus *iskay kuti* or two times. A more specific Quechua term for place is not used, the Spanish-based term *sitia*, being used instead.

4. There is evidence that a *hacienda* at Pincos existed as early as 1650 (Jimenez de Espada 1965: 14).

5. Doughty's (1970) discussion of migrant clubs in Lima demonstrates how the dual organisational principle is applied in the urban context.

# 3

# Women's Space in a Men's House: the British House of Commons

*Silvia Rodgers*

## Introduction: The Premiss of Invisibility

This chapter suggests that the House of Commons at Westminster shares many features with the Men's Houses of certain primitive societies, where the male/female dichotomy is at its sharpest, and where the women are confined to the domestic space and are excluded from the Men's House – the centre of the public domain. The attempt to draw parallels may at first glance seem too far-fetched, since the House at Westminster does have a space of sorts for women: out of 635 seats for members, 19 are currently occupied by women (see Figure 3.1 and, for comparison, Figure 3.2). I was drawn to this comparison, however, after reading the literature on other societies, and from my observations, conversations and interviews with members of the House of Commons, of both sexes and of the two main parties. References by MPs to the precincts of the House as 'a male preserve' were made with a regularity that demands attention. The House is, after all, the central political insti-

**Figure 3.1:** Space Occupied by Women in the Membership of the House of Commons 1980

**Figure 3.2:** Women (18 years and over) in the Population of the United Kingdom, 1979. Numbers supplied by David

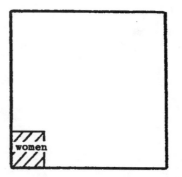

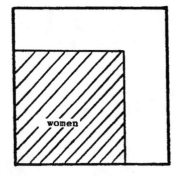

tution of this complex society, the pivot of the nation's legislation, and the reflector and generator of social changes.

Before analysing current material from and about Westminster I want to give some comparative material: one from a distant and tribal society, the other from British history.

Tribal societies across the world rigidly exclude women from Men's Houses and ritual secrets and their model for a male is sharply characterised by aggression, public display and self-confidence. The model for a female is equally familiar: the complementary one of submission, dependence and competence in the domestic sphere.

One such Men's House is that of the Iatmul culture of New Guinea and its very vivid description by Gregory Bateson (1967) evokes the atmosphere of the Chamber in the current House of Commons. After that comes a brief description from the old House of Commons before it was burnt down in 1834. This was a time in British history when the models of the sexes corresponded particularly closely to those of the tribal society described, where women were given a *space for listening but not for seeing or being seen.*

### An Iatmul Men's House in New Guinea

In his account of the ceremonial Men's House of the Iatmul culture of New Guinea, Bateson likens it first to a church and then to a club. It is 'a splendid building with towering gables at the ends' (1967: 123). It has the appearance, the atmosphere and the taboos of a church, but instead of 'austerity' or 'meek devotion', there is 'pride and histrionic self-consciousness' (ibid.: 124). The greatest Iatmul men are those who not only have material or esoteric achievements, but who also have the dramatic and debating skills to hold the centre of the political stage.

As a symbol of the chief ritual and political activity, the Men's House *is* a political stage. 'The debates are noisy, angry, and above all ironical.' It is also a club-house where men meet and gossip but one 'in which men are not at their ease but conscious of being in the public eye, in spite of being separate from their womenfolk'. Entry into the Men's House of the Iatmul is strictly forbidden to women, but they are expected to listen outside when the men are preparing for the most important rituals. The preliminary flute music is played 'in the knowledge that it is listened to by the women who are standing outside. The men are extremely conscious of the unseen audience of women' (Bateson 1967: 128). There are occasions when some women participate in public ritual, but they are *never* allowed to enter the Men's House. The idea of a woman setting foot inside is linked to the phrase, 'breaking of the screens'. When women are found inside the Men's House in this society, it is a symbol that the community has disintegrated (Bateson 1967: 135).

The contrast in male and female emotional expression among the Iatmul has a parallel contrast in spatial location. The men occupy themselves with aggressive and public activities 'which have their centre in the ceremonial house' while the women quietly carry out the mundane activities concerned with food preparation and child-rearing 'which centre around the dwelling house and gardens', the domestic space (Bateson 1967: 123)

## The British Men's House at Westminster

The structural opposition of male/female in Victorian England has many similarities to that described of the Iatmul of New Guinea. In the nineteenth century the public domain was controlled by men. Ideally the women's role was confined to the domestic and the private, although some women were active in a variety of economic and peripheral political spheres. The Old House of Commons was burnt down in 1834. A contemporary account, written before the fire, describes the House of Commons as having a chamber that was overcrowded and which had no public galleries. It advocates a new design and states

> Ladies in recent years had listened to debates concealed in the roof-space, peering down through the central ventilators in the ceiling of the House . . . . The ease with which they heard was used against such a method of ventilation . . . . The ladies then must have new accommodation. (cited by Port 1976: 13)

After the fire in 1834, the building was redesigned, with the new House still basically a Men's House with no provision for women *inside* the Chamber. The role of women who were wives or friends of the political elite was acknowledged in their spatial assignment to the peripheral Ladies Gallery.

The present House of Commons, rebuilt after the Second World War, was very closely modelled on the New House designed by Barry and Pugin in the nineteenth century. A brief outline of the spatial layout of the central area of the Chamber might be useful (see Figure 3.3). The floor, the operative area of the Chamber of the House, is divided into right and left.[1] This classification of physical space, as seen from the Speaker's chair, derives from the cultural map of political power. Those in government sit on his right; those in opposition, on his left. Factions and minority parties sit in more or less defined areas. The despatch box is the place of confrontation between the government and the opposition. Order is kept by the Speaker, assisted by the Clerks at the table.

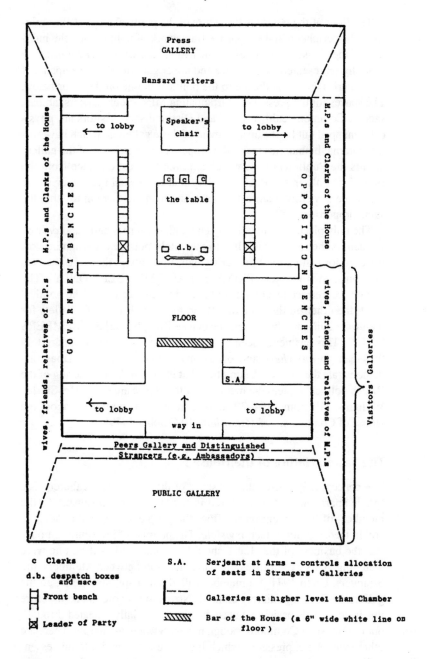

**Figure 3.3:** Layout of Chamber of House of Commons, with Galleries above

The floor of the House is the centre of the political stage at Westminster. The peripheral and supportive framework of politics, and the interface of the House with the rest of the nation, and with other countries, is spatially represented by the outer and upper galleries. The occupants of the galleries are the audience to the political drama on the floor below. The spaces for the press, non-participating MPs, spouses, peers, ambassadors, Commonwealth visitors and Distinguished Visitors are physically mapped out by the arrangement of these galleries, which have further internal boundaries marked by ropes. The largest part of the gallery area is the Public Gallery, which is at the furthest distance from the floor. It is only in the Public Gallery that the sexual symmetry of the electorate is visibly manifest: women and men are there in roughly the same proportions.

The only place used by all women members across party and *only* by women, is the toilet which lies immediately outside the Chamber, off the corridor behind the Speaker's Chair. In addition, there are two sets of rooms, each marked 'PRIVATE, LADY MEMBERS ONLY'. The one on the Terrace level tends to be used by the women of the political right, the other on the principal floor, by the political left. Toilets for men were built into the original design and simply marked 'MEMBERS ONLY'. This has never been changed. New women members are told they can go *anywhere* and occasionally make mistakes. Does this demonstrate the implicit assumption that in the symbolic ordering of the British political system the members of the House are men? Mrs Shirley Williams, MP from 1964–79, writes, 'it tells one quite a lot about the House of Commons. . . .' (*Guardian*, 10 October 1979).

## The Sacred Nature of the House

The conceptually self-contained space of the central political arena is a 'place apart', and as such sacred in the Durkheimian sense.[2] To the members of Parliament on the floor the people sitting in the galleries are, in theory if not in fact, *invisible*. The premiss of invisibility implies that the business of the House should be conducted as if no one were watching. This exemplifies the basic division between Members and Strangers. Up to 1971 if a member called out 'I spy Strangers', all the galleries were immediately cleared. Nowadays a vote is taken before this is done. This basic dual classification is spatially repeated throughout the House of Commons though not everywhere as sharply. There are other symbolic expressions which introduce the sacred into this essentially political space: not only as a place apart but in other ways in which the notions of the sacred and the religious are perceived.

*The Speaker:* without his daily procession and prayers, the Commons sitting cannot start. The prayers are witnessed by members only. The Speaker with his ritual regalia, esoteric knowledge, and experience of the House, symbolises the continuity of Parliament. Though a Member of Parliament, he is, in his role of mediator, essential to the order of the House, and above party politics. Through his prayer he is the link to the established religion. A member's entry and exit into the chamber is marked by a bow towards the Chair.

## Parliamentary Privilege and Immunity

Parliamentary privilege provides a barrier of immunity and rights by which MPs are protected from certain categories of actions. This protection is regarded as essential to the proper functioning of the institution. The concept dates from the reign of Edward the Confessor and was given statutory recognition in the Bill of Rights (1689).

*Membership of the House:* Every MP has successfully passed through an election which is a corpus of rigorous *rites to passage*. The ultimate incorporation into the new status of MP is a ritual on the floor of the House (the most sacred area), which is charged with awe and emotion, particularly for the initiant.

*Architecture:* The House was rebuilt in the nineteenth century in the neo-gothic style, as were churches of the same period.

The configuration of symbols suggests, then, that the House at Westminster has certain essentially sacred aspects. That the House also accommodates the profane and can be seen as a noisy and even bawdy club, will be shown later in this chapter. I shall anticipate this by interposing a few typical words from a male MP at Westminster which echo those of Bateson on the Iatmul: 'the House is fine if you are at home in a London club or a miners' club, and if you are as tough as old boots and enjoy the ribaldry of the House'.

## The Tiny Space for Women

For the audience in the galleries, the most striking feature, apart from the small size of the chamber, is the virtual *absence* of women, shown up by the occasional presence of one. Women are consequentially conspicuous by their scarcity rather than by their individual styles in dress and hair. In England, since 1918, women over thirty have had the right to vote. Since 1928 when the power base for the House, the electoral register, became open to both women and men, they have had *equal* franchise. It was also in 1918 that some women were given the right to fight to sit as equal members with men inside the House of Parliament.

The first woman MP did in fact enter the House in 1919.[3] Instead of the steady increase of women MPs which might have been expected throughout the subsequent sixty years, the House has stayed almost exclusively male. The space for women reached its maximum in 1964 with 29 women members. At present it has shrunk to 19.

This poses a contradiction. The House which itself legislated for women to participate on equal terms in this centre of politics, which has legislated for equal rights throughout society, including the Sex Discrimination Act in 1975, remains severely unbalanced in its representation. The last sixty years have seen significant changes throughout society, including some improvement in the rights of women. Yet this legislature which both *reflects* and *generates* social change appears perpetuated as essentially a male precinct. Is this cultural lag, this contradiction between theory and practice, an inherent fault in the House, in the structure of the political system? Or does it derive from the society at large? I shall return to this puzzle at the end of this chapter.

As noted, the House does have a legitimate space for women – a space in *theory* equal to that of men. In *practice*, it is less than 3 per cent of the total space. Nevertheless it is a legal space for women, however tiny, and since May 1979, for the first time, a woman has occupied the top space. Do these facts negate the analogy drawn with the Men's Houses in exotic societies which exclude women from these centres of political activity? Or does the inescapable fact that the space for women is resistant to growth, and the constantly recurring reference to 'this man's club',[4] justify at least the question: '*Is* it a Men's House?' and if it is, 'How is it maintained as such?'

## The First Woman MP and Those Who Followed

The first woman to enter the House was Nancy Lady Astor, an American by birth. She took her husband's constituency in 1919 when he went to the House of Lords. Although she could be said to have come into the House as a male surrogate, she tried to secure a firm place for women within this core of British politics. She devoted her time to women's causes and when, in due course, she was joined by other female MPs, extended herself across party boundaries to make women friends. But her attempts to form a *Feminine Fourth Party* failed. Her female colleagues saw themselves primarily as party politicians, and as persons, rather than as women, and preferred to apply themselves to broader issues.[5] Extracts from the diaries of one of Nancy Astor's male colleagues, Sir Henry or 'Chips' Channon, provide a revealing view.

Chips Channon was an American who became a British national, and in 1935 an MP. His deep desire to be accepted as part of British tradition, British society and the British House of Commons required him to conform to the commonest denominator of the dominant category. His anomalous status and his attempts to be more British than the British, rather than reducing the validity of his diary (as suggested to me at the seminar) make it a particularly useful tool with which to illuminate the ideal. He had to learn the symbols and applied them more closely to the traditional ideal than his more secure colleagues. He could well see in Nancy Astor a threat to his own acceptance: both were American by birth, both had joined the same sector of British society. He might be classified with her, who had transgressed the traditional norms of the House of Commons, instead of those with whom he wished to be categorised.

Nancy Astor, as the first woman MP, must indeed have been a symbol of threat to his whole cosmology, of which the male integrity of the House – 'this tawny male paradise' – (Channon 1967: 129) was the core. In this he is like a member of the Men's House in New Guinea, to whom a woman inside the Men's House signifies the collapse of the community. His diary shows how this early antipathy to her develops into perceiving her as a witch; the following phrases are in chronological order:

18 April 1934: 'She is a queer combination of warm heartedness, originality, and rudeness. I find her anti patica [sic]' (p. 31).

24 February 1936: 'She rushed about like a decapitated hen' (p. 59).

8 May 1940: 'Lady Astor rushed about, intriguing and enjoying the smell of blood' (p. 246).

4 December 1941: 'How I loathe the interfering termagant' (p. 313).[6]

23 March 1944. ' . . . this mad witch is still loved by her husband after nearly 40 years of marriage' (p. 390).

## Reclassifying Women

### Women as 'Matter Out of Place'

The impression gained from recorded comments by Nancy Astor and from entries in Channon's diaries and other accounts of that period,[7] is that neither Nancy Astor, nor her female colleagues were ever accepted as *women*. Some were more or less tolerated, and perhaps accepted, as *honorary men*. As *women* it seems, they were (and are) regarded as 'matter out of place'. This phrase has been used by Mary Douglas (1966), for things from one category found within the domain of another category. Such intrusions are seen as a threat to the purity and integrity of a category; and as elements that pollute, they have to be dealt with or removed. This section of the paper will be concerned with the devices used by the members at Westminster to cope with the pollution or contamination of their own category.

The men of New Guinea protect the boundaries of their Men's Houses by the deterrent of violence. Contamination by the presence of women is controlled by the threat of rape and assault. The Members of the House at Westminster cope with the intrusion of women by more subtle strategies, each one effectively a re-classifying or de-classifying device.

Common practices include attempts to throw doubt on a woman's femininity, to question her legitimacy in the House, to place her on a different plane of reality. Nancy Astor, when she first entered the House, was treated as invisible: 'Men whom I had known for years would not speak to me if they passed me in the corridor' (Brittain, quoted in Vallance 1979: 23). Even today, women in the present House are seen as alien, as children or as unreal. None of these categories has the legitimate right to be in the House. These extracts from conversations exemplify the ways in which some male MPs reclassify women members:

> She was small, scruffy . . . an odd-ball . . . like an alien from another world.
>
> [She was] so young she was like everybody's daughter.
>
> She is very nice, but so unreal, and she did such funny things like having a baby and now she is gone.
>
> [The women are] a rum lot.

There are, of course, women who are successful in the House and who have to some extent been accepted by the men. This accommodation has in part been achieved by their symbolic reclassification (1) into the category of men, or (2) onto a supernatural plane, or (3) into both categories. Reclassification into the category of men is usually marked by the epithet 'honorary man'and is accompanied by references to characteristics deemed to be male attributes. These range from clarity of mind to the capacity to drink beer. Other women are regarded as not having the required qualities of the female stereotype such as softness, warmth and reticence, but rather as being tough, ruthless and aggressive. Presumably, these attributes qualify a woman for the category 'man'. Some women members who are no longer in the House are elevated to the supernatural plane, by being relegated to mythical times. For example: 'There will never again be ones like Barbara Castle, or Dame Irene Ward, or Joan Vickers who defeated Michael Foot.' I have shown how Nancy Astor, who succeeded as a feminist rather than a parliamentarian, was described as 'witch' and 'termagant'. These creatures, unlike the supernatural categories reserved for women who are or were acknowledged as 'men', are female and have powers that are negative. How Mrs Thatcher is classified, both into the male and the supernatural categories, by her colleagues inside the House will be discussed later. By these reclassifications, the members of the Men's House would seem to be saying that women, as women, cannot succeed inside the House.

## Nature/Culture at Westminster

I agree with Hastrup that though there is no clear-cut opposition between nature and culture it is nevertheless helpful to use this dichotomy as an analytical tool. I shall follow Ortner who reshapes the duality into: nearer to nature/nearer to culture. Ortner shows how the physiological functions of women are often used by society to exaggerate the dichotomy of nature/culture. She argues that it is by their special *reproductive* capacities that many societies place women nearer to nature, while men's *productive* activities afford them a place nearer to culture. The physiological function relevant to this paper is child-bearing. This is woman at the epitome not only of her femininity, but of her 'natural' creativity. A woman Member of Parliament who is pregnant is creative concurrently as a woman and as a 'man', and this is too powerful and threatening to be acceptable to the House of Commons.

The ways members of the House react to a colleague's pregnancy are particularly revealing of some of their underlying feelings towards the women. These feelings are seldom expressed directly. They are communicated obliquely in joking and other forms of verbal behaviour. As I have tried to show, devices by which women members are reclassified are ways of maintaining the illusion that the *integrity* of the House as a male domain is kept inviolate. A woman who is visibly pregnant, or known to be breastfeeding, is at her most explicitly female. There is no way in which she can be classified as anything but a woman. The reactions to *pregnant* women members in the House indicate how portentous is the confusion of the domestic with the public. Having said that the categories of nature and culture cannot be kept discrete, I shall suggest that the efforts to do so in this domain are probably as tenacious as in any social context.

The reaction of some women members to a colleague's pregnancy is no less extreme than the men's. Why should women be so hostile to another woman's pregnancy and breastfeeding? Women whose success has been geared to the male construct have discarded the symbols by which they would be anchored into the traditionally female domain of domesticity and nature. Perhaps they fear that if one of their women colleagues openly combines the public symbols with the female and domestic ones, they themselves will be at risk of being seen as the women, which on some levels they, of course, are. Their position in the dominant category is after all a tenuous one. To be seen to share a room with someone who is breastfeeding her baby could lead to being identified, by association, as a 'woman' and as such 'out of place' (see Channon's fear of identification by association, Channon 1967: 11).

What, in practice, are the reactions of members to the pregnancy of a colleague? And how is it experienced by the pregnant woman herself? From my interview with one MP who was pregnant during a recent Parliament, it seemed that no concessions had been made even when she was seven months pregnant and obviously tired. The only people who had tried to help her during one of those long late-night sittings were one backbench MP and one Minister, both due to retire. The latter had been persuaded by his *wife* to let the pregnant MP lie down for a rest in his ministerial room. When the Minister's driver opened the door he mistook her for a possible terrorist.

The government Whips had promised her that they would be co-operative and arrange 'pairing' for her so that she could occasionally take an evening off. In the event, this promise was not kept. In all fairness, it must be pointed out that at this politically critical time even members near to death were not being 'paired'. Nevertheless I gained the impression that the pregnancy was not treated by the majority of her colleagues with sympathy. For some whom she herself regarded as being behind the times, it was even an embarrassment. She had to return to the House when the baby was seven days old, because (as before) there was no 'pairing'. The knowledge that she was breastfeeding provoked sniggers from some men. It drew overt and covert hostility from some women members. When one of them saw the husband with the baby enter one of the rooms marked LADY MEMBERS ONLY, she requested the nearest policeman to deal with 'all sorts of strange people in there'. Others accused her of 'letting the side down'. The pregnancy and what followed had been fraught. She confessed to dreading the prospect of enduring another while she was a member of the House.

The reactions of her female colleagues form a continuum spanning the open hostility described, covert resentment and tolerance that is often somewhat ambivalent. The latter categories of attitude were expressed as 'not having minded too much', perhaps because 'the baby was a pretty one', or because the MP herself had been liked. She was criticised for having gone 'too far'. This applied particularly to her campaign for a creche in the House: 'Before you know it, there'll be ten of us all having babies here!' She was praised for getting the 'worst of the pregnancy over' during the recess. This was contrasted with the pregnancy of another woman MP a few years back, who had apparently walked about the House 'so huge that everyone had been frightened that she would give birth within the precincts of Westminster'. It sounded ominous and a desecration, though some members cannot recall this phenomenon.

Some male MPs, even those with small children, tended to regard this pregnancy as an 'odd' or 'a funny thing'. Some feared that the pregnancy might disturb *other* members because it was not 'normal' to the House: 'it would be like having someone around who is not equal to the rest and expects preferential treatment'.

Other women MPs have been pregnant while in the House. The crucial difference is exemplified by Lady Tweedsmuir in 1947, as described by her contemporary, political opponent Jean Mann:

> She [Lady Tweedsmuir] probably created a precedent by attending and taking part in debates right up to a few weeks of the birth of her child and fooled everyone about the pregnancy. The women MPs saw her looking bonnier than ever . . . . Moreover, she would sit watching to catch the Speaker's eye for hours, even in the seventh month. [They concluded she was not pregnant.] But shortly after the House broke up for the recess the press announced a daughter for Lord and Lady Tweedsmuir. (Mann 1962: 18, 19)

### The Fear of Childbirth within the Precincts of Westminster

If classification is organised within the nature/culture framework it follows that a birth on the very central space of politics would be more than grossly 'out of place'. A plethora of enthnographic examples indicate that places of birth are commonly treated as areas endangered by natural and supernatural forces. It is not within the scope of this chapter to elaborate this, only to make clear that in those societies the rest of the community is often protected from these sites of power and danger, by various forms of ritual isolation.

In some societies the husband is thus excluded from the child-bearing process and everything involved with it. In others, the ritual takes the positive form of the *couvade*. The *couvade* is the term given by Tylor (1865) to the various ways in which the prospective father is ritually linked to his pregnant wife and to the birth process. There are several interpretations. What is of relevance to this discussion is that pregnancy in the House of Commons is 'nature' moving into the space reserved for 'culture' at its most polarised, in the same way as the *couvade* is 'culture' (symbolised by the father) moving into the space reserved for 'nature' when most explicitly creative and feminine. The *couvade* is then the mirror image of pregnancy in the House and as such illuminating. The father may be excluded from the very moment of the birth, but his ritual link lasts from when the birth is impending until the baby is a few days old. The father is crucial for the physical and metaphysical well-being of the child until its integration into society. Significant for my thesis is that the *couvade* requires him to *relinquish his key symbols of manhood and culture*. Otherwise, by the presence of the father, the place of nature would simultaneously become a place of culture. The danger of this fusion of categories is reduced by the surrender of the symbols of culture.

When an MP is overtly pregnant, or breastfeeding on the precincts of Westminster, the two categories of nature and culture at their most polarised, where culture is most explicit and powerful, occupy the same space at the same time. Since no symbolic concessions are made to avert or reduce the potential danger, as in the *couvade*, the fear engendered by the (albeit remote) possibility of a birth on the precincts is explicable. It is pertinent that the recent case of pregnancy referred to above was widely publicised, not only within the House but throughout the country, by an extensive press coverage. In contrast, Lady Tweedsmuir had kept her pregnancy well hidden from men and women MPs. She participated in the procedures of the House as usual, and did not expect any concessions. The symbol of her femininity at its most creative was kept to the private domain, and never intruded into that most public domain, the House of Commons.

## Joking Behaviour and Excessive Courtesy

Jokes often relieve the tensions of parliamentary occasions. They are also used to undermine the arguments of senior politicians. Otherwise, men are not unkind to each other, and their jokes would not exploit any physically eccentric features of a male colleague. Jokes, and even jeers, are, however, used to diminish the category of women when the reclassification device is found inadequate. All members are in theory equal regardless of their physical attributes. Ribaldry based on the physiological and anatomical features peculiar to women is an attempt to mark out the invading category as unsuitable, and to render it harmless and ineffective. Douglas points out jokes which 'bring forward the physiological exigencies to which all moral beings are subject', as being a 'universal and unfailing technique of subversion' (Douglas 1968: 95). They are a particularly cruel and appropriate weapon in the Chamber of the House where self-confidence is at such a premium. Douglas writes 'all jokes have a subversive effect on the dominant structure of ideas' (ibid.: 95). I suggest that jokes are also the method by which a dominant category defends itself against a disadvantaged but threatening category. In the House, the dominant category, in an attempt to reinforce its own boundaries, makes jokes which tease out the sexual features peculiar to women. Jokes are the symbolic and acceptable way of indicating that one particular woman, or a group of women, have no legitimate place in this area of politics and authority. Some members, however, whose ideology allows them to say overtly what for their colleages must remain covert, do not need to resort to joking.[8]

Most of the joking behaviour is directed at individuals who seem to be particularly resistant to the reclassification devices. For example, whenever one particular woman rises to speak, she is greeted by several of her male colleagues mimicking her in high-pitched falsetto tones. Another, known to them all as the '47-year-old Virgin from Barchester'[9] has to face a tougher and more embarrassing barrage of thinly veiled obscenities. There was one occasion, however, when the joking, which included a great deal of jeering, was focused onto a *group* of women. Inside the Chamber women avoid sitting in groups, but on one day during the debate on the Abortion Bill Amendment Act they did.[10] A deeply felt and shared concern led to a physically contiguous space being occupied by – variously estimated – seven or nine women members of the party of the political left. As they sat on the back benches they were the target of ribald jokes. These ranged from: 'Where are your hockey sticks' to 'Who is the Madam?' Men consistently sit in groups according to their point of view, or special interest, without provoking attention. Why was the group of women treated in this way? Probably because not only had they coalesced into a visible and effective category but had done so, not on a party political issue, but on a women's issue.

There is yet another method of undermining women MPs, and one which is classified by the participants themselves with joking behaviour. It is the display of excessive courtesy, and is apparently evidenced in the corridors rather than on the floor of the House.

### Women against Women

It should by now be clear that it is not only men who reduce the symbolic space of women inside the House. If I select one interview, it should be seen not as anecdotal but as encapsulating the attitudes of some other women members. This particular MP emphasised that she was not used to *working with women 'except as my secretaries'*. She preferred those directly responsible to her (whether in business or in government departments) to be men. She explained that in general, women tend to be 'diverted by minutiae' rather than to 'see a thing as a whole', whereas she herself valued organisational abilities above all else. She could not criticise Mrs Thatcher for having formed an all-male cabinet. She volunteered that the House was 'very much a man's club'. She enjoyed being of it.

In classifying herself so strenuously as a man, she somehow resembles the women who came into the House after Nancy Astor. Some of those women, too, appeared to have concurred with their reclassification as 'men'. Margaret Bondfield, the first woman member of a government, and then of a cabinet in 1929, did not seem displeased when Bernard Shaw, on the occasion of her adoption for a marginal, rather than a safe seat, wrote to her, ' you are the best man of the lot. . . . ' Nor did she object to being referred to as 'He' in a recital of documents when she was first a Minister (Vallance 1979: 52). Perhaps these women reasoned that if they excelled themselves as men, they would show that women were as good as – if not better than – men. Then there is a category of women, and it includes the MP quoted above, which agrees with the male construct. I suggest that this contributes to the devaluation of women and the concomitant reduction of their symbolic space. They realise that to achieve success within a male domain women must learn to manipulate the male symbols (see S. Ardener 1975: xv; 1978: 20). But, and it would follow, they think that it takes both longer to learn (see below), and also an exceptional woman, to excel at this manipulation inside the male domain which itself contains, ideally, exceptional men.

Others cherish their positions as anomalies. This affords some advantage as well as power (see below), and considerable satisfaction, and even pleasure. To be the only woman may at times feel uncomfortable and 'out of place', but it is also a visible measure of success. The only woman at the top may be unwilling to relinquish her loneliness, in case it diminishes the uniqueness of her achievement.

In the earlier period it was only Nancy Astor who disregarded the male framework of values, in which women's and children's issues are banished into the unimportant corners. It has been suggested that some of the younger members of the current and the last Parliament are more sure of their identity as women and thus less likely to defer to the male value system. From my own material – and it is very incomplete – the evidence is conflicting, and nowhere more so than in the attitudes to pregnancy.[11]

## Power and the Most Secret Places

As has been noted, women MPs comprise only 19 out of the total of 635. Yet in spite of the reclassification device, the effective and symbolic space of women is enlarged out of proportion to their share of the physical space. They are disproportionally conspicuous by their uniqueness, by their inherent and compounded anomalous nature, by the kind of person they have to be. To reach the House in the first place, and then to withstand and even flourish in this male club a woman has to be able to perform well in public. A woman who is inarticulate in terms of the dominant structures of this society would not put herself forward as a candidate, and if she did, she would not be selected.[12] Men say that once in the House women are not disadvantaged. On the contrary, they say, the leader of a party who allocates the places of power would remember all the names of the women MPs, but might overlook, or even muddle up, the male MPs. Since 1924, possibly with a tactical eye towards the female electorate, leaders have indeed given women a place in government. In the House this is symbolised by a seat on the front bench. With some exceptions, however, women are usually placed in departments dealing with women's issues. Education has been represented more frequently by a woman than any other department. This suggests that the traditional role of a woman as the educator and socialiser of children in the *home*,[13] has been transferred to the *public* domain.

It is a striking fact that the chief offices of state, the ones most valued within this male construct, have never been held by a woman. These departments handle the most secret material. They are responsible for finance, law and order, and relations with foreign powers.[14] One Minister, when asked why no woman had ever been Chancellor of the Exchequer, Home Secretary or Foreign Secretary, replied with the tautology: 'None of the women are senior enough.' The exclusion of women from the top secrets seemed as natural and as obvious as in the exotic societies of New Guinea and elsewhere. Other posts seemingly reserved for men are the jobs of Leader of the House and the Chief Whips of each party, which are concerned with the running of the business of the House. Bearing in mind the sacred nature of the House discussed earlier, it is interesting to note the explanatory phrases which were given for the exclusion of women from these offices: 'A woman may be Prime Minister, but she would never be able to have one of the jobs which deal with the internal arrangements by which the House conducts its affairs.' She would not be 'on the right wave-length for the heart of the mystery'; 'certain aspects of that inner mystery within a mystery could never be fathomed by a woman'; 'that inner sanctum which no woman could penetrate'.

## The Paradox of a Woman at the Top

Since May 1979 Margaret Thatcher has occupied the top space to the right of the Speaker. Does this fact invalidate my theme of the House as a Men's House, a male domain? It is important for this paper to distinguish how she is seen by the public from the way she is perceived from within the House, and to concentrate on the latter. Occasional backbench comments nominating her as 'the best man they've got' points only inadequately to her reclassification.

My contention is that Mrs Thatcher has not only gained entry into the dominant category but has also been embraced by various supernatural categories. This concurrent membership has created her as an anomaly of considerable power. 'Attila the Hen', a nickname coined by immediate colleagues, subsumes a plethora of categories. It is said that Mrs Thatcher herself has fostered the analogy to Queen Elizabeth I, the Virgin Queen of Divine Right. It has also been implied by those from within, that she takes the role of Queen, rather than of *prima inter pares*. Another appellation, which she encourages, is that of the 'Iron Lady', a term coined by the Russians. As it stands, the epithet evokes the Iron Chancellor, Bismarck and the Iron Duke of Wellington. Its transformation into the 'Iron Maiden' (as Joan of Arc, rather than the instrument of torture), not only by the press but within the House, echoes the myriad of anomalies contained in the original title in 'Attila the Hen';[15] 'Colleagues find her style somewhat unnerving', writes a lobby correspondent (Adam Raphael, *Observer,* 7 October 1979). I suggest that though a woman has occupied the most politically important space since May 1979, the essential nature of the House as the Men's House has not been altered.

## Where is the Boundary of this Men's House?

In 1936, Florence Horsbrugh, MP and Minister, described 'this citadel of male prerogatives' as defended by 'some fortress wall' (Vallance 1979: 102). The final part of this paper will attempt to locate this wall.

So far, all my material points in one direction. It can only be encoded as the message that men desperately want to keep the House as a male preserve. This is grossly misleading, of course, and I must now redress the balance. The original Bill – enabling women to sit in the House – was passed by an all-male House in 1918. Subsequent legislation which indirectly makes it easier for women to stand as parliamentary candidates has been introduced by male-dominated cabinets and passed by a male-dominated House. There are many individual men and women who, while seeing, and possibly enjoying the House of Commons as a man's club, express a genuine regret that it is one. Some cannot understand why it has continued as such; some would like to see more women in the House; and some expressed the wish particularly to see more women who had grown-up children. One male MP who 'would like to see hundreds of women in the House', blamed women for not putting themselves forward.

He is probably mistaken. A senior woman politician forecast that the number of women in the House will *decrease* even further, and the House *revert* to being purely a male domain. She blames this on the increasing work-load and hours, and also to the essentially male atmosphere of the House. It was during those long late-night sittings, when there was a 'smell of wool and sweat' that, to use her own words, she, as a woman, had felt 'out of place'. Several of her female colleagues share her view. But empirically the evidence that the House itself is a deterrent is in doubt; it almost points the other way. Women who have lost their seats make every effort to return to the House of Commons, in spite of having experienced the atmosphere and conditions.

That the House itself does not deter some women from coming forward is supported by the figures for the 1979 election. Out of a total of 2,576 candidates, 206 were women, and 19 were elected. Although the number of women contesting seats was higher than ever before, the sex ratio of candidates was still only 1:13, and the ratio of women to men *elected* only 1:33. The figures bring with them two further questions: *Why* is there this considerable sexual asymmetry in *both* figures? Why do the proportions change? In these questions lies the clue to the effective wall. The barrier which maintains this as a male precinct would seem to be determined partly by the national headquarters of each party, but its main siting is at the level of the constituency parties, where small groups of active party members select the candidates for Westminster. Each MP is not only a symbol of the party, but is at the same time a symbol of his constituency, a geographically and demographically defined unit of the United Kingdom. The personal name of an MP is only uttered by the Speaker when he calls upon a member to speak. Otherwise, every member is referred to by the name of the constituency.

Elizabeth Vallance (1978) points to the difficulties facing women when selection committees are choosing a candidate for a safe seat. Women I have interviewed would agree with her. One of the reasons given by constituencies, for this discrimination in favour of men, is their reluctance to risk a safe seat. They say: 'People don't vote for women'. According to recent opinion polls, and electoral results, evidence for this is – at best – ambiguous. Were it true that the electorate is reluctant to vote for women, it would make more sense to give women the safe seats and let the men fight the more difficult and critical marginal seats. And it is a nice irony that the women as the marginals of society, fighting the marginal seats, are thus the determinants of power. It is after all the marginal seats which decide which of the contending parties takes power.

Research at national and constituency levels might indicate how many women present themselves as potential candidates, and how the small selection committees, which are composed of both men and women, arrive at their choice of a candidate. Why, for example, does it appear that they consider that a woman should pass through a greater number of *rites de passage* than do the men, by fighting elections for marginal rather than safe seats? Leach (1961) has pointed to *rites de passage* as being 'markers of time'. It seems on this circumstantial evidence that the selectors think that women take longer to learn than men.

In British society the roles of women and of men are in a state of flux. The House of Commons has legislated, at least from 1918 up to now, towards changes in these roles. For the Iatmul of New Guinea the ideology and the identity of the Men's House are not in conflict with the ideology of the society, with its sharp dichotomy of the sexes. But in our society the traditional polarisation is no longer the unquestioned norm of the Victorian era. Contextually, then, the House of Commons sits uneasily.

## Conclusion

The space occupied by those who, by election to the House of Commons, enter the category of 'women MPs' is tiny. It has, as yet, not been satisfactorily explained why an enlargement of their political space, though jurally and ideologically feasible, does not happen. It cannot be accounted for by the usual discrepancy between the ideal and what happens on the ground; the gap in this case is too great. The ideations of power must be examined at various levels. Perhaps the tiny and tenuous space alloted to women MPs indicates that underneath our ideals, which are jurally and otherwise expressed, there still lies the belief shared with other societies, that women should not be prominent in positions of control and power in the public domain. Further research on the phenomenon of the British House of Commons as a 'Men's House' should now focus on the perimeters located in society,[16] in particular at constituency level. We have seen here how women who succeed in entering the political stage are reclassified. That this is of only partial and transient efficacy is borne out by the sustained repetition of the reclassifying processes. It is a pity that these processes are often reinforced by the tacit concurrence of some women members. Finally, we might suppose that an increased space for women in a future House of Commons would make reclassification even more difficult, and if the space were large enough, reclassification would become redundant, as the balance of dominance changes.

## Postscript

I wrote this paper in 1979 when Mrs Thatcher had just come to power. Now, sometime after she has left office, after a general election and after the election of a new Speaker, is a good moment to look again at the space that women occupy in the House of Commons. Has it increased after more than a decade of a woman Prime Minister? And have other events, especially the formation of a new party in 1981, and the regular televising of the Commons since 1990, made any difference?

There have been changes, but few. In a slightly enlarged Chamber, the percentage of women Members is higher but still only 9 per cent. Women still tend to come into the House in marginal seats. According to one woman Tory MP, the older women on selection committees 'prefer a man to look up to' (Stephen Castle, *The Independent*, 2 December 1990). Doors in the House of Commons marked 'MEMBERS ONLY' are still men's lavatories. The House of Commons is still repeatedly referred to as a men's club, a gentlemen's club; only recently, before the replacement, it was referred to as the bawdy playground of a boy's school, with Mrs Thatcher the tomboy in charge (*The Times*, 30 November 1990). Women are still reclassified. Julia Langdon, not a Member but a political journalist, was greeted by one MP with: 'Julia, my dear boy, how are you?' (*The Guardian*, 9 September 1991). An article in *ELLE* (July 1991) asks its women readers, 'Have you got the balls to be an MP?'

To bring small children into the House of Commons is still seen as inappropriate. Harriet Harman was told children were not allowed in the Family Room. This room is within the main part of the House, whereas the terrace where children are allowed skirts the Palace of Westminster on its riverine aspect.

Television has shown everyone how small is the space for women Members, but also that by that very fact and by what they wear – mostly primary colours – women make this space more visible. A grey suit on a woman is rare. When, on 25 June 1991, Mrs Thatcher announced in the House that she was going to retire at the next election she wore a shocking pink suit which eclipsed everyone and everything else. All eyes were drawn to that pink figure even before the cameras made clear who it was. Her choice of colour also symbolised her declared intention to head a faction that would oppose the government, perhaps only on one issue but a major one. As she also opposes the official opposition, whose colour she was sporting, she has accrued yet another anomalous feature.

As for the other anomalies: the Falklands campaign secured her as a warrior queen and member of several categories. The image of 'Attila the Hen' was embellished with the symbol of feminine eroticism in Western culture: François Mitterand recognised Mrs Thatcher as having the eyes of Caligula and the lips of Marilyn Monroe. A cartoon in *The Times* (Peter Brookes) depicted her as Oliver Thatcher to illustrate an article by Conor Cruise O'Brien that compared her to Cromwell (3 February 1988). There are enough testimonies, both private and public, that her colleagues feared her as a termagant with more than natural powers. In private some commentators confess to her magnetism as a woman.

During and after the battles to topple and then replace her, we were offered a feast of her anomalous identities. But the supreme epithet of anomaly was uttered three months later, when one Minister forecast her future role as 'the tribal figurehead, a sort of female Willy'. This was a reference to Lord Whitelaw (Colin Brown, *The Independent*, 7 March 1991).The not uncommon fate of women whose power has waned and about whom others feel guilty – guilt in this case is due to having so abruptly toppled her – is to be cast as witch. Although there is little evidence of this so far, John Pinnear in his Westminster Diary in *The Independent* detected a Wizard of Oz mood of 'Ding dong the witch is dead' (7 December 1990), and Robert Harris' article in the *Sunday Times* (18 November 1990) is headlined 'Thatcher is for burning now'. An allusion first coined by her when she said in the House: 'The lady is not for turning!' Michael Jones refers to her 'talons' (30 June 1991).

Her attitude to women in general has evoked criticism. Her legislation or absence of it, is seen to adversely affect other working mothers; the absence of any other woman in her cabinet was noted. In the last summer of Mrs Thatcher's government, the 300 Group which has done much to bring attention to the low percentage of women in Parliament, invited her to address their tenth birthday lunch on 18 July 1990. She accepted and they were delighted. She cut the birthday cake – not with a cake knife but the ceremonial sword they provided – and she voiced her support for the aims of the Group, but then devoted the substantial part of her speech to praising the family and introducing new measures to make errant fathers pay family support. On the whole she is regarded as not having done anything to increase the space for women either in politics or other professional areas.

At the end of her reign – her style was often likened to that of a reigning monarch, including the use of the royal 'we' – Isobel Hilton concluded that Mrs Thatcher was no more a feminist than was Boadicea. After 'her chariot thundered past . . . the watching women [were left] . . . far behind and spattered with mud' (*The Independent*, 26 November 1990).

John Major, Mrs Thatcher's successor, may drive a more down-to-earth vehicle, but when he formed his first Cabinet that oval table in the Cabinet Room had not a single space for a woman. After protests from some of his own Party – not by any means all – Mrs Lynda Chalker got from him a kiss and apparently a promise. The promise could not be honoured after the election in April 1992, as Mrs Chalker had lost her marginal seat. She was transferred to the House of Lords but remained in her old job. However, John Major has given two of the chairs at the Cabinet table to women – Mrs Virginia Bottomley and Mrs Gillian Shephard.

The space for women in the top stratum is enlarged even more significantly. That almost sacred space, the Speaker's chair, is now occupied by Betty Boothroyd, famed for having once been a dancing Tiller Girl. Though she is neither a wife nor mother, it is difficult to see her as anything but a woman. Nor has she sought to disguise her femaleness by donning the traditional wig. Nonetheless, since her election, I have heard comments about her voice being peculiar, not like a woman's but rather gruff and even bullying.

Occupying the space for women Members may, in general, be getting more congenial. Joking behaviour can still be sexist but it has become less harsh since the sessions have been televised. And even out of range of the cameras and the public gaze, there are signs that sexist overtones are diminishing. To Emma Nicholson's delight, her male colleagues 'insulted me as a man' by telling her that her views were 'unsound' (BBC4, 11 January 1991).

There is hope from other directions, too. Over the last ten years there have been developments that may eventually lead to an increase of women in the overall parliamentary space. The Social Democratic Party, formed in 1981, introduced a rule requiring a minimum of two women and two men on every short list of parliamentary candidates in each constituency. The Labour Party has followed this example. It also has three women Shadow Ministers, but then there has long been space for women in a Labour cabinet. Mrs Margaret Beckett has had enough support to stand for Deputy Leader in 1992. There is talk of banning men from some Labour Party selection altogether, though this has been criticised as sexist and not practical.

But it is PR (Proportional Representation) that would be the single most crucial factor for getting women into a Parliament. Except for France, all countries within the European Community and in Scandinavia have both PR and a higher percentage of women legislators than Great Britain (information from the 300 Group). This applies even to the Catholic member-countries of the Community where in certain respects female emancipation lags behind that in the United Kingdom.

The point is that to get more women elected a Party need only put women on its lists of candidates and that not to do so is now seen as too blatant a discrimination.

Of course, in some countries, Norway for example, where the percentage of women in Parliament is particularly satisfactory – 38 per cent – additional factors contribute. Norway has PR, but also social policies that include paternity leave and a Labour party that requires a minimum of two women out of five candidates and two men out of five on any short list. Its leader, Mrs Gro Harlem Bruntland, who has been Prime Minister twice, surrounds herself not with men but women: indeed, half her Cabinet are women (Isobel Hilton, *The Independent*, 18 February 1991). But for Great Britain, PR may be a long way off. The Liberal Democratic Party have campaigned for PR, Charter 88 (a multi-Party organisation) has taken it up and there is increasing pressure for it within the Labour Party. A public opinion poll in April 1991, conducted by Mori for the Rowntree Trust, indicated that 50 per cent of the public favour PR with only 13 per cent against; the rest don't know. The Prince of Wales too has been reported as being in favour of PR. But the Conservative Party is against it.

When, as in Norway, it becomes normal for a woman to be an MP, it brings great self-confidence to women. I had been blind to the barrier formed by lack of self-confidence until I watched the SDP and then the SDP-Liberal Alliance and now the Liberal Democrats try their best to get more women candidates. It is this barrier which starts forming in childhood that stops women from putting themselves forward in the first place, and reinforces the boundary of the selection committees.

What has emerged as another disincentive for women standing for Parliament is not a fact but a myth. The myth is that, for the backbencher, the House is a gruelling place on account of the hours it sits. The myth is perpetuated by Members anxious to make the House appear more macho and heroic in order to impress the voters. This deters women from entering and ironically the myth is also propagated by those very women Members who are campaigning to increase the space for women inside the House of Commons. It is quite obvious when one watches the proceedings on the television and sees the empty benches, that the hours the House sits are no reflection of how many hours each member sits.

Plans to change Parliamentary hours into a more conventional 9–5.30 working day have been discussed for decades. Now reformers – they include Harriet Harman, one of the women MPs – who want to get more women into the House of Commons, are trying to effect similar changes. Perhaps they will have second thoughts. The hours of parliamentary sittings may have been tailor-made for male barristers to attend court but they are the ideal flexi-time to suit a mother with small children (see Silvia Rodgers, *The Times*, 28 June 1991).

## Notes

1. The other spatial framework within the House of Commons, which is based on the dichotomy of Right and Left, is constructed to accord with the ideological polarities of the political parties. For the wider significance of this particular dual symbolic classification see Herts and Needham in Needham 1973.

2. Comments by Keith Hope and Shirley Ardener during the seminar led me to re-evaluate the extent of the sacred nature of the House of Commons.

3. Countess Markiewicz, though elected in 1918, did not take her seat.

4. It is important to note that the level at which these references occur is always *within* the House. Outside and at some distance from the House, the House might be seen more as a bisexual place.

5. Collis 1960, Sykes 1972. Eleanor Rathbone, who entered Parliament in 1935 as an Independent, said: 'We can never have a woman's party because of politics' (Mann 1962: 20). Rathbone, as Lindsay Charles pointed out, led a determined campaign to ameliorate conditions for women and children. Other women too have been instrumental in this area of legislation, not always by virtue of the portfolio allocated to them.

6. The two COED definitions are: (i) imaginary deity of violent and turbulent character; (ii) brawling, overbearing woman.

7. I realise that (to support my thesis) I am drawing on material which spans a gap of over sixty years. It is, however, recommended by members of the current House, with the Channon diaries singled out as evoking the present atmosphere of the House as a 'male institution'.

8. Sir Ronald Bell MP said in the debate on the Second Reading of the Sex Discrimination Bill, 26 March 1975: 'Differentiation by sex, . . . in general physical and mental characteristics is observed not only in man, . . . but throughout animal life. The polarisation of function, interest and attitude has been strongly marked at all stages of our development' *Hansard*, vol. 889, col. 591). To him the Bill was 'evil' (ibid., col. 593).

9. Age and place are fictitious in order to disguise her identity.

10. Elizabeth Vallance was the first to draw my attention to this event. Her account appears in Chapter V of her thesis (1978) and book (1979).

11. The recent (November 1980) formation of the '300 Group' designed 'to get more women into Parliament' suggests that women in and around politics will in the future be more willing to help other women get into the House.

12. No member of any 'muted' category (as formulated by E. Ardener, 1972; 1975a) could hope to flourish as an MP without adopting 'verbal fluency' in the code of the dominant category (S. Ardener, 1975, p. xiv; 1978, p. 21).

13. A striking example of this role is in Tamara Dragadze's paper in this volume.

14. Interviewed during the spy-case – the 'Blunt affair' – Lord Gordon-Walker, ex-Foreign Secretary, said that constitutionally the Secret Service need only report to the Home Secretary. It was up to the Home Secretary to report to the Prime Minister (BBC 4, 'World at One', 21 November 1979). The Prime Minister speaking in the House on the same day said: 'It was for the Home Secretary to decide whether the PM should be informed' *Hansard*, vol. 973/4, col. 407).

15. My own unpublished paper, 1979.

16. Some research along these lines has been done in the United States (Kirkpatrick 1976).

# 4

## Essential Objects and the Sacred: Interior and Exterior Space in an Urban Greek Locality[1]

*Renée Hirschon*

### Introduction

This paper examines aspects of the relationship of urban Greek women to their immediate physical environment through investigating the house, its interior arrangement and its immediate surroundings. The house is obviously an appropriate focus for the analysis of female activities and spatial organisation – the 'woman-environment' relationship (an area usually called 'man-environment studies', see Rapoport, 1976) – for the domestic *locus* of Mediterranean women in general has become a truism. Most often it carries implications of deprivation and of exclusion from the mainstream of life, but these negative and pejorative connotations may be questioned (Sciama, this volume, Hirschon 1985) for, as we shall see, in their domestic activities Greek women are concerned with the most vital aspects of physical and social life.

The case of Yerania is an interesting one. The houses were originally designed as units for single family residence, but they have been progressively subdivided through time. This arose from a complex of social, historical and political factors, among the most important being the provision of dowry for a daughter's marriage. Here, dowry takes the form of separate living quarters in the parental home. Nevertheless the independence of each nuclear family or 'household' is maintained; it is manifested in the creation of a separate kitchen, the realm of each housewife.

Most houses are thus shared between several households related through women, or have been in the past, and they are characteristically overcrowded. In this context, certain recurrent items of household furnishing might seem to an observer to be eminently unsuitable. We find, on consideration, that, although they serve some obvious practical functions, their particular form and their placing in the house can only be understood through the realisation of symbolic attributes and of their 'sacred' connotations. Here the presence of the 'sacred' is embodied in the large dining-table, the double-bed and the *iconostási*, some of the 'essential objects' of Yerania homes.[2]

In the wider context of social life the fundamental dichotomy of the 'house' and the 'road', the inner and outer realms, is the point of orientation for interaction between women in the neighbourhood. This spatial and symbolic division is mediated, however, by two items – the kitchen, which is the diacritical marker of each conjugal household and the exclusive area of each married woman, and the movable chair. The latter is taken out in the late afternoons when people sit on pavements passing the time in conversation and observation of neighbourhood activity. The opposition between 'inside' and 'outside' is bridged through these two 'marginal' items. On the one hand, food brought into the house is processed by the housewife in her kitchen; on the other, social exchange takes place through the extension of the inside realm as the chair is moved out onto the pavement. The association of women with spatial arrangement and objects in the home, and thus with the symbolic order, is seen to be an integral part of their daily activities.

Yerania is a poor district of the city lying a few miles north of the harbour of Piraeus. It was established in 1928 as part of a massive housing programme for over one and a half million refugees from Asia Minor who fled to Greece in the early 1920s. The refugee settlements are today totally integrated in the physical fabric of the city and can be distinguished only where the original housing remains. In Yerania there has not been much rebuilding despite the great number and variety of modifications which have taken place over five decades, and the standard size and pattern of the houses provides a base line for comparison. In the face of severe economic constraints, modifications to living space have made manifest, in material form, the priorities of each family which were ultimately culturally defined (Hirschon and Thakurdesai 1970).

The original structures were prefabricated, single-storeyed houses ('prefabs') made from panel board under pitched tiled roofs. They were semi-detached, containing two separate houses, mirror images of one another, under one roof. Each house had two main rooms (3.2m x 4m), third smaller room intended as a kitchen (2m x 3m) and a toilet (Figure 4.1), and was set in a courtyard, the size of which depended on its position in the block. The 'prefab' district as a whole covered about 80,000 sq.m over 32 blocks. The crowded conditions characteristic of the locality were already apparent from the earliest days: 550 Yerania houses contained over 650 families at the outset. In the next forty years, densities increased and few houses remained in single-family occupation over this period. Though census figures indicate a decline in density in the late 1960s there were still over 1,000 households and a total popula-

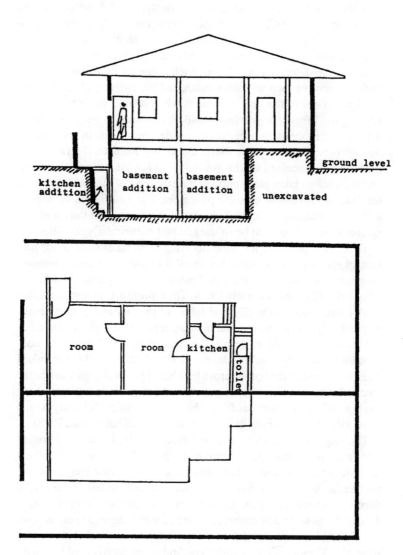

**Figure 4.1:** Yerania House

top – Section showing basement and kitchen additions
bottom – Plan of original house

tion of 3,500 persons in 1971 ('National Census', Statistical Service of Greece, unpublished).

## The Dowry in Yerania

The subdivision of the houses for several households and the continual pressure on living space must be understood as a response to the custom of providing daughters with dowry on marriage. Yerania houses have thus to be seen in the context of wider cultural features and conditions. In Greek society it has always been customary for the bride's family to provide some form of material wealth for the new household/family. The exact nature of this wealth varies depending on the community – fields, olive trees, poplars, sheep or gold coins, besides the household items themselves (linen, kitchen equipment). But in the city, and increasingly for rural families, the girl's dowry is categoric and explicit. It should be a 'house' (*spíti*) or more accurately, separate living quarters (Loizos 1975). Obviously there is much variation: a wealthy family may provide a villa in spacious grounds in an Athenian suburb or a penthouse apartment on the slopes of Mount Lykavittos. More usually, in the middle-income range, a dowry residence is a three- or four-roomed flat in one of the residential areas around the city centre, its exact size and appointments determined by their means. For some families who have capital and own a plot of land a possible solution is the construction of a small family block of flats of two, three or four storeys, each floor being a self-contained apartment. The parents' home with unmarried children will be on the ground floor, the oldest daughter (properly the first to marry) takes the first-floor flat as her dowry, the second floor goes to the second daughter, and so on. Observant visitors to the city are sometimes puzzled by the many unfinished buildings with their protruding reinforced concrete rods, and many of these cases can be explained by the unending obligation of Greek parents to provide housing for their female offspring. The resulting pattern, a vertical arrangement of older and younger families is also to be found in Yerania, not through increasing the height of the building but through underground excavation and the creation of basement rooms (see below).

Two interesting consequences result from the emphasis on a separate residence as dowry. First, the considerable capital outlay entailed in providing a daughter with a dowry appears to have affected family size, and acts as a most effective means for limiting the number of children after two daughters are born. Girls are seen as a heavy financial burden, an economic liability, and are wryly referred to as *grammatia*, literally 'promissory notes', but more aptly rendered as 'mortgages'. Certainly, family size has decreased in Yerania over four decades, as elsewhere in

Greece in recent times (Safilios-Rothschild 1969). Secondly, the provision of a house as dowry results in the physical clustering of families linked by female kin, so that households related through women live in close geographical proximity, even in the same dwelling. In Yerania, the co-residence of households related through women under the same roof has interesting repercussions on family relationships (see Hirschon 1983).

Economic constraints have always been severe in Yerania and the housing situation has been complicated by legal issues related to the 'refugee' status of the original inhabitants (Hirschon 1989: 70–76). The provision of dowry, therefore, posed specific problems and it was fortunate that these prefabricated houses facilitated the rearrangement of living space. By excavating under the house it was possible to create basement rooms and in this way almost to double the family's living area (Figure 4.1). So effective a solution was this and so great was the need to provide additional rooms that over 80 per cent of the houses have been modified in this way (based on a sample survey).[3] Even so, a daughter's dowry is usually not more than a portion of the family plot, one room or possibly two, either in the original prefab house or in the courtyard where a small house could be constructed (always illegally and often by the family members themselves). The general pattern which has emerged is one of subdivision through the generations: the ground-floor residence is parcelled out between married daughters together with any courtyard additions, while the parents' quarters are invariably in the basement. Far from being ideal for the infirmities of old age, their residence in the basement is based on the rationale of parental sacrifice, the subordination of comfort to the interests of their children. Although the basement rooms are not considered suitable as dowry in themselves, they have allowed for the provision of a 'dowry house' for daughters, adapted to the particular features of housing in this locality. As is common elsewhere in the city, bonds between mothers, daughters and sisters are maintained through physical proximity. The local group is composed of parents, unmarried children, married daughters and sons-in-law. This does not, however, constitute an extended or joint family, but a grouping of co-resident independent families, for marriage creates a separate nuclear family headed by the husband whose authority over his wife and family is undisputed (Hirschon 1983). The autonomy of each conjugal unit is revealed not only in the conduct of everyday life, but also in a physical and particularly graphic form, by the separate kitchen.

## The Kitchen

Besides the need to provide separate quarters as dowry for daughters, marriage entails another priority in the allocation of living space in the

Yerania houses. This is the creation of a separate kitchen, however small, for each married woman. The close kinship relationship between co-resident housewives, that of mothers, daughters, sisters, and the chronic pressure on space in these dwellings, might suggest that food preparation and cooking could be a communal task, or that a single kitchen would be shared by the co-resident families. On the contrary, however, each nuclear family has its own separate cooking area; since most of the houses are subdivided, there are commonly two or three kitchens on any one plot, and even four or five.

The original kitchen provided in the Yerania prefab, a small room of 2m x 3m, has of necessity been converted into a living or sleeping area (in none of the houses studied was it used solely for cooking). The kitchens created subsequently were notably small in size, accommodated in nooks and crannies, in basement alcoves, stairways and even partially excavated under the sidewalks. Their average size is around 2 sq.m, several being no more than 1 sq.m, but a number were more spacious at around 5–6 sq.m (sample survey).

The space then is conceived of primarily as a cooking area; the kitchen is not for communal or shared use, nor is it for family activity. There was only one case of a shared kitchen known to me, between mother and two married sisters, the three households being closely united in a state of open conflict with another family co-resident in the same house. The shared use of kitchens and the communal preparation of food by women who are not kin occurs in other Balkan societies where households are based on patrilocal extended families, and co-operating women are related by marriage to brothers (in the Serbian *zadruga*, among Sarakatsani shepherds). In Yerania, however, marriage confers independent status upon each woman regardless of her close kin in the same dwelling: the autonomy of each household is a central tenet of social life with the kitchen its physical marker.

The significance of the kitchen must not be underestimated in spite of its minimal size. Since its primary use is for cooking, the kitchen is the domain of the housewife, for in Yerania food is handled and prepared for consumption solely by the women; rarely do men even purchase food, which once supplied to the home is the concern of the women. In this community culinary ability is highly prized, being one of the main criteria for assessing a woman's worth. Food, its provision and preparation occupies the housewife's thoughts and actions for much of the day (Hirschon 1978: 82–84). Interestingly, the emphasis on preparation of food by women is highlighted in the case of edible raw foods – the abundant fruit of Greece, for example, usually eaten once a day, is never served 'untreated' in its 'natural' form. Oranges, apples, pears and peaches are not offered whole from a bowl but are first peeled and sliced, then offered on a platter by the woman of the house whose task this is.

As Lévi-Strauss has suggested, the transformation of the raw into the cooked represents a conversion process from nature to culture. The association of women with nourishment, the concept of the woman as a source of sustenance and her enduring association with food is a theme running through Greek culture (and indeed may have universal expression, cf.Ortner 1974: 80). Transposing the nature/culture opposition to the context of Yerania, it is the woman who, in dealing with the raw 'natural' substances of the 'outside' world, acts as the agent in the cultural process and by extension, the man is designated to 'nature' through his activities outside the home.

The transformation of food takes place on a daily basis in the tiny kitchens of the Yerania homes which provide in this sense the space where the 'inside' world, that of home and family, intersects with the products of the 'outside' world. The kitchen can thus be seen as a zone of transition: it is significant in this respect that the kitchens, among the many modifications in Yerania houses, are always added externally, tacked onto living areas. The association of pollution and cooking may be inferred from this external location of the kitchens (cf.Raglan 1964: 44,75); certainly, if nothing else, a marginal quality is suggested, as one might expect. The kitchen conveys a sense of its ambivalent character in its peripheral location while in the emphasis on a kitchen for every household it is the physical expression of central cultural notions relating to the family as a unit and to the woman's role within it. It has therefore the force of a major 'condensed' symbol (Douglas 1973: 29–30). Something of the ambivalent character of the kitchen is shared, albeit in a less emphatic way, by the standard chair common in these houses (see below, pp. 81–82); both link the 'inside' with the 'outside' and provide, or cross, the threshold between these two worlds.

## Interiors

Several striking features characterise the present state of Yerania houses: in the first instance continual pressures have resulted in the creation of new living areas, and calculations show that there has been an increase of built-up floor area by about 117 per cent. Since only 18 per cent of the structures have been demolished and rebuilt (in 1972) this has come about mainly through unauthorised modifications and additions to original dwellings. The excavation of basement rooms and the construction of extra rooms in courtyards are two common solutions which, as we have seen, are specifically related to the need to provide dowries for daughters, and separate kitchens for each married woman.

Despite the increase in living area, pressure on space has always been extreme, and a second characteristic feature of Yerania is that the original rooms have in the vast majority of cases changed to multipurpose use. The original kitchen has been converted into a bed/living room, while the two main rooms, originally provided as a reception and bedroom respectively, most often accommodate both these as well as other functions. They are simultaneously bedrooms, living-rooms and food-storage areas, but most important, the main room is presented as a formal reception room. The mixture of furniture displayed in these crowded rooms indicates the various uses, producing an immediate impression of highly congested, functional confusion which suggests a haphazard approach to the problems of living space.

This impression of impractical disorder is reinforced by the fact that much of the furnishing is unwieldy; it conforms to a standard pattern. One might expect that pressure on space would have long ago produced a practical attitude with foldable tables, convertible beds and easily stored items (as found in Japanese homes). On the contrary, space-saving furnishings are far from common: the housewife who was complimented on her spacious reception room with its low coffee-table instead of the large dining-table was embarrassed, explaining this inadequacy – they were saving for the full dining suite, for 'How can you receive people into your house without it?'

The main room, into which the newcomer is ushered on the first visit, is thus inevitably crowded: typically it contains the central dining-table, six matching chairs, a buffet-display cabinet filled with rows of glass and china, one or two sofa-divans (beds for children) and a clothes alcove in a corner (Figure 4.2). Alternatively a main room may contain the central dining-table, its six chairs, a single bed, a wardrobe, the refrigerator and some occasional chairs and tables. In a home with even less space, the main room may contain the double-bed of the couple, the dining-table, chairs and a wardrobe. The most important item of furnishing, however, is the central dining-table, where all formal gestures of hospitality are performed. In terms of frequency and duration of use, this room may be a child's bedroom or food-storage area, but in terms of significance it is the formal reception room and is presented and preserved as such by the family.

It is only after several visits to these houses that one begins to discern a pattern underlying the apparent lack of order. In the face of functional confusion there is a remarkable persistence of vision based on a sense of symbolic clarity. Extreme pressure on space has dictated the coincidence of several functions in each room, but if the Yeraniots could have

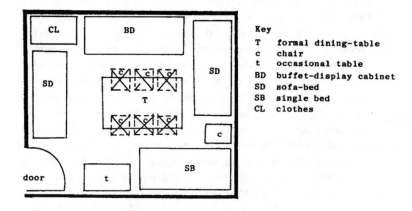

**Figure 4.2:** Reception Room (with other uses)

their way, there would be separate rooms for reception, for sleeping, eating and food preparation. These rooms must be understood, therefore, as reflecting two different levels of perception: on the one hand there is the mundane, everyday use, on the other the ideal or symbolic form, and this latter predominates and is expressed in the central dining-table/suite.

There are also other objects which recur regularly in the Yerania home. These 'essential objects' without which the home is incomplete are, besides the large dining-table, the double-bed, the *iconostási* and the standard wooden chair. Their particular significance, as we shall see, is that they evoke a dimension beyond practical or rational considerations in the organisation of space, for each, in a different way, provides a link with the metaphysical realm through its sacramental associations, thereby embodying a 'sacred' quality. And each item has a specific connection with the activities of the woman of the house.

### The Dining-table

A formal dining-room suite *trapezaría* is held, ideally, to be an essential part of every home's furnishing. It is an important item in a girl's dowry (which does not consist only of a 'house' but also of most of the furnishing and electrical appliances). A properly equipped house is one in which hospitality can be offered in an appropriate fashion, that is: centred round a large table. In fact, over two-thirds of the houses had the large dining-table (average proportions 1.3m x 1.5m x 0.8m), if not the complete suite, including six chairs and a buffet-display cabinet. A large sturdy table could of course provide a useful working space (for ironing, food preparation) but in the present arrangement of Yerania homes it is not used in this way, since the kitchens are now situated away from the main rooms (which alone can accommodate an item of furniture of this size). Thus in most homes a smaller folding table which has a purely utilitarian function is found in the kitchen, or the room nearest to it. Its purpose is stated graphically by the bright plastic covering, usually printed with designs of fruit, fish on a platter or other edible items. The dining-table, in contrast, is always covered with a textile cloth of fringed velvet or hand-embroidered cotton.

The room with the large table is used for the formal reception of strangers to whom the housewife offers the customary *kérasma* (a home-made sweet preserve, a small cup of coffee, a glass of water). It is also used for festive meals (celebrations of family life-crisis rituals such as baptisms, weddings, funerals), and on the name-day of a family member. It is significant that the preparation of a formal meal is idiomatically expressed as 'we make a table' (*kánoume trapézi*) or 'making a table' (*kánontas trapézi*), which suggests that the ritual offering of hospitality through food and drink in some sense 'constructs' the table. The physical object is revealed to be somehow incomplete for only through a functional enactment, in the expression of its symbolic correlates, does it fully 'become' itself.

Since the dining-table is not used on a daily basis but irregularly on formal family occasions and when strangers are received into the house, it should be understood as a ritual object and not simply as a three-dimensional item occupying an unnecessarily large area of floor space. The table evidently represents values beyond those of practical necessity alone; it has symbolic significance comprehensible in the wider context of Greek beliefs. In Orthodox Christian practice, the Eucharist or Communion Service, in which the common participation in food and drink is sanctified, is the greatest sacrament, and, like every meal, the formal festive meal is in fact patterned on this sacramental act.[4] Significantly, in Yerania houses, an icon of the Last Supper hangs on the wall near the table and, before eating, the sign of the cross is customarily made. At all meals bread is served; pieces which remain are not thrown away, and in other ways it is treated as a special substance. The table in Yerania, as the place of the formal meal, becomes endowed with the symbolic attributes of the activity, and itself becomes imbued with 'sacred' elements.

The table's other use, for the reception of visitors, is similarly suggestive of its symbolic function. In many cultures and since antiquity among the Greeks (Hocart 1969: 78), the stranger has received special treatment. Whether this is to be interpreted as a response of fear or of reverence (cf. Pitt-Rivers 1977: 162), or whatever other reason (cf. M. Herzfeld 1987), hospitality in Yerania involves an invitation into the home, an area normally closed to outsiders as well as to neighbours and casual acquaintances. The stranger to whom hospitality is offered is an 'extraordinary' being, for through his or her presence in the home the divide between the 'inside' and 'outside' worlds has been bridged.

The dining-table must be seen therefore as the embodiment of a set of notions interweaving the divine associations of commensality, family unity, the values of hospitality and the opposition of 'inner' and 'outer' realms.

## The Double-bed

In Yerania homes, each couple has a double-bed, its size and immoveability remarkable features in the context of available space. The double-bed may occupy as much as a third of the room's area and never less than about 20 per cent. It is highly significant that it is never used for extra seating; people are ushered onto sofa-beds, or extra chairs are brought in, but the double-bed is treated as an object 'set apart' (Durkheim 1976: 41). Furthermore, it is the centre of a ritual.

Before the Greek wedding ceremony, one evening is spent in communal celebration around the double-bed which the couple will share. Young people are invited to the new home 'for the bed' (*yia to kreváti*). They gather round as the bed is made up by young unmarried girls, friends and relatives of the couple, and as one man attempts to undo it, the sheets are struggled over. Once made, the visitors throw money onto it, and then a little boy is brought and dumped on the bed amid cheers. Sweetmeats and drinks are then served. These ritual actions suggest the farewell to virginity (the young girls, the struggle for the sheets), the wish for prosperity (money gifts) and offspring from the marriage (the little boy), and they underline the role of the double-bed in the marriage. As the *place* of conjugal union, in itself a bond of sacramental significance, the double-bed is also a sacred place. This bed symbolises the unity of the marriage, for to sleep in separate beds or for one spouse to leave the bed because of a row is considered a serious violation of the relationship.

The prevalence of these large beds is explicable in the context of ideals relating to marriage, procreation and conjugal unity, and its sacred character is revealed in the initiatory rituals as well as in the avoidance for mundane purposes such as seating.

## The Iconostási

Every home in Yerania has its *iconostási*, a shelf on which icons and other sacred substances are kept. The icons vary in number, while the degree of attention paid to this area depends on the religious commitment of the housewife. The oil lamp suspended in front of it may be lit every evening by devout women, or only a few times a year at major religious festivals, or, as in the homes of most of the older women, every Saturday evening. Each house in Yerania is a religious community, the spiritual world being present in the family abode, and, though the *iconostási* does not take up any floor area, it is a place – or sacred space – of concentrated spiritual presence. The *iconostási* should properly be in an eastern corner, preferably in the bedroom. In Yerania homes it is obviously found in a room of several purposes but its position matters far less than the fact that no house is without one and that through this presence, the house itself 'becomes a temple' (Raglan 1964; du Boulay 1974: 38, 54; Stahl 1976). The responsibilities for religious acts fall on the woman of the house; she is the intercessor for her family, caring for the spiritual needs of both living and dead members. Her role as intercessor is patterned on that of the Mother of God and her devotions in the home and outside parallel the role of the priest in the community's church.[5]

## The Standard Chair

The kind of chair referred to here – wooden, straight-backed, rush-seated and uncomfortable – is familiar to all who know Greece. It does not stack or fold and yet these chairs predominate in all Yerania houses. They are sturdy, small and lightweight, which may account for their popularity, which is undoubtedly reinforced by customary seating habits and convention (Thakurdesai 1974). Once again the presence of these chairs strikes one's attention, not because of their size this time, but because of numbers. Households are well-endowed with chairs – an average of three chairs *per head* was calculated. One household with three persons, however, had sixteen chairs, another of four persons had thirteen. These are interesting figures in themselves, even more so in the light of the poverty of the inhabitants and the crowded rooms. One might expect that chairs have little importance under these circumstances but closer observation reveals that chairs are among the 'essential objects' of the Yerania home because they are used in everyday contact with the world beyond the house. These chairs are brought out onto the pavements every afternoon during the warmer months (up to eight months of the year) and here the social life of the community has its public expression.

## The Exterior

The neighbourhood as social space is primarily an area of communication and of reciprocal exchange where the relative prestige and rank of families is assessed. In this part of the city, neighbourhood life is well developed and of marked character, and the neighbourhood, like the house, is the particular domain of female activity. Thus women are the chief agents and actors in the exchanges through which the reputations of families are estimated. Women are both the assessed and the assessors in the competitive relations between families in the neighbourhood. The maintenance of the home is obviously a crucial area of competence and together with it the housewife's attentions must also include part of the pavement and street. This area, extending from her wall roughly to the middle of the road, is swept once or twice daily and, as if to establish clear boundaries, some women even mark the pavement edge and lamp-posts with a neat line of whitewash. Since the house is closed to outside scrutiny, a woman cannot demonstrate her housewifely abilities directly. Thus the pavement and the street are 'annexed' as extensions of the home so that any neglect of this external area suggests incapacity within the home itself.

Contacts between women are vital in connecting unrelated families, the exchanges creating a pool of information linking families throughout the district. These unscheduled and spontaneous meetings take place during the morning and afternoon, but depending on the time of day, are very different in style and form.

### Mornings on Foot

During the morning, women meet in the vicinity of the home and these meetings have a transient and contingent appearance. They stand in small groups on street corners and pavements as well as in the neighbourhood shops, passing the time of day on apparent trivia. Domestic chores, food preparation, laundry, ironing and other matters of a routine kind are discussed, their significance resting in the way each woman conveys to others her commitment to domestic duties, her diligence and efficiency. Morning meetings must be brief though – a woman who loiters can only be neglecting the household chores which should fill her morning hours. Thus the contacts take place under the guise of some other activity such as buying fresh bread and shopping at the local grocer (cf. Bailey 1971: 1–2). Grocery shopping is particularly revealing as a pretext since many items purchased on a daily basis (sugar, rice, dried beans, tinned goods) are imperishables which could be more efficiently – but far less sociably – provided through a weekly shopping trip. It is quite in order for a woman to visit the grocer once or twice a day to obtain such items and in the process exchange a few words with whomever she meets. Women, therefore, far from being in total seclusion, manage to combine a high degree of social interaction outside the home with their primary obligations as housewives.

### Afternoons on Chairs

Afternoon gatherings are different in several respects. Though still informal and spontaneous, they include men as well as visitors from other neighbourhoods; the rhythm is leisurely, contacts last longer and conversational topics are broader. Significantly, too, the orientation of the group is not inward, as in the case of the morning groups of women but outward, directed towards the street. Passers-by are observed and stories and bits of information are told about them. Now the scene can be likened to an open-air theatre with the spectators seated on the pavements, though the spectators are also actors and part of the action (Thakurdesai 1974).

It is during these afternoon gatherings that the chair makes its appearance outside the house. At this time of day the woman is expected to have completed her housework and must 'take the air' (*na pári ayéra*) sitting outside her house for some hours. She comes out with a chair and a piece of crochet or embroidery, and sits facing her own door (inward) until she is joined by a neighbour or friend. Another chair or two are brought out and the seated group then begins to grow, facing outwards. A spare chair is usually available too as a foot-rest for the tray of coffee-cups, and it may be offered to any newcomer to the group.

The emphasis on sociability in this community is marked; it is an absolute dictate of neighbourhood life and cannot be avoided. To withdraw from patterns of social exchange requires conscious effort, incurs some cost and has little value (Hirschon 1989: ch. 8). The movable chair brought out by the housewife signals her participation in these values but the offer of a seat to any particular person is voluntary and not obligatory. As passers-by stroll along they greet those seated outside the houses, and if the offer of a chair is not forthcoming they move on. Thus the seated groups on pavements are based on selection, while in the brief morning gatherings, contact is indiscriminate, for any woman may join a standing group.

One can see then how during the afternoon the pavement takes on the aspects of the home, its barriers relaxed but not eradicated. It could be said that 'The house enters the street' for the chair, an item of *indoor* furnishing is brought *outside*. The offer of a chair to an outsider establishes an extension of the domestic realm – of the 'inside' world – in the street, temporarily reducing the sharp distinction between the 'house' and the 'road', or outside world. The chair crosses the threshold, mediates in space, and provides a bridge between two separate realms. In this way the chair and the kitchen space have a common aspect, fitting into the gap between the separate realms of 'inside' and 'outside'.

## Conclusion

This analysis of interior and exterior space in Yerania is founded upon the notion of the house as an exclusive precinct, that of the family, closed to outsiders except under special conditions such as the formal granting of hospitality. Neighbours who are involved in frequent interactions outside their houses seldom enter one another's homes. The house is thus to be understood as conceptually opposed to the 'road', an image for the 'outside' world, so that by extension a dichotomy of 'inside' and 'outside' is inferred. Although it is itself perceived as a locus of positive values, the house and the family would exist in potential isolation were it not for the clearly defined code of neighbourhood conduct, emphasising sociability, openness, and requiring frequent interaction from residents in the locality. Injunctions to sociability are explicit; in its absence social life and hence social existence itself ceases (cf. Hirschon 1978: 76). The woman's role in promoting contacts and in creating relationships throughout the locality centred upon her activities in the neighbourhood are thus to be understood as vital in maintaining social life. The object in which social contact beyond the home is embodied is, as we have seen, the movable chair which bridges the separation of the 'house' and 'road' by moving from 'inside' to 'outside'.

Movement across the threshold takes place in the opposite direction too, for food is brought in to be processed first in the kitchen, and then served in the house. The kitchen is thus a marginal zone where the conversion of 'outside' products occurs, and where the two realms intersect. In their activities in the kitchen, the women prepare food which on the one hand provides nourishment, and thus physical life itself is sustained through their efforts, while on the other they offer food at the table where, as we have seen, fundamental symbolic values are expressed.

The 'essential objects' of Yerania homes have been shown to represent central values in the lives of Yerania families – the double-bed represents marital stability, the dining-table reveals the importance of commensality and hospitality, and the *iconostási* marks the presence of the religious or metaphysical dimension in the home.

It is striking that Yerania homes are excessively crowded, largely as a result of the dowry provision for women which also accounts for the concentration of female kin in a dwelling. In spite of the continual pressure on space, kitchens are not shared and notions of practicality and utility do not appear to be foremost. In the choice of furnishing, for instance, we have seen that certain 'essential' objects recur whose practical functions are secondary to their symbolic correlates. The 'essential objects' are set apart for special use, having sacramental associations, and partake of the quality of the 'sacred'. This manifestation of the metaphysical realm pervades the organisation of Yerania homes so that, in the organisation and use of physical space both within and beyond the home, the interplay of 'sacred' and 'profane' become evident. It is suggested that these houses can only be understood within a context of thought where sacred qualities permeate the objects and activities of everyday life. They are not to be seen simply as physical structures for they are patterned on the ideal world and 'rational' considerations are apparently subordinated to concerns of a symbolic kind.

In the creation of living quarters (the dowry) and the provision of domestic space (the kitchen) a primary consideration is the role and position of the woman in her family of marriage. In the life of the family, whose head is the husband, she is paradoxically the central figure through her association with 'essential objects' and hence the sacred dimension, while in the social exchange of the neighbourhood her role in mediating the opposition of 'inside' and 'outside' realms is crucial and unifying. The understanding of interior and exterior space, its use and organisation at the micro-scale, is dependent therefore upon specific attention to the most important elements of a woman's daily life.

# Notes

1. This paper is based on material collected for my DPhil during fourteen months' fieldwork conducted in the early 1970s as well as on a three-month survey done with S. Thakurdesai, an architect, to whom I am indebted for numerous insights, technical expertise and diagrams. Much of the material is now published in Hirschon 1989.

2. It is well to emphasise that at the time of fieldwork the modern Greek state was organised in a non-secular framework. Church and state were not distinguishable in many areas of life (marriages and divorces were conducted by ecclesiastical authority, education and national festive occasions were joint concerns of Church and state, identity registration was through baptism). The separation of 'sacred' and 'profane' was not evident therefore in the most public and official aspects of life and this was a striking feature of life in Yerania. 'Sacred' is used here to denote a state of being 'set apart', as well as having sacramental attributes.

3. A detailed survey of the 62 households was undertaken as part of the fieldwork; much of the quantified data presented here is based on this survey.

4. Among Sarakatsani shepherds 'the sign of the cross is made before the members of

the family share in the communion of their common meal' (Campbell 1964: 341). du Boulay notes that in Ambeli the meal is an 'act of communion' (1974: 54–5).

5. The importance of these religious activities is multifold; in particular, their involvement in religious observances takes women out into the wider community where they have an obvious and defined 'public' role as representatives of the family. The notion of domestic confinement and deprivation is not borne out when this sphere of life is analysed (see Hirschon 1980). This, and other issues raised in this article have been further explored for rural Greece in Dubisch's excellent edited volume (1986).

# 5

# The Problem of Privacy in Mediterranean Anthropology

*Lidia Sciama*

The Giants, enchained under the mountains by the frightful religion of the thunderbolts, learned to check their bestial habit of wandering wild through the great forest of the earth and acquired the contrary custom of remaining hidden and settled in their fields . . . . The virtue of the spirit began likewise to show itself among them restraining their bestial lust from finding its satisfaction in the sight of Heaven, of which they had a mortal terror. So it came about that each of them would drag one woman into his cave and would keep her there in perpetual company for the duration of their lives. Thus the act of human love was performed under cover, in hiding, that is to say, in shame, and they began to feel that sense of shame which Socrates described as the colour of virtue . . . . In this guise marriage was introduced.

(Vico, 1725, trans. Bergin and Fish, 1968)

## Introduction

Vico's mythical account of the beginnings of settled life and of the origins of marriage clearly suggests a most appealing set of themes for our anthropological discussion of women and of their social space: patterns of human dwelling, love, shame and matrimony are universally, if infinitely variously, interrelated. Their connections, which become particularly evident as we read ethnographic accounts of Mediterranean societies, are therefore taken for granted in the discussion to follow. The main theme of this chapter, however, is one particular aspect of the social and psychological tendencies related to different forms of dwelling and of social life, namely, *privacy*, that is, the need for individuals, families or other social groups, to separate themselves from others at various times, or for certain well-defined activities.[1]

Indeed the wish to be 'private' at times and the feeling that some actions are more appropriately performed in private than they are in public seem to be almost universal, yet the concept of privacy has no precise and uniform content; it is therefore very difficult to define, whether in ethical, psychological or simple linguistic terms.

Feminist debate – which, on this topic, is closely related to Marx and

Engels's views on the origin of the family and of property – has in a way made the problem more complex; women, some feminists argue, are almost universally confined to private spheres, both in social and in economic terms, while men have access to more rewarding public spheres.

While this statement clearly contains much truth, it also raises a host of fascinating problems so that, even if we leave aside the major question of the origins of private and public domains, the need is felt for more precise and culturally specific evidence. Indeed as we quickly learn from reading ethnographies, the aspects of life people wish to shield from public knowledge are very diverse, so that while in one culture it may be felt strongly that food consumption should be private, in other cultures sexual activity or open shows of affection are considered strictly personal, while in others yet, friendship or patron-client relationships may be surrounded with great reserve or even secrecy.

Secondly, in as far as we may argue that there has been some development from a rather crude and hazy perception that individuals should have a right to privacy (possibly parallel to the development of the legal notion of 'person', see Carrithers, Collins and Lukes 1985) the movement has by no means been a simple and homogeneous one. Thus, although we might expect women to be more strictly confined in less developed or simple peasant societies, surprisingly we find that exclusion from men's spheres is sometimes more significant in societies with well-developed institutional structures than in those which are more remote or less fully absorbed into the state system (cf. Engels 1884; Sacks 1975).

What is more, social spheres outside those of the home and family which, if we adopt a simple private/public dichotomy, should be defined as public, are themselves, in many instances, eminently 'private'. No simple private/public distinction, therefore, will help us to understand the actual 'choreography' of social life, the sentiments and values attached to private and public spheres, or the positions and relative statuses of women and men in different cultures.

The aim of this chapter is, then, primarily to illustrate, on the basis of ethnographic evidence, different notions of privacy. Two main threads will be developed: one is an attempt to understand 'privacy' in the context of English society. The second, based on a comparative treatment of sexual separation in two Greek communities and in Oxford and Cambridge collegiate society, is mainly a criticism of the private/public opposition, particularly in studies of the lives of women in the European Mediterranean.

Careful descriptions of spatial arrangements in different societies – whether in everyday life or in the performance of ritual – are frequently found in good ethnographies. Important theoretical landmarks were Durkheim and Mauss's *Primitive Classification* (1901–2) as well as Hertz's essay 'The Pre-eminence of the Right Hand' (1909; 1973 transl.). These works showed (a) that dual classification is almost universal and (b) that spatial conceptions which may map out small lived-in spaces, villages or tribal areas, but which in many instances concern the entire cosmos, frequently correspond to moral, social and hierarchical notions.

> Society and the whole universe [Hertz writes] have a side which is sacred, noble and precious and another which is profane and common: a male side, strong and active, and another, female, weak and passive; or, in two words, a right side and a left side. ([1909] 1973: 98)

The polarity between right and left, for which the human body provides 'the most readily available image' or 'natural symbol' (Douglas 1970: 17), is therefore invested with ethical value and is frequently coupled with other basic distinctions – above all that between male and female. Male/female and right/left oppositions can then be seen as basic co-ordinates for systems of social classification.

The clearest example of a 'total' system of classification which is fully expressed in the arrangement and division of the house, is Needham's analysis of a typical Purum dwelling (1969: 87–88); there domestic space is divided along right/left: male/female lines. The notions of 'male' and 'female', moreover, are metaphorically extended to persons associated respectively with the father as wife-giver (e.g. extended to his unmarried children) and with wife-takers and affines (including married daughters and prospective bridegrooms). What is more, superior value is attributed to house-areas and objects associated with right/male and inferior value to those associated with left/female.

Thus, as ethnographers have frequently reported, sexual divisions in the use of house, temple, village or city space generally correspond to different conceptions of the moral natures of men and women. As a consequence, women's spaces may be variously perceived as either the most sacred, or the most polluting and, literally, 'sinister' or, in some instances, as both together (cf. Steiner 1967). Spatial arrangements of the house or compound, therefore, often carry great symbolic significance, as do other spatial distinctions studied by anthropologists, such as those between the 'inside' and the 'outside', the neighbourhood and the village, or the village and the bush.

One opposition, already noted by Needham in his Purum material, which over the last ten years or more has been widely applied cross-culturally, is that between private or domestic, and public social spheres, and consequently some of the negative values attached to domestic spheres in some communities have similarly been extended to other societies where this may be less appropriate or not fully justified. For instance, as Reyna Reiter writes, 'There is a sexual geography to the way people use space within the village as well as outside of it. Throughout the Mediterranean area a distinction is often made between private and public spheres' (1975: 256). Or, as Rosaldo argues,

> An emphasis on woman's maternal role leads to a universal opposition between domestic and public roles that is necessarily asymmetrical; women, confined to the domestic spheres, do not have access to the sorts of authority, prestige and cultural values that are the prerogatives of men. (1974: 10).

A period of fieldwork in Italy as well as my re-reading of ethnographies in which the private/public opposition is used for purely descriptive and analytical purposes, however, has led me to question the value of its polemical use in sociological studies of the European Mediterranean.[2] Consequently I would like to suggest that, since the notion of privacy, as well as being subject to great cultural variation, is somewhat ill-defined even within our own society, definition of social spaces as private should always be explained in terms of their particular contexts; and, furthermore, that values attached to private and public spheres cannot be generalised since they vary in accordance with other factors, both of a material and of a moral or ideal nature.[3] My criticism of the private/public opposition in Mediterranean anthropology, therefore, is based first of all on a very simple linguistic argument, concerning the vagueness and ambiguity of the concept of privacy itself; secondly, it is based on an argument of an empirical nature, that is, on the simple observation that Mediterranean people themselves do not seem to regard privacy, for which some of them have no noun, in the same way that the English do.

Finally, a clear distinction should be drawn between 'privacy' and 'individualism' (cf. Lukes 1973). Indeed although the two notions are in many ways interrelated and, particularly in its individual and Western connotations, privacy can sometimes be regarded as a corollary of individualism, 'privacy' and 'private spheres' are more often used in anthropology, because of their wider reference, since they clearly concern groups as well as individuals. Moreover, the fact that they refer to physical spaces and objects (Vico's 'caves' as opposed to 'forests of the earth') as well as to moral attitudes, makes it possible for them to be analysed through study of the organisation of space in different ethnographic settings. Finally, we must keep in mind that complete individual privacy is only indirectly relevant to social anthropology, which studies interaction of groups and individuals. (Similarly philosophers of language have debated the problem whether a private language is a language at all, if language is a form of communication.) The area which, to my mind, is of great anthropological interest is the borderline between the private and the social and the ways in which privacy itself is patterned or organised in different societies. Thus states of mind, such as 'brooding', 'longing', 'grieving' or 'ecstasy', which, in some societies are considered to be private experiences *par excellence*, are nonetheless culturally styled and delimited.

## Words and Meanings

'Privacy' derives from the Latin verb *privare*. It soon becomes clear, as we look at a number of dictionaries, how *privare* is given some strangely different and contradictory translations. Since, as we shall see, these reflect ambiguities inherent in the concept of privacy itself, the best rendering of *privare* is the most unspecific, 'to set apart', 'to exempt'. The 1969 *Oxford Latin Dictionary*, on the other hand, lists a number of possible translations, such as 'to bereave', 'to deprive', 'to rob of anything' as well as 'to free', 'to release', 'to deliver'. It is then clear that *privare*, as well as its adjectival forms *privus* and, later, *privatus*, do not in themselves necessarily imply any negative or positive connotations, but, insofar as they usually refer to an indirect object, they are good or bad, depending on whether one is deprived of (a) public honours, offices and wealth, or (b) painful obligations, debts or other afflictions. The most important, and socially revealing, aspect of the word's development in English is the formation of the noun 'privacy', which came powerfully into literary, and, later, into common use in the sixteenth century. This clearly has no parallel in Latin itself or in other neo-Latin languages. Like other abstract notions, however, the concept is still as indefinite and problematic as the Latin *privatus* and *privare*. Indeed, while changing attitudes to privacy have led to changes in the organisation of the lived-in environment, which would certainly fascinate the social or architectural and landscape historian, the concept of privacy itself has remained strangely fixed and still retains all the implied ambiguities and contradictions of its Latin equivalent.

A clear illustration of the difficulties of giving 'privacy' a precise definitional content arises from its recent legal discussion, and, particularly from a comparison of its legal history in England and in the USA (Pratt 1979). For, while a person's 'right to be let alone', based on English common-law traditions, has had legal recognition in the USA since as early as 1890, in Britain, offences against privacy are treated as trespass.

Alternatively they may be regarded as violations against property (whether material or intellectual), or as instances of damage against reputation. Since the turn of the century, however, and despite the fact that right to privacy always was recognised 'de facto' in the common-law tradition, there developed a strong popular movement demanding that it should be given formal recognition in the law (Pratt 1979: 1–16). (The movement, at first motivated by concern with indiscretions committed by the popular press, gained force after the Second World War through realisation of the dangers of government intervention in totalitarian states, while during the 1960s people feared that bugging devices and data-storing computers might destroy individual privacy altogether.) But when, in response to that demand, the government specially appointed a committee of philosophers, legal experts and political thinkers, despite a great deal of research and reflection, one of the major themes of the committee's *Younger Report* (1972/73) was its 'inability to define satisfactorily what was meant by privacy' (quoted in Pratt 1979: 195).

Thus, as it clearly appears from some of the wry observations of the *Younger Report*, the problematic nature of privacy and in particular the fact that disputes over privacy often concern principles and sentiments, rather than more tangible realities such as property or reputation, places it clearly outside the scope of British legislation because of the latter's traditionally concrete and empirical approach to justice. A second – but paradoxically even stronger reason – is that (as Pratt writes), where the British are concerned, in comparison with Americans, 'privacy inheres more in the character of the people and thus requires less protection from governmental institutions' (1979: 16). Yet, granted that it may be stronger in Britain than in the United States, a self-conscious respect for privacy is undoubtedly widespread throughout Protestant Anglo-Saxon and Northern European society.

Anthropologists' discussions of private as opposed to public domains in other cultures often reveal a great deal of emotional commitment to the notion of individual privacy as freedom, and one of the topics most commonly touched upon in retrospective accounts of fieldwork is the extent to which they were allowed to retain, or had to forego, any degree of privacy. Thus, to mention one of the most famous instances, when Evans-Pritchard arrived in Nuerland, he was somewhat dismayed by the fact that he was hardly ever left alone (1940: 14). Women anthropologists first working in Mediterranean countries have often remarked on the fact of having to be chaperoned and to take lodgings with a family or with an older single woman, since living alone would not be considered proper (Golde 1970). At the other extreme, Clifford Geertz (1973) relates how, on arriving at a Balinese village, he was so studiously avoided that he began to doubt his own reality until contact was made through his participation in an important village event, the forbidden cock-fight.

Anthropologists' accounts of difficulties at the initial stages of fieldwork in, literally, finding their 'proper place' in a new home or village and of their transition from the position of guest to that of family member, are often very informative aspects of ethnographies – and, not least, because, due to the current discussion of its ethical significance in their own countries, some of them are deeply concerned with the fact that their research often does involve breaking other people's privacy. The rights and wrongs of getting to know people's customs and homes are therefore abundantly discussed, and indeed a chronicle of anthropologists' social blunderings might contribute some clarification to our own apparently hazy, though deeply rooted, concept of privacy in our own society.

It is, in any case, an interesting contradiction that, while anthropologists are sometimes disturbed by lack of privacy in some simple societies, and their writings imply an understanding of privacy as freedom, some deprecate the existence of private feminine spheres, to which women are confined, and where privacy is interpreted as deprivation, robbing, bereavement.

To conclude, the most important observation we may be able to add to Pratt's minimal definition of privacy as 'the right of an individual to control information about himself and the right to a private sphere' (Pratt 1979: 13), in the light of anthropological insights, concerns the relativity of the concept since the right to be 'let alone' is upheld by human individuals or groups, and something or somebody is always said to be private in relation to something or somebody else. Thus in suburban England, a son's or daughter's room in their parents' home is private in relation to the house (or he or she may so regard it); the house is private in relation to the neighbourhood and so on, through ever widening circles and through more inclusive social groups. Privacy can then be seen as a continuum, and it may be very difficult indeed for the anthropologist, faced with the complexities of human interaction, to say at just what point the private turns into its opposite, the public. Thus in any given society, a number of different and even opposed institutions, such as families, age-groups, secret societies or colleges, may overlap and include the same individuals, while the same places may be private sometimes, but public at other times (cf. S. Ardener 1978: 32).

It follows that, while in some societies privacy does have its own symbolic markers, so that ideas and values related to it can be precisely described by an attentive observer (Eco 1973; Hirschon, see above), in other instances, social attitudes may be more elusive or heterogeneous, and require careful study of people's ideas and behaviour. The anthropologist's first task, therefore, if he wants to adopt the private/public opposition as an analytical tool, especially in a complex society, is to identify the individuals and the social units, as well as the particular activities, for which privacy is considered important.

If we leave aside a purely spatial approach, there are two ways in which privacy may be studied (cf. Pratt 1979: 13). The first of these is simply by observing which actions are actually performed in isolation or in a state of separation from part or all of society. The second concerns the way in which communication takes place. Thus, while a society in which everyone tells everything to everyone else is not logically inconceivable, most ethnographers clearly show that people are in fact very selective in respect to what they communicate to whom (and when) and what actions they perform in the presence of others. For the purpose of this paper, however, action and communication need not be separated, since actions reveal and communicate, while the passing of information can itself be viewed as a form of action, as it is always embedded in a context of pragmatic concerns.

This, I trust, will be shown in the following section which concerns two Greek societies described by Campbell and du Boulay.

## The Home, Marriage, Privacy and Secrecy among Sarakatsani Shepherds

The Sarakatsani are a group of transhumant shepherds, living in Continental Greece, North of Corinth. In summer they graze their sheep and goats on the mountainous district of Zagori, while in the winter they move down to the coastal plains and valleys (Campbell 1964: 7). The shepherds' social life too varies with the seasons. In the winter, herding groups (*stanis*), formed by two, three or four related families, spread over a very large area and *stanis* become more concentrated and turned in on their own affairs so that individual shepherds are then isolated from contacts with non-related people. In summer there is 'greater awareness of the community and of its life'; herding groups break up into smaller units, families live in houses or huts in the village and women are left at home, while men graze their herds in the pastures above, individually or in couples. 'Winter in the plains is a kind of exile; the return in spring to the mountains of Zagori is the return home' (ibid.: 8).

Sarakatsan social groupings are, as Campbell writes,

Extremely simple. . . . The most restricted unit is the most important. . . .
This is the *family* [my italics] whether in its elementary or extended form. . . .
The shepherd normally has no membership in other social groupings which
might conflict with his exclusive duties to the family. (ibid.: 8)

Indeed the most important feature of relationships between families is
their mutual competition, lack of trust and hostility. As a consequence,
'The Sarakatsan family is not only a domestic association . . . it is also a
corporate group, owning in common all significant property and acting
together in political matters' (ibid.: 37). It is at the same time 'a religious
community with its own "sacra", icons and other objects, since through
reference to a divine model a man or a woman in family life participates
in a reality that transcends individuality' (ibid.: 37). Each individual,
then, sees the community as sharply divided into his kin, and those who
are not his kinsmen and from whom he can only expect hostility and
aggression. The kinship system is a cognatic one, yet

[t]he absence of a unilineal principle of descent does not prevent Sarakatsani
from having a very strong sentimental interest in their patriline and a formal
preference for those kinsmen who are related through the father, especially
those who bear the same name. (ibid.: 47)

Affinal relations, on the other hand, provide an intermediate category
between kin and non-kin; they are the necessary strangers with whom a
family has joined to 'form new blood', but it takes a very long time for
Sarakatsani to develop any real confidence in their affines, since they
are regarded as ambivalent and potentially treacherous. Indeed the
extent to which patrilineal kinship acts as an organising principle
becomes very evident in the *stani*'s winter arrangement, when, as
Campbell writes, 'brothers build their homes next to one another with
the huts of cousins and other relatives on the periphery' (ibid.: 20).

Sarakatsani women actually do most of the building; they help shepherds build sheepfolds, as well as the simple thatched shelters for the men
who guard their ewes at night; they erect huts for the cheese-maker, who
establishes himself in their vicinity (ibid.: 20–21), and 'except in the case
of rectangular huts the men help the women to erect the posts and cross-
beams, the building of the hut is entirely the work of women' (ibid.: 33).

Indeed the shepherds' dwellings are extremely simple and compact.
A family of six or seven adults may live in a hut with a diameter and a
height of fourteen or fifteen feet, and with a central hearth (ibid.: 33).
Sleeping arrangements are similarly simple, since the whole family generally share one room, sleeping on rough-woven woollen blankets.

Marriage is patrilocal and the bride's separation from her family of
origin is emphasised in the marriage ritual by the fact that, when the

wedding feast, which customarily follows the ceremony, is celebrated in the groom's hut, no member of the wife's family is allowed to be present. During the first two months of marriage the couple is given some degree of privacy, sleeping together in a temporary hut which has been built specially before the ceremony, or in a store-shed in which a space is cleared to arrange their accommodation. The bridegroom is excused from shepherding for eight days and is 'thus able to sleep in privacy with his bride. . . .' (ibid.: 66).

Although it is thus recognised that it is desirable for the bride and groom to be physically separated from the family during the first few weeks of marriage, a man's sexual relations with his wife are by no means considered to be a private and secret matter. On the contrary, his sexuality, which is a means for increasing the patriline, is very much a matter of concern for his relatives and, as Campbell writes, any difficulty he might encounter is discussed with his brothers, who offer him advice and solidarity. Clearly, during the early days of his marriage, a man's loyalty towards his family is put to a hard test: he must not show any overt affection towards his wife. What is more, about two months after the wedding he must return with her to share the family hut, since prolonging the period of privacy would appear as a kind of desertion and a breach of solidarity. From then on, therefore, intercourse will take place rather quietly and surreptitiously when the rest of the family has gone to sleep (ibid.: 66–67).

Despite the men's unshakeable belief in their own superiority and their firm control over their wives, daughters and sisters, women are by no means physically confined to their huts. Often they must walk miles to fetch water or they must wander some distance away to graze their goats, but all their movements take place under the surveillance of a brother or of an older male member of the family.

During the early stages of marriage, a wife is seen as a threat to the unity of the husband's extended family and since easy contact with her own family of origin is regarded as a potential source of quarrels and an obstacle to her incorporation into the husband's kinship group, brides whose parents live some distance away are preferred to the daughters of neighbours. A bride is therefore not allowed to see her parents until the second Sunday after the wedding and, when the visit takes place, she is always accompanied by her husband and by some of his relatives. As Campbell writes,

> A sister or brother's wife of the bridegroom sits close to the bride and attends her every moment so far as good manners will allow. However, the young wife generally succeeds in whispering a few of the desired details into the ear of her mother or a sister. (ibid.: 137–47)

Such circumspect and suspicious behaviour, then, clearly shows the Sarakatsani's distaste for any relations with people outside of their kin group.

But what relevance does all this have to our discussion of the problem of privacy? If we accept that privacy may be regarded as a continuum, so that something may be private to an individual, to a family, a neighbourhood, or any larger social unit, until it gradually turns into its opposite, that is, the public, we see that, where Sarakatsani are concerned, the outside terms 'individual' and 'social' or 'neighbourhood privacy' have become quite irrelevant, while the only significant term remains the family, whether elementary or extended. Our privacy line, which may be conceptualised as a spectrum, then segments so as to produce a configuration which is interestingly different from patterns we find elsewhere, and, above all, in Protestant Western societies, since very little value is attached by Sarakatsani to *personal* privacy, while *family* privacy and even secrecy are thought to be of paramount importance (ibid.: 33). It therefore seems that, where the individual is concerned, just as it is impossible or very unlikely for a man alone to survive in economic terms, so it would probably be pointless for him to withhold information or to separate himself in sentiment or thought from his family group.

The important notion that determines how communication takes place among Sarakatsani is *trust*. As Campbell writes, trust is 'an axiomatic value . . . which is never questioned' (ibid.: 111). Given that life outside the home is nothing but competitive and hostile, a shepherd has to rely on his kinsmen for information about business, about grazing grounds or about the qualities of possible marriage partners. In economic matters, too, a man expects co-operation only from his kin whom he may ask for a loan without feeling humiliated. Above all, should there arise the need for a vengeance killing, a man can turn only to a young brother or cousin (ibid.: 39–43). A man's kindred, which is often dispersed, then acts as a very effective information network through which news can travel with remarkable speed and decisions are deliberated upon with a great deal of secrecy and circumspection.

## Privacy and Respect

One more aspect of the Sarakatsani's social life which bears some relation to the problem of privacy is their notion of respect, as it is expressed through a number of customs ruling the behaviour of family members both inside and outside the home. Thus,

> A wife must show respect to her husband before strangers at all times . . . .
> From the age of thirteen a daughter is expected in front of strangers to show

[her] father respect by standing when he sits and helping her mother to wait on [him] and his guests. (ibid.: 151–59)

Respect is even more crucial in the relationships of fathers and sons. When a boy leaves school at thirteen and begins his working life as a shepherd under his father's direction and authority, he must be careful to show his father respect (ibid.: 159). As he grows older, a boy must avoid behaving in ways which symbolically emphasise independence and sexual maturity and which would place him and his father in a position of social equality, therefore

> if he is under the age of twenty, he does not smoke or drink ouzo in his father's presence. Similarly he does not swear or make coarse remarks or jokes about sexual matters before his father. If a youth is sitting in the village coffee shop when his father enters, he unobtrusively gets up and leaves. (ibid.: 160)

Here, too, as in many other instances in Sarakatsan life, the presence of strangers is crucial in making respectful behaviour imperative, since any public show of disrespect would diminish the father's authority and make him an object of ridicule. Conversely, after the son returns from his military service, the father will try not to intrude when the young man is having a drink with his age-mates. Thus, although Sarakatsan men are at all times aware of being their families' representatives and champions, fathers' and sons' mutually respectful behaviour, which clearly is in keeping with their agonistic conception of social life, involves some recognition of the need for a man to be alone when mixing with people outside the home.

Where women are concerned, on the other hand, the position is quite the opposite; it is not customary for women to go about on their own and the presence and companionship of a mother or sister is always thought to be a source of safety and support. Clearly women are more closely associated with the hut and its immediate vicinity than shepherds. Most contacts and negotiations with the outside or public world of villagers, tax officials or politicians are conducted by men, and only men handle money and make decisions. What is more, a woman will not eat with her husband at the table at times when the home is, in a way, made more public by the presence of non-related visitors.

These facts, together with other aspects of women's lives such as the strictures of their honour code and the negative position assigned them in Sarakatsan symbolic classification, have led interpreters to see their exclusion from public spheres as the ultimate deprivation. The women's domestic existence, however, may in fact not be the most severe aspect of their lives if we consider it in the full context of their material circumstances and of the outlook they share with their husbands. Clearly their way of life is above all a consequence of Sarakatsan pessimism with regard to relationships outside the kin group. Indeed a man too has to undergo some trying behavioural adjustments when he goes out into the public arena and it is only 'while in the privacy of the family hut . . . [that] a man is able to relax, to laugh, to give affection and to receive it' (ibid.: 191). If, as is clearly shown throughout Campbell's treatment of Sarakatsan values, the most significant dividing line in their conception of society is that between kin and non-kin, and if kin are associated with all that is good, holy, comfortable and reassuring, while non-kin are competitive, hostile and deceitful, then women's lack of independent social contacts outside the home and the family can hardly be regarded as 'deprivation'.

The extent to which the Sarakatsani value and respect private above public spheres is most eloquently expressed in Campbell's discussion of sanctions against eavesdroppers or intruders:

> The hut or house is inviolable. No stranger may invade it without an invitation. Similarly whatever takes place within the sanctuary of its walls is private and sacred to the members of the family. This understanding makes possible the warmth, affection and easy intercourse of family life secluded from the public gaze. (ibid.: 292)

To conclude, given the shepherds' harsh living conditions, their gloomy pessimism about relationships with non-kin and their high respect for the home and the family, the fact that Sarakatsan women, whose lives are beyond any doubt very strenuous and hard, may remain free from involvement in business or bureaucratic dealings, can only allow the more positive interpretation of *private* as 'free from affliction'. To interpret it otherwise would be, I believe, a most extreme form of ethnocentrism.

## Lying and Privacy in a Greek Peasant Community

Juliet du Boulay's study of a Greek village offers a new and interesting example of ways in which privacy is maintained under different environmental conditions, in a Greek peasant society.

The villagers of Ambéli, like the Sarakatsani, hold a pessimistic view of relationships outside the family. Although they do have a notion of 'friendship', and friendships are in fact developed in the village to a much greater extent than among shepherds, relationships between non-kin are always thought of as potentially disappointing and are regarded as ambiguous and impermanent. As du Boulay writes, they are essentially relationships of practical expedience, and so they lapse when

expedience lapses (1974: 213). In Ambéli, too, therefore, a strong dividing line is drawn between kin and non-kin. Trust, the necessary condition for confidence and honest communication, is almost exclusively
invested in the family and household events are therefore best not
divulged. The notions of privacy, reserve and secrecy are, then, associated with a person's kin group, but since families overlap with other families, and kinship becomes diluted at the edges of the kindred, trust and
solidarity are felt to be strongest and most enduring at the household
level.

Undoubtedly this greater emphasis on household as distinct from kin
group is also related to the villagers' more stable existence compared
with the Sarakatsani's transhumant way of life. By virtue of their continued residence in Ambéli, moreover, the villagers have a very high
level of interaction on a face-to-face daily basis – a fact which, as we
shall see, creates some contradictory pressures between silence and
communication, openness and concealment. Another relevant datum is
the fact that the villagers' behaviour, like the Sarakatsani's, should ideally be ruled by adherence to a very strict and impossibly demanding
honour code, in particular where women's sexual mores are concerned.
Prestige in Ambéli is assessed on the basis of the extent to which people
succeed in living up to (or appearing to live up to) the society's value-
system. People therefore compete for position in an ideal hierarchy, as if
a limited and in some way divisible amount of prestige were given collectively to the village population, and families rise or fall in relation to
other families in a continual reassessment of their relative worth, so that,
while people are very much concerned to protect or increase their own
standing, they are at the same time very anxious to do other families
down by observing any fault or item of misdemeanour which might tell
against them.

Given the villagers' curiosity about other people's behaviour and
their need to conceal their own household affairs, how do they preserve
any measure of individual or family privacy? The answer is simple,
although it is at the same time fascinating in terms of all its implications: by lying. The inhabitants of Ambéli thus lie,

> to conceal some failure of oneself or one's family to live up to the highest
> requirements of the social code . . . to conceal unintentional failures – such
> as poverty . . . or the fact that a proposed marriage has not succeeded because
> the son or daughter in question has been turned down. Both are intimately
> associated with the notion of family honour. (du Boulay 1976: 400)

Lies, however, can also be used to attack 'others by false imputation . . .
[T]his type of lie, that slanders another, automatically breeds a further
one . . . the lie to avoid trouble or quarrels'. Finally lies can be told for

material gain, for sheer love of concealment or love of secrecy or of mischief (ibid.: 400–3).

Here du Boulay's subtle and detailed analysis of concealment and lying in Ambéli clearly shows the methodological advantage of understanding the nature of secrecy and of identifying the areas of life people prefer to keep private in different cultures. Her work thus fully bears out the relevance to anthropologists of semioticists' views about the essential relation between lying and signifying. Indeed, in Eco's words, 'Semiotics is in principle the discipline studying everything which can be used in order to lie' (Eco 1976: 7). The lies people tell in Ambéli are then as revealing as some of their true statements and their accurate study can contribute as usefully to our understanding of the community's rules as the study of other, whether true or unverifiable, statements. Thus, to quote Eco again,

> A theory of codes must study everything that can be used in order to lie. The possibility of lying is the proprium of semiosis just as (for the Schoolmen) the possibility of laughing was the proprium of man as *animal rationale*. (ibid.: 58–9)

Indeed, as du Boulay points out,

> The Greek word for 'to deceive' is the same as that meaning 'to laugh' and may be interpreted freely as 'to have the laugh of' – an interesting indication which makes the connection between lies, deceit, mockery and laughter still more apparent. (du Boulay 1976: 399)

Thus, while mockery is in the first place a sanction, when people use deception to initiate some elaborate and whimsical make-believe situation, what they are in some sense laughing at is really society itself with its impossible strictures and demands. Therefore, although lying clearly evades an almost universal moral injunction, it appears from du Boulay's analysis that, as far as Ambéli is concerned, it does fulfil some useful social functions, since it 'reconciles the need of the individual to break the code on occasions, with the need for subscription to the moral code, which is vital if the code is to survive' (ibid.: 404). The social code is thus maintained, despite the pressures of social change, since

> The lie as a mechanism for sheer concealment . . . serves a vital function in reconciling the need for individual families of the community to lead a private life with the sanctions (curiosity leading to mockery) which must operate if the moral code is to have force. (ibid.: 404)

As du Boulay emphasises, Ambéli, like many other village communities, is in a state of transition, but one is nonetheless impressed by the conservative force of the code and of its metaphysical underpinning, given the frequency and the wholeheartedness with which rules are broken. Indeed this is only made possible through the villagers' amazing ingenuity and through their cunning way of achieving privacy through secrecy and deception.

## Privacy in Cross-cultural Perspective: Oxford and Cambridge Colleges

A comparative reading of ethnographies shows the difficulties we may encounter when we attempt to study different cultures from the standpoint of a universal distinction between private and public spheres. Particularly, general remarks about feminine social spheres in the European Mediterranean appear to be incorrect when they imply reading in the lives of Mediterranean country women some of the characters of women's privacy in our own, post-industrial milieus (loneliness, powerlessness, lack of opportunities for 'transcendence', and so on).[4]

A brief comparison between attitudes to private spheres in Oxford and Cambridge's collegiate society with those of the Greek shepherds described by Campbell should further illustrate my point about the concept's relativity and ethnocentricity. I shall therefore introduce a few observations on women in our academic society, making it quite clear at the outset, however, that these do not have the systematic nature of fieldwork[5] and that they concern mainly one category of women, those who, whether they do or do not have academic careers of their own, are defined as 'wives' in relation to their husbands' colleges.

Some of the topics discussed in the section on the Sarakatsani, namely the men's relations with non-related men and the women's avoidance of public life, will provide the main line for my argument, but I should like to emphasise that, given the presence of some common elements which make comparison possible, the object is that of highlighting differences rather than elaborating on the theme of some perceived similarities.

As we have seen in the second part of this chapter, relations between shepherds who are not mutually tied through kinship are characterised by competitiveness, lack of trust and hostility. Academics too are, by the very nature of their careers, similarly competitive, but in the college setting their anxiety to distinguish themselves above others is tempered or sublimated in an atmosphere of shared values, intellectual achievement and conviviality[6] from which their wives have until recently been excluded, except on specially appointed and relatively rare occasions. Naturally this has led to a sexual separation of space, which provides a basic analogy between Greek women and English 'academic wives' through their common exclusion from the men's social spheres.

Clearly, where Oxford and Cambridge are concerned, such separation is directly linked to a long-standing monastic tradition and to a deeply-rooted preference for a celibate existence in a well-organised, all-male society of scholars. Some of its underlying ideal elements and rationalisations, however, also bear interesting analogies to Greek views on the nature of women.[7] Indeed, to return for a moment to Sarakatsan shepherds, the most telling aspect of their symbolic classification is its association of the female sex with intellectual and moral weakness and with all the more sinful and negative aspects of life. It is therefore of some relevance to note how the shepherds' views on women, like other Greek popular conceptions, present a clear resemblance to Aristotelian notions about human nature and generation, which in the course of time have been absorbed throughout Europe, and which are now so widespread, both at the level of folk and of academic culture, that it would be fruitless to examine them in terms of influence and diffusion, except in well-defined literary and scholastic contexts.

It is none the less remarkable that the influence of Classical ideas contributed to shape English mores even more markedly than they did the customs of other European countries. Indeed, as Bolgar writes,

> During the later part of the eighteenth and most of the nineteenth century, the Classics that were taught in the schools and Universities . . . were used to inculcate a taste for rhetoric in France, patriotism in Germany, and a *public school morality in Dr Arnold's England*. (1977: 367. My italics.)

It should therefore be no surprise to find that English attitudes too bear some resemblance to those held by Sarakatsan shepherds: since they both contain a common core of diffidence and misogyny, and are often expressed through similar imagery and analogous idioms.[8]

Observation of women's attitudes in Oxford and Cambridge shows that many of them perceive men's colleges as vaguely hostile and somewhat puzzling institutions (see Gallie 1968). Thus colleges are generally regarded by the women as part of their husbands' public professional domains, since they provide opportunities for the creation of wider networks than those formed through university departments, as it is often in colleges that fellows meet members of other faculties, gather useful information on academic politics and do their professional entertaining. The men themselves, on the other hand, generally describe their colleges as private, and indeed they certainly are private in legal and economic terms. It follows that, if we consider some of the more traditional colleges as settings for social life, the private/public distinction becomes quite blurred and both terms only have relative meaning, since, while sets of rooms may be entirely private, colleges are clearly more public than homes, but infinitely more private than the city's streets or department stores.

Unlike most university departments, Oxford and Cambridge colleges offer meals to their fellows, and, but occasionally, to their wives. Although in recent years there has been a tendency for the midday meal to be a fairly informal and relatively hasty one, evening meals are often gracious and strongly ritualised ceremonial occasions. Therefore, since, as E. M. Forster sensitively observed, 'one belongs to the place one sleeps in and to the people one eats with' (1978: 217) – and, as anthropologists, we don't need to emphasise the spiritual dimension of the sharing of food and drink – the wives' daily exclusion from the college table has often been a matter for disagreement and discontent, with wives feeling hurt and with some college fellows persistently defending the rights and the professional advantages of their exclusive dining customs.

While all women were excluded from men's colleges the position of wives was related to the all-pervasive sexual divisions in English society, and it was, on the whole, either taken for granted or discussed as one of the many facets of Oxford and Cambridge life. At the present time, however, following years of pressure, women academics are admitted to share full rights in most colleges if they achieve the required level of distinction to obtain fellowships in 'open competition' with male candidates. The dividing line, therefore, is no longer a uniform one between women and men, since the sexual division has given way to a new and equally rigid one based on academic excellence and achievement. Given the enormous imbalance in the numbers of suitably trained male and female candidates and the fact that the wives of college fellows are not necessarily themselves academics, however, admission of women to fellowships has made little difference, or only a negative one, to those in the position of 'wives'.

But to pursue our comparison with Sarakatsan shepherds a little further, where Oxford and Cambridge are concerned, the exclusion of wives from college life certainly cannot be put down to a strict code of sexual honour and to men's fear of sexual competition which lies behind the Sarakatsani's shielding of their women from mixed social occasions. Moreover, the shepherds' belief that they are far superior to women in dealings with the world outside the home, which is comparable to confidence often expressed by some members of colleges that they are more suitable than women to their professional calling, clearly is in keeping with their harsh environment and with the evident value of physical prowess in coping with their work and with the hostility of other shepherds, while no compelling ecological reasons can be invoked to justify similar attitudes to sex-roles in today's Britain. There are, to be sure, good practical and economic reasons for not having wives – or, for that matter, the husbands of female fellows – at college meals, but where wives are concerned, their exclusion is still perceived as offensive, because practical arguments are often mixed with archaic misogynist ones, still tied to a past which is too close or too painful. It is, for instance, often stated that, if colleges were freely open to wives, 'the level of conversation would be lowered'[9] and the character of social intercourse would be bound to change for the worse. Such remarks clearly reflect negative attitudes towards domestic life (and wives are thought of as totally absorbed in and completely moulded by their domestic roles) which clearly differ from Sarakatsan attitudes to their homes and which show how fellows either genuinely value college above home, or sometimes profess to do so.

Indeed social relations which take place in the carefully selected and cultivated environments of Oxford and Cambridge, by contrast to those which occur on the Zagori mountains, are idealised; they are associated with intellectual achievement, spiritual pride, high-mindedness and good taste. Far from suggesting any analogy with those masculine public domains described by anthropologists, which are mainly characterised by negative reciprocity, some colleges offer images of privacy more often associated with privileged domestic milieus, but which are clearly more conducive to intellectual work than most present-day households. Finally, but perhaps most important of all, the Sarakatsani's belief in their superior ability for rational thinking and in the wisdom of their division of labour, as well as their pessimistic views of social relations are shared by their wives, whereas, in contemporary England, women's and men's conceptions have become increasingly divergent and are often in conflict. Thus, to express this in structural terms, while the Sarakatsani's main opposition is that of family/strangers, a don's social life is based on two couples of opposed terms: (a) college/strangers and (b) family/strangers. His wife's conception of society, on the other hand, is usually ruled by only one dichotomy, that of family/strangers. Wives therefore find themselves among strangers in respect to those very institutions which constitute a prominent and valued part of their husbands' social lives. Consequently many wives who, unlike their husbands, do not have access to alternative social spheres to those of their homes, feel their positions as anomalous and contradictory, since it goes counter to the ideology of sharing spiritual and intellectual companionship, now prevalent in English society, and only too frequently upheld by moralists and politicians. Thus, unlike Sarakatsan women and unlike Victorian 'academic wives', 'those gifted and capital creatures . . . who fortunately for their husbands were trained to self-sacrifice'[10] (Annan 1955: 252), many of them do not share the ethos and the psychological conceptions of the men to whom they are, on the other hand, tied in marriage.

## Conclusion

The passage from Vico's *New Science* quoted at the beginning of this chapter is in itself a mythical account of the origins of privacy: dwelling in caves, then homes, arose not only out of a need for shelter, but out of an essentially psychological need, at the basis of culture, to make love and found families in private – and not through fear of beasts or other men, but through the fear of Heaven. Indeed, as we have seen, the connection between 'shame' and 'home' is particularly strong in Mediterranean cultures, so that Vico's account, as well as possibly containing some universal psychological truth, is certainly true to his own Southern Italian experience.

Alas, what Vico did not tell us in his explanation of the origins of human dwelling is how women may have felt about being dragged singly, each one into one cave and kept there 'in perpetuity'. Over the last twenty years or more, however, women, as well as anthropologists, have been very sedulous in trying to understand through research and introspection their own and other women's position in society. Yet, as often happens in the incipient stages of a new field of study, there may have been a tendency to overgeneralise some otherwise useful analytical categories. Thus, general statements about women in relation to private and public spheres often prove untenable when applied in different ethnographic settings. Above all, and surprisingly, the opposition of women-private-deprived/men-public-privileged may be more appropriate to some sections of North European and American society, with their positive attitude to the world beyond the family, and with the state, or other institutions, like universities and colleges, taking up the position of patrons and distributing means to support individual freedom and initiative, than to the Southern Mediterranean. Therefore, while 'private' and 'public' remain important sociological key terms, the relative and culture-bound nature of their contents make it imperative that differences and ambiguities should be taken account of. That may be the reason why a wholly individual *cri de coeur*, such as Virginia Woolf's *A Room of One's Own*, with its own hesitancies and contradictions, possibly tells us more about women and about the character and rhythms of *their* privacy than some otherwise excellent ethnographies – and hence the need that, when we do set out to study other women, in other cultures, we should fully discard our own biases.

## Postscript

Acceptance of the feminist dictum 'the personal is political' was in my case purely the fruit of experience. In a truly Blakeian sense, it coincided with my loss of innocence. It all happened in Cambridge, England, during the early 1960s. When I arrived there as a young married woman (or, as I was sometimes referred to, as D's Italian wife) after completing an MA in English at Cornell University (USA), I was, for the first time in my adult life, quite aimless and without any clear prospect of future employment.

As I wandered round colleges I was struck by the numbers of notices forbidding access to parts of their buildings and gardens: *'Private'*, *'No Visitors allowed beyond . . .'*, *'Fellows Gardens'*, etc. Such notices must, of course, be familiar in all parts of the world and especially in places where power, whether political, economic, or mystical is held and transacted. However, in Cambridge, my sense of puzzlement at their frequency deepened when, planning to register as a PhD student, and having asked a professor if I could attend a course of lectures in his department, he firmly answered, 'that is not possible, because University and college activities are strictly private'. As he explained, 'to attend lectures, members of the University are required to wear a gown, but since you are not a member you have no right to do so, *ergo*, you can't go to lectures'. And he closed our conversation with warmest wishes for my husband's career.

The interview had left me with a sense of anxiety at such unexpected exclusion from activities I had hitherto held to be entirely natural, since they had been my full-time occupation. I would have no place in those institutional structures within which I had habitually interacted with persons with whom I felt some intellectual affinity and shared a common pursuit. As the professor, little mindful of sociological subtleties (and confusing ascribed and acquired statuses) had explained, the university was like a family, but one to which you had to be elected. And, alas, in his opinion, neither my American qualification nor my proposed field of study, 'Social Aspects of the Italian Novel from 1920 to 1960', held any promise that such an event would ever occur. However, uneasiness, surprise, and a lack of familiarity with Cambridge ways made it difficult for me to see clearly the contradictions and the misinformation with which he, as well as others after him, greeted all my enquiries.

As I was learning about Cambridge traditions (a topic never exhausted among academics), I was at the same time beginning to understand ways in which social categories are formed and sometimes become crystallised. In this case, the main divide, and the one that had the most direct impact on my daily existence, was one due to sex and marital status. (In those days, one did not yet think in terms of gender but more usually in terms of roles – in ways which often went with facile stereotyping.)

In the 1960s Cambridge University was generally described as a highly elitist institution. Intellectual values were dominant. Overlooking the fact that earlier selection by census and class made it so that most eligible candidates for academic positions were predominantly middle- or upper-class males, it was sometimes described as a meritocracy – a gloss that gave its successful members full license to view anyone outside their circle and most educational qualifications from other universities with overbearing disdain.

A few women did hold academic jobs, but most senior members of the university seemed determined to maintain its exclusive and predominantly male character; it was not, as one of the university's distinguished members, and later recipient of the Nobel Prize, once flippantly stated, *because* they were women, but just because they were silly and ill-educated. In this instance, persistent reference to 'academic wives' as a category may have derived from a fear that, with growing numbers of women graduates, a challenge might come from very close quarters, that is, from those wives who were themselves qualified for university posts. On the other hand, the husbands of women academics, although in a similar structural position, did not cause any concern, since they were comparatively few, and were usually active in their own professional spheres. Labelling 'wives' as a category, then, served admirably for the purpose of qualifying, keeping at a distance, controlling, and, above all, excluding them. At the same time, it separated 'mere wives' (as the women often described themselves, sometimes in irony and sometimes in abject humility) from the few women in academic positions. Restlessness on the part of some of the women seemed to bear little or no positive result: change was obviously a long-term project. My loss of innocence, then, was not in learning the facts of love, but learning about sexual antagonism, destructiveness and academic contempt, as I was slowly becoming acquainted with an unfamiliar division of labour – one which, as older women indicated, required greater humility, dedication and forbearance than I had ever known in my Mediterranean days.

Discussion of 'private' and 'public' as descriptive and analytical terms first came to my attention when in the 1970s I began my training in social anthropology, and my comments were a spontaneous 'response from the native'. At that time structuralists seemed confident that binary oppositions neatly summed up the moral values and outlooks of different cultures and provided a key to their understanding. Public/private were thus often linked with right/left and male/female, and usually viewed as positive/negative. In accounts of Mediterranean life, private spheres, mainly associated with women and with domesticity, were generally reported to have been considered inferior to public spheres which were the preserves of men, and in which economic and political power were visibly held and transacted (Peristiany 1965; Pitt-Rivers 1954, etc.). As other, somewhat later, ethnographers showed, however, for women the house was both a 'locum of power' (Hirschon 1978) and 'a stronghold of essential values', a 'focus of family loyalty', an 'image of salvation' and 'agent of redemption' (du Boulay 1974: 256). Descriptions of women's informal economic and religious power within the home thus seemed to provide examples of reciprocity and complementarity possibly less asymmetrical than those observed among Oxford and Cambridge academics.

As Davidoff points out, a distinction between private domestic spheres and the workplace was most strongly developed in Victorian England, and was indeed a strong feature of Northern European thinking in the nineteenth century (1979: 64–65). Might the opposition of private/public, then, have been transposed on to Mediterranean (mostly village) societies without sufficient attention being given to nuances in the use of space and in attribution of value? And might not accounts of the superiority of public male spheres in the European Mediterranean be partly a projection of Anglo-Saxon attitudes, for instance, might it derive from a disaffection with domesticity widespread in post-industrial and urban areas? Or might not reports of sexual stereotyping, of constricting role-structures, and of the control of women, be due to an underlying tendency to view those societies as less civilised 'others', and at the same time obscure realities much closer to home? (M. Herzfeld 1987b: 59–61).

Description of the seclusion and protection of Mediterranean women within the confines of the family then appeared to me like a reflection (albeit an upside-down one) of women's exclusion from prestigious professional spheres in the industrial north of Europe, and in developed urban areas of the Mediterranean itself. In my comparison of aspects of the lives of the wives of dons in Cambridge in the 1960s with those of Sarakatsani women – both strong examples of long-standing misogyny – I tried to show the the difficulty of drawing firm boundaries between domains, and the mistakes that can derive from assuming that 'private/public' is homologously linked with other dichotomies or oppositions. For example, while traditional colleges, as places dedicated to intellectual values and academic endeavour, are naturally thought of as 'male' and 'public', they are only 'male' insofar as until recently they excluded women, and they are in fact strongly defensive of their privacy (as privilege). They, at the same time, offer comforts usually associated with domesticity, in ways which some women consider as a usurpation of their traditional prerogatives as wives and as hostesses (Sciama 1984: 61–62; S. Ardener 1984: 36–38).

Neither 'public' nor 'private' can then be used as fixed analytical terms or readily be associated with negative or positive values, while the domains they describe are never as clearly bounded as some of the literature implies. In the economic sphere, the dichotomy has in general obscured the significance of households both in terms of production and of exchange while a definition of backstreets and neighbourhoods as 'private' merely based on the fact that they are often frequented and apparently dominated by women (Reiter 1975: 13–15) fails to note that such places usually act as filters between the family and the community (Hirschon 1978 and 1989, *passim*) and are no less interesting to the observer of social and political life than are the men's cafés, main streets and *piazzas* of cities and villages.

Whether Strathern's observation that 'in terms of Western classification' public/private, political/domestic and social/individual 'form coherent ideational sets' (1988: 70–74) may hold true throughout Europe should, I think, remain open to question. In the context of an anthropology that purports to reflect upon the categories of our own as well as of other societies, variations in the ways by which the privacy of individuals, families, or institutions, is protected – and whether its consequence is privation or empowerment – are certainly important issues and still pose a challenge for fieldworkers.

# Notes

1. As Simmel writes, 'Comparative anthropological data do not seem to exist in a form that crystallizes out the aspects relevant to questions of privacy, nor have correlations of these aspects with other social and cultural elements been given any extensive study' (1968: 481). By contrast, the distinction between public and private morality, most dramatically put forward in Machiavelli's *The Prince*, has always concerned moral philosophers. (For a recent example, see Stuart Hampshire 1978.)

2. The opposition of private-women/public-men clearly is related to the Marxist distinction between private and public economic sectors. In particular the general assumption that women exist entirely within a 'private' sphere is based on Engels's understanding of the difficulty of reconciling women's domestic roles with integration of their labour into a wider, and trade-unionised section (1972 ed., pp. 152ff). Space does not allow me to discuss the analytical validity of the Marxist distinction; I should, however, like to suggest that its application to aspects of life other than economic ones may obscure some broader or more subtle (and non-sexist) distinctions underlying different private/public formations in a variety of cultures. Indeed, according to its radical feminist critics, a rigid private/public opposition itself reflects a bourgeois conception of society.

3. Clearly it would be incorrect to assume that 'private' and 'public' may be universally opposed, or universally coupled with 'female' and 'male' and viewed respectively as negative and positive values, or associated with the spatial distinction between left and

right. For example, while Sarakatsani do associate female and male respectively with left and right and with negative and positive values, their symbolic classification is not expressed in the organisation of house-space (cf. Needham 1979: 55–70).

4. This view of women's lives is most eloquently expressed in Simone de Beauvoir' s *The Second Sex* (1949). See also Judith Okely's work on English girls' boarding schools (S. Ardener, 1978) and Hilary Callan's article on diplomats' wives (S. Ardener, 1975), but for interesting Mediterranean comparisons, see Rocco Scotellaro (1972) and Ann Corneliesen (1977).

5. They were collected over several years in Cambridge. It should be added that rules are now changing in many colleges, so that the situation I am about to describe may soon cease to exist. However, they may retain some historical interest.

6. Several of my informants, however, maintain there is *no* competition in colleges and that emulation only takes place in university faculties. Yet, while it is true that college fellows ideally form a society of peers, a great deal of competitiveness, albeit controlled, is very often shown in their frequent assessment of the rightness of their colleagues' claims to distinction. Moreover, when there arises the possibility for advancement within the college itself, as, for example, when a college headship becomes vacant, the undercutting of possible rivals could happily equal the slanderous gossip of the villagers of Ambéli.

7. Compare F. P. R. Just, 1976, 207–8.

8. It may be of some interest to note that one of the first topics discussed by members of one of Cambridge's early nineteenth-century essay clubs was 'Has woman, since the Fall, been the cause of more good or evil to mankind?' (Peter Allen 1978: 2).

9. Notice the fear of pollution in the often repeated commonplace 'they [women] will speak of nothing but nappies and babies!' When I first arrived in Cambridge I was surprised that intelligent people could be so repetitive. It took me some time to realise that the remark, often reiterated at 'ladies' nights', involved an element of ritual and an attempt to keep order and re-establish boundaries between categories which were threatening to break down (cf. Douglas: 1966).

10. The full quotation is as follows: 'Pleasure was identified with happiness and happiness by both their favourite philosophers, Mill and Green, with self-realization . . . [T]heir goals nevertheless were so clear and their purpose so single-minded that they were apt to sacrifice other valuable things to achieve them. Self-realization was not extended to those capital creatures their wives. Fortunately for their husbands they were trained to self-sacrifice'.

# 6

# Sexual Prohibitions, Shared Space and 'Fictive' Marriages in Shi'ite Iran

*Jane Khatib-Chahidi*

## Introduction

This chapter is an attempt to give a description of the reality of both sexual segregation and interaction for the ordinary Moslem with particular reference to Iran, where the majority of the population belong to the *Ithna Ashari* ('Twelver') branch of Shi'a Islam.[1]

Although most Western observers are familiar with the Islamic pattern of living which, with varying degrees of severity, stresses the separation of men from women, they are often not so familiar with the laws upon which the separation is based and mixing permitted, nor with the elaboration of these laws and the customs associated with them, which justify the actual behaviour witnessed in Moslem countries today. Fundamental to an understanding of social interaction between the sexes is the Islamic ruling on the forbidden categories of person for marriage. Those men and women whose *kinship*, as defined by the jurists, represents an impediment to marriage are permitted to be on familiar terms with each other and share the same physical space; those not related in this way, should avoid each other's company. The impediment of *kinship* to marriage in Islam provides the rules upon which restrictions of marriage partner *and* social interaction between the sexes are based. Taken in conjunction with additional categories of excluded persons, moreover, the forbidden categories in their entirety represent a comprehensive attempt to avoid all extramarital sexuality which, in Islam, is strictly prohibited.

I shall first indicate briefly what sexual segregation and mingling normally entails. I shall then elaborate upon the forbidden categories of person for marriage in Islam. Next I shall relate these laws to the actual household in Iran, its composition and its allocation of space. Following this are the exceptions to the rule, where it will be seen that either expected social behaviour between the sexes is modified to permit more informal relationships between potential marriage partners who are likely to find themselves within the same physical space, or the ruling itself is 'manipulated' to enable additional persons of the opposite sex to share the same space in a legally approved manner.

I shall give but brief consideration to the life-style of Shahs, tribal chiefs and wealthy landlords in Iran because, as in many societies, the way of life of ruling elites is not always representative of the life-style of the population at large; neither shall I consider practice in the rural areas since, although it sometimes corresponds fairly closely to practice in the towns (cf. Wright 1978) it also exhibits great regional variation, whereas the life-style of the urban-dweller, wherever the town may be situated, exhibits greater homogeneity.

My terms of reference are wide and deliberately so: I go from traditional to modern life-style, from province to capital, from the relatively modest household to the more affluent, from the customs of the devoutly religious to those of people who may never say their prayers. I do this for two main reasons: during the 1970s in Iran, traditional patterns of living subsisted side-by-side with more modern ones. Within each extended family of, for example, three generations, there were often wide discrepancies in religious practice, wealth, education and social status as reflected in the occupation of the head of household of each nuclear unit. Secondly, if we take as an arbitrary date, 1965, when I first went to Iran, it seemed to me that the life-experience of most urban women, rich and poor, had a basic similarity: their lives, passed mainly in the home, revolved around family and household occupations. The wealthy certainly had more in the way of material comfort than the poor but it was a difference of *degree* rather than *kind*: the wives of landowners, army officers, minor government officials and labourers had much in common with one another. By 1978, however, this difference in degree *had* become a qualitative one: the 'modern', educated, emancipated young Iranian woman had little in common with her working-class counterpart and, what is more, rarely had any form of social contact with her. Yet, it is my contention that, despite the changes that appeared to have radically altered the way of life of many of the middle and upper classes in that period, the *underlying* religious rulings and their associated social norms inculcated in childhood were still very much in existence, sometimes in modified and distorted form. For the rest of the urban population, both life-style and the legal-religious principles upon which it was based had remained largely unchanged during the same period. To this I will allude in my conclusion to the chapter.

For Islamic law I have relied mainly upon Querry's translation into French of the work of Sheikh Nadjm ed-din Aboul Qassem J'afar ebn Ali Yahya, entitled *Sharāy'eh al-islam fi masāel al halal val harām*, whose interpretation of Islamic law is widely accepted by *Ithna Ashari*

Shi'ite Moslems. The teaching of present-day religious leaders in Iran on the matters dealt with in this chapter remains substantially the same as that of Sheikh Nadjm ed-din (A.D. 602–676), as can be seen from references given to Khomeini's works. I have tried, wherever possible, to refer the reader to Xavière's translation into French of extracts of Khomeini's writings published under the title of *Principes politiques, philosophiques, sociaux et religieux de l'Ayatollah Khomeiny*. I have had to supplement this, however, from Khomeini's *Resāleh touzi almasāel* which is only available, as yet, in Persian and Arabic. My principal sources, apart from these, are my own experience of Iranian family life in Iran and abroad and fieldwork done over several summers in Kerman which was not, however, directed towards this specific topic.

## The Reality of Sexual Segregation for the Ordinary Moslem in Iran

Veiling and confining women to the home have served in practice to ensure that as far as possible the only men and women permitted social interaction are those between whom marriage is forbidden: they are said to be *mahram* to each other. *Mahram* is the legal term denoting a relationship by blood, milk, marriage or sexual union which makes marriage between persons so related forbidden. It is a permanent prohibition which remains unaffected by divorce or death. *Mahram* also has a wider meaning: uppermost in the mind of the average Iranian when the term is used is the fact that *mahram* persons are those with whom one can mix freely and be on informal terms. Unlike our English prohibited degrees of kinship for marriage, which until recently existed for the most part as little-read notices in the church porch, these degrees form an integral part of most Iranians' upbringing, whether they come from a strictly religious family or not, because their social behaviour is based on them. A child grows up knowing that it is quite acceptable to be in the company of such persons of the opposite sex, to joke with them, kiss them and show affection towards them. A man and wife are *mahram* to each other as a result of their marriage. Familiar behaviour, however, is unacceptable towards *na-mahram* persons. *Na-mahram* literally denotes any person of the opposite sex whose kinship does *not* represent an impediment for marriage. By extension *na-mahram* is sometimes used to denote people of the opposite sex whom the speaker does not know.

For the devout Moslem any sharing of space with *na-mahram* persons is to be avoided as it could lead to illegal sexual intercourse outside the bonds of marriage, which is forbidden to all Moslems. The prohibition upon illicit sex extends even to looks and gestures, according to some commentators (Querry 1871: 642, 669). Practising Moslems would, for example, consider their prayers nullified if they looked at a *na-mahram* person while praying and this aroused sexual desire; for the more scrupulous, the mere looking, without the desire, would be sufficient for them to feel they had to repeat their prayer.

The wealthy Moslem of the past was able to ensure this segregation of the *na-mahram* from the *mahram* by confining all the womenfolk of his household to the harem and placing eunuchs to guard them (*Encyclopedia of Islam,* new edn. 1971, vol. III: 209). For the ordinary Moslem, however, it neither was, nor is, practicable to do likewise. His household is not likely to be either so big or so self-contained that he can insist upon such strict confinement of all the women, including mother, sisters, wife, daughters and servants. Outside the house certain observances might ensure the minimum of contact between these women and *na-mahram* males: one side of the street used to be designated for women's use in Iranian towns and cities; the public baths were used at separate times by men and women; public libraries in some provincial towns in 1978 only allowed women access on one day a week. Even in recent years in the provinces the wearing of the *chador* (veil) in public was considered obligatory by most self-respecting women and girls, especially if they were natives of that town. Very rarely would any woman from a 'good' family go out alone in the provinces even for household shopping, which was often done, either by the husband if the family had no servant, or by the husband and wife together, or by the wife with a female companion.

Although stories are told of wives – mainly urban-dwellers who have moved away from their own home area on marriage – being confined to the one marital home all their lives, this was not typical. It was more usual for women to be confined, as far as possible, to a number of houses. With the permission of the head of the household, which could be withheld according to Islamic Law, the women of the household were allowed to visit other women in their homes and receive their visits in return. Amongst middle- and upper-class Iranians whose houses were large enough to allow for special rooms for entertaining guests, frequent all-female gatherings were held in them; the men would use the rooms for their all-male gatherings on other occasions. Judging by the memories of many older Iranian women, the social life they led in this largely women's world often compared favourably in richness and variety with that which they were experiencing in Tehran during the 1970s.[2]

Yet there were situations where it was impracticable to adhere to strict segregation from *na-mahram* persons. Inside the house not all relatives were *mahram* to each other. Servants were employed in even relatively modest households. It was not always possible to ensure that a suitable *mahram* relative was available to accompany a woman if she was travelling. The death of a man meant his widow, while remaining permanently forbidden in marriage to *mahram* kin as a result of her marriage, became a potentially available marriage partner for *na-mahram* persons living in the same household or for frequent visitors to the family, her previous married status having made her temporarily forbidden in marriage to all other men. Shi'a Islam, as opposed to Sunni, has a mechanism for dealing with such varied and awkward situations: through marriage contracts and the kinship which ensues, the space shared by men and women standing in a *mahram* relationship to each other can be opened to others for whom it would normally be forbidden amongst religious households in Iran.

## Forbidden Categories of Person for Marriage in Shi'ite Islam

As interpreted by Shi'ite Islamic jurists, the Koranic *surahs* relating to the forbidden degrees of kinship for marriage (IV. 23–25), can be divided into four categories of *mahram* persons.

*Blood relatives*: marriage or legal sexual union (concubinage) is prohibited between a man or woman and their ascendants or descendants in the same line, their full or half-brothers and sisters, and their maternal and paternal aunts and uncles of whatever generation (Querry 1871: 656).

*Milk relatives:* the same rules as for blood relatives apply in the case of 'fosterage' where a woman suckles another's child. The feeding of the child at the breast is considered as creating the relationship of mother and child between the two. By extension, the 'milk-mother' *and* her husband, by whom she became pregnant and who is 'owner of the milk', become *mahram* relatives of the same order within the natural genealogy of the suckled child, just as this child becomes assimilated into the natural genealogy of the milk-mother and her husband (the 'milk-father') (Querry 1871: 661; Altorki 1980: 234ff.). The relationship extends, as in the case of the natural one, to the ascendants and descendants in the direct line, to brothers and sisters, and aunts and uncles, whether they are real or milk-kin resulting from *their* having been suckled by a woman other than their own mother. The relationship does not affect the siblings of the milk-child or the relatives of the milk-parents towards each other: thus the milk-mother can marry the brothers of the milk-child, and her relatives do not become *mahram* to the siblings of this child. The father of the suckled child, however, cannot marry the daughter of the milk-mother or the daughter of her husband, whether real or milk. He may marry the milk-mother's milk-daughter, but it is not recommended (Khomeini, n.d., pp. 392–98, articles 2464–97).

*Relatives by marriage*: marriage and concubinage are prohibited between a man and the ascendants and descendants in the direct line of his wife or concubine, whether they are already born or to be born, and whether they reside in the same house or elsewhere. The same prohibition applies for the wife or concubine with regard to the man's ascendants and descendants in the direct line (Querry 1871: 666).

In the case of marriages which are not consummated the man and woman are subject to the same prohibition concerning ascendants. However, although the woman and the man's sons (that is, his descendants) are permanently forbidden in marriage to each other, the man can marry his wife's daughter provided that his marriage with the former has been terminated (ibid.: 666).

*Relationships arising from illegitimate sexual unions*: the same prohibition as for blood relatives applies in the case of illegitimate sexual unions which result in the birth of illegitimate offspring (ibid.: 656). It extends to illegal sexual intercourse without issue where the prohibition is the same as that for relatives by marriage (ibid.: 666, 668). Fornication between nephew and aunt prevents a future marriage between the nephew and his german cousins (ibid.: 668). The prohibition can even come into force by illegal looks and touches according to some Shi'ite commentators. In this case the prohibition operates upon the woman (object of the looks and touches) and the father or son of he who committed the act, but it does not extend to the mother or daughter of the same woman (ibid.: 669).

Homosexuality incurs the marriage prohibition between the man who committed the act and the sister, mother and daughter of his partner in the act (ibid.: 672; Khomeini 1979: 126). If the homosexual act takes place after the marriage, the marriage remains unaffected, whereas in the former case, the marriage becomes null and void (Khomeini 1979: 127).

Apart from the categories of person mentioned above *who are all mahram* (excluding descendants of the wife in an unconsummated marriage), a man is also forbidden to be married to two sisters at the same time. He can, nevertheless, marry his wife's sister if he divorces his wife or she dies: sisters-in-law and brothers-in-law are *na-mahram* to each other and potential marriage partners, only temporarily forbidden by virtue of an existing marriage.

## Penalties for Infringement of These Laws

Marriage to a *mahram* person automatically renders the contract null and void; consummation of the marriage thus becomes the illegal sexual act of *zinā* compounded by the fact that it was committed with a *mahram* person and, therefore, incestuous (*zinā bā mahārem*).³ All sexual intercourse between persons who are not in a state of legal matrimony or concubinage is forbidden (*harām*) in Islam. The term *zinā* denotes the illegal sexual act which could be fornication, adultery, incest or rape. Adultery is sometimes described by the addition of the word *mohseni*.

In the Koran it is stated that *zinā* should be punished by flogging – a hundred lashes for both the man and the woman (XXIV.2). In another passage where only adulterous wives are mentioned, it is said that they should be 'kept in houses' until they die (IV.19). In practice, flogging has been administered for fornication; for adultery, women have sometimes been immured and, in later times, stoned (Levy 1931: 170). The Prophet is said to have ordered a woman to be stoned because she was Jewish; she was punished according to Jewish law which exacted the death penalty for both the man and the woman (Leviticus XX.10). The author of *Sharā'yeh-al-islam* (Querry 1871, 1872) states that the penalty for *zinā* is incurred if the guilty party knew of the prohibition, committed the act voluntarily and was a major. Stoning should only be exacted in the case of adultery if the guilty spouse, man or woman, admits guilt four times on four different occasions, or the illegal act has been witnessed by four males, or three males and two females. If the accused, before production of testimonial proof, repents sincerely, he or she should not be punished. Those guilty of an incestuous marriage, that is with *mahram* kin, who consummate it not knowing of the interdiction, should not be punished; those who knowingly commit incest should be put to death. According to one tradition the crime of simple incest is punishable by beheading, preceded by flogging, and that of adulterous incest by stoning, preceded by flogging. The argument for this distinction is made on the grounds that each case is complicated by another; in the first it is incest *and* fornication and in the second incest *and* adultery. To Sheikh Nadjm it seemed that beheading was sufficient in both cases (Querry 1872: 482–90).

## The Composition of the Iranian Household

When we examine the actual composition of the Iranian household, as one might well expect, it is these *mahram* relatives (consanguinal and affinal resulting from marriage and, in the past, concubinage) who were, and still are, those most likely to occupy the same physical space within the Iranian household, or to be the most frequent visitors to the household.

Traditionally, in village and town alike, the household, at a certain period of its development cycle (to use Goody's 1958 phrase), would often comprise a cluster of nuclear families. While parents were alive, their sons would bring their wives to live in the parental home where they and their children would have a separate room, rooms or house, within the same compound as the parents. This pattern of household has not entirely disappeared even in modern Tehran. Amongst the wealthier, 'westernised' Iranians, parents have had additional houses built in their large gardens in the north of the city or invested in a block of flats where the parents occupy one and married children the others. The main change in this respect is that it is often married daughters – not just married sons – who occupy them.

In the past, therefore, and in the present day in villages and provincial towns, grandparents, unmarried or widowed grandfather's sisters, unmarried and widowed paternal aunts, the sons of the paternal grandparents and their wives and children might well all be within the same physical space, often eating communally. In addition to these there would be resident servants. Those engaged as wet-nurses and dry-nurses on the birth of a child would remain in the household for years acting as a kind of nanny, their own young children sometimes also with them, being visited by members of their own family and going on periodic return visits to their own homes. The number of persons within the household would be increased further by the visits of relatives, especially the maternal kin of each generation represented within the household, and those of daughters with their families who had left the household upon marriage.

## The Allocation of Physical Space in the Iranian Household

In the past the allocation of space within the house reflected the need to accommodate such large numbers of people. Visitors, if relations, rarely paid brief visits and rooms were not normally set aside for one use. The absence of furniture in the main living areas facilitated the transformation of living areas during the day into sleeping areas at night. Carpets were the only essential furnishings, on which one slept and sat and on which the meals were served, a cloth being placed over the carpet for this purpose. Mattresses and bedding were rolled up during the day and stored either in rooms especially designed for this purpose, in alcoves built into the walls, or, wrapped in large pieces of material, they would serve as cushions placed against the walls. To this day in the provinces it is frequently only the guest room that contains furniture. Personal belongings were kept in trunks, boxes or carefully tied-up bundles and were the only privacy the individual had. Not that privacy is very often sought within physical space in Iran where to be alone is tantamount to being lonely.

The more affluent landowner, high-ranking government official or successful merchant of forty years ago might have lived in a house as depicted in Figure 6.1.[4] He needed to be wealthy because it comprised virtually two houses in one and necessitated keeping two groups of servants, one for the family quarters, the *anderun*, who would be mainly female, the other for the *birun*, mainly male. *Na-mahram* male visitors would be entertained by the men of the household in the *birun*. The *birun* also served as an office for landowners and politicians. Female visitors would be more likely to go to the *anderun*. Their presence in this area would mean that male members of the household who were *na-mahram* to them and considered adult[5] would retire from the family group in the *anderun*. The cooking for both areas would be done in the *anderun* but shopping for the household would normally be undertaken by male servants of the *birun*. Since the *birun* was situated at the main entrance to the house and not all such houses had a separate entrance to the *anderun*, visitors to the *anderun* would be seen as they passed through the outer courtyard, just as the womenfolk of the *anderun* would be seen by members of the *birun* when they left the house. Here we have a way of life approximating to that of the harems of the Islamic Empire but on a smaller scale. Sexual segregation is marked and the women living in such a household were frequently more secluded than their less wealthy counterparts living in similar urban areas. It is in this type of household that polygyny might have been practised, although its occurrence in Iran in this century appears to have been rare.

Turning to Figure 6.2, we have a more modest house plan that is typical of many old houses still in existence in the provinces and in the older quarters of Tehran. The families that occupied and still occupy such houses range from the relatively affluent to the less well-to-do urban dweller. The head of household could be an army officer, civil servant, merchant or artisan, although in modern Tehran the first three would be more likely to have moved to a recently-built house or flat in one of the more fashionable suburbs of the city.

As can be seen, the entertaining area, like the *birun* of the wealthy man's house, is situated near the front entrance on one side of an enclosed courtyard that may thus have rooms on three sides opening into it. The family area is situated at the furthest end, opposite the main entrance. The rooms to the left will serve as extra sleeping areas for unmarried children, and married ones with their families if still living in the parental home. All these rooms might be raised from ground level by a few feet to allow for a semi-basement storey to the house. Here

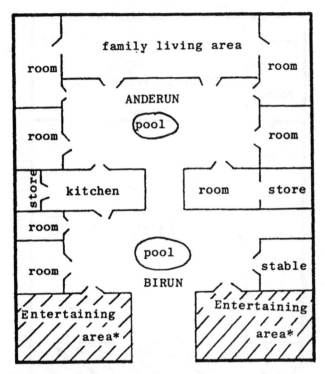

*Traditional men's area
NB. Hatched areas in these diagrams indicate where *na-mahram* male visitors are entertained.

**Figure 6.1:** Traditional House of Wealthy Family

would be the kitchen, storage rooms for water and provisions, and the lavatory. The entertaining area in this house would be used by both men and women if the guests were members of the extended family. In the past and present times, for more religious families, *na-mahram* male visitors to the house would be entertained in this area although the women of the family might use it when they were entertaining larger numbers of female visitors who were *na-mahram* to the men of the household.

The courtyards with their centrally-placed pools were, and still are, focal points. In the traditional house all rooms open out into and have a view of the courtyard (there are not necessarily interconnecting doors between the rooms). The courtyard thus affords the most common, visible-to-all arena for social interaction and household activity, besides offering additional sleeping space in the hot summer months. All per-

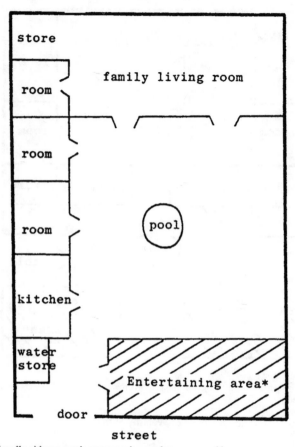

**Figure 6.2:** Traditional House of Average Family

mitted visitors to the family living area can be seen coming across it;[6] in the evenings informal entertaining takes place here; during the day the vegetables for the meals will be prepared in the open air by the women-folk of the household; the washing and washing-up used to be done next to the pool, dishes and clothes being rinsed in it because, until recently, this might well be the only place where a tap could be found.

Again, this aspect of physical space is not altogether absent in the modern Tehran flat (Figure 6.3). Here we find that an almost universal feature of apartments is a relatively large, central hall with rooms open-ing out into it. The hall serves as the family living quarters where the family spend most of their time, where the table and chairs for family

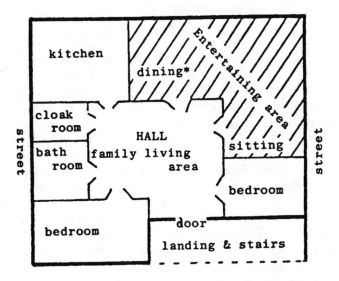

*In modern times often a 'mixed' area but in religious families used by men *or* women

**Figure 6.3:** Modern Tehran Flat

meals are found and where the television is placed; it is also where all social activity with close friends and family takes place. In addition it has features of the old courtyard, in that it is through the hall that one must pass to go from one room to another and through which guests must pass to gain access to the entertaining area. This latter area contains all the best furniture, carpets and bric-a-brac. It is often larger and always more luxurious than the family living area of the hall, but it will only be used for more formal or large-scale entertaining. Although the prohibitive cost of land in Tehran has meant that most young couples can only aspire to renting a flat, the necessarily more limited physical space of the flat still reflects traditional ways of living. It also exhibits the weakening of the prohibitions over the sharing of space between *na-mahram* men and women since, whereas the courtyard enabled the family to see the visitor to the house without the visitor seeing them, the family living-area of the hall means the seeing is reciprocal. Moreover, friends as well as *mahram* relatives now share this space. Nevertheless, many of the more religious of the older generation will forego the interest of seeing *na-mahram* visitors to the household by retiring from the hall to another room where the 'strangers' will not come.

## Exceptions to the Mahram Principle

### The Na-mahram Relatives

Although persons of the opposite sex standing in a *na-mahram* relationship to one another should and could withdraw from each other's presence to a different area of the house, this was rarely rigidly adhered to when these persons happened to be relatives by blood or marriage, except in the most religiously-minded families which, in any case, had methods of dealing with this situation (see below). Cousins – father's brother's children – might well be resident members of the extended family households. Father's sister's children and wife's brother's and sister's children might well be frequent visitors. Cousins were, and still are, considered as ideal marriage partners, particularly the father's brother's daughter. Marriages between them are referred to as being 'knotted in heaven' and thought of as a form of miracle by many devout Moslems. These feelings would appear to overcome legal-religious injunctions against mixing with *na-mahram* persons. This, in conjunction with the fact that, traditionally, girls were often married before reaching puberty so either left the home or remained in it as married women, which thus made them forbidden in marriage to any other man, presumably satisfied religious principles.

Similarly, in the case of brother- or sister-in-law, the husband's brother and husband's wife might well be residing within the same household. The wife's sister might well be a frequent visitor. Actual practice, as in the case of cousins who often mix freely with one another, does not conform to *na-mahram* principles. The husband's brother may enjoy a relaxed relationship with his brother's wife and the husband with his wife's sister. In the latter case it is particularly striking: a man will jokingly refer to his wife's sister as his *nān-e-zir-e- kebāb* ('the bread under the *kebāb*') which is considered as the tastiest part of the dish since all the meat juices which have dropped from the *kebāb* during cooking will have been absorbed by it. Again here, there seems to be a relaxation of the *na-mahram* principle, which, in its turn, affects observed patterns of behaviour.

For those who would consider such informality as illegal there are recognised procedures for making the *na-mahram* relative *mahram*. If, for example, a man wishes to make his sister-in-law *mahram* to him, he can marry an infant girl for a few days (see below p.125 for temporary marriage). He then gives his infant wife to his sister-in-law to suckle for the required number of times or for twenty-four hours. The sister-in-law thus becomes the milk-mother of his wife and like his mother-in-law, a *mahram* relative (Khomeini, n.d.: 398, article 2493).[7]

*Making the Na-mahram into Mahram – 'Fictive' Marriage*

Marriage, according to Islamic Law, is a civil contract, subject to the same regulations as other contracts,[8] the validity of which does not depend on any religious ceremony. Neither does the validity of the contract depend upon consummation of the marriage[9] although non-consummation and refusal to have sexual intercourse by the husband are grounds for divorce for women. The legal guardian of a minor has the right to conclude a marriage contract on behalf of a minor or anyone not considered as having reached the age of discretion.[10] Shi'ite jurists, contrary to the practice of some Sunnites, refuse the girl the right to ratify or dissolve a marriage contract when she reaches maturity, and maintain that the consent of the guardian renders every act of a minor legal and valid (Baillie 1805: 312; Querry 1871: 650).

In addition to the 'permanent' (*nikah*) marriage with up to four wives at any given time, dissoluble upon divorce, Shi'a Islam recognises 'temporary' marriage contracts. The Arabic term for these is *mut'ah*; in Persian they are more usually referred to as *sigheh*, which denotes both the *form* of the marriage contract and the *woman* who becomes the 'temporary' wife in such contracts.

For Shi'ites this temporary marriage is a legal contract, like the permanent one, but there are important differences between the two. The contract must contain a precise statement of the period of time it is intended to last. This can be anything from an hour to several years, at the end of which time the contract automatically expires. The contract is not subject to dissolution by divorce but it can be dissolved upon the mutual consent of both parties although, according to Ameer Ali (1965, 361) some Shi'ite jurists say the consent of the husband alone is sufficient. Omission of mention of duration can make the contract a permanent one (Querry 1871: 694). If the marriage settlement by the husband (*mahr*) is not given – it can consist of anything, even a handful of corn – or if any expression implying the idea of possession by sale, as an offering or rent, enters into the contract, then in both cases it becomes null (Querry 1871: 689). The contract can be concluded by the partners themselves if they know the correct formula (*Encyclopaedia of Islam*, 1936, Vol. III: 775), but since it is recommended that this should be in Arabic (Querry 1871: 647), a mullah is often called upon. A minor girl requires the consent of her father or guardian to contract such a marriage. It is declared abominable for a man to marry a virgin who has no father but it is only discouraged if she preserves her virginity (Hollister 1953: 55–57; Querry 1871: 691). The husband does not require the consent of the wife *not* to have sexual intercourse.

The temporary marriage confers legitimacy on any children born of the union, but whereas the children inherit, the wife cannot, as she does in the permanent contract according to Shi'ite Law. There is some dispute over whether it is admissable to put a clause in the contract to enable the spouses to inherit from each other (Querry 1871: 695). The wife does not have the right to maintenance, although the Shi'a of India regularly include the right to maintenance in the temporary contract, and the falling incidence of such marriages has been attributed to the inability of present-day Shi'ites to meet the expense (Husain 1976). Khomeini states such a wife has no right to maintenance even when pregnant (1979: 129).

For the Shi'ites who advocate its practice, temporary marriage in its 'real' form as opposed to its 'fictive' form – with which the present paper is more concerned – is commonly seen as beneficial in that it prevents the birth of illegitimate children. In order to establish physical paternity the temporary wife is supposed to abstain from another contract with another man, on expiry of the first contract, for forty-five days.[11] Critics of the custom – who include many devout Moslems in Iran – are more likely to see it as a form of legal prostitution. The devout Moslem, however, is likely to make good use of the institution in its strictly nominal form to facilitate the sharing of space with na-mahram persons inside and outside the home in a legal manner.

Other semi-permanent and, in the natural course of events, na-mahram members of the household in even the moderately well-to-do Iranian family, are the servants, male and female, and nannies. Even in the 1970s in Iran – and in all probability its incidence will increase dramatically now – servants in Iranian houses where there were devout Moslems of a more scrupulous nature were made into mahram relatives. The servant has a temporary marriage contracted for him or her with one of the blood relatives of the head of the household, usually an infant son or daughter. A mullah will normally be called upon to pronounce the formula which will stipulate any length of time. The stipulated duration, however short, is of little importance as provided the mahr has been given, the mere agreement to the contract by both the servant and the legal guardian of the minor puts the servant into the forbidden category of kin for marriage for the principal members of the household. The servant thus becomes either the son-in-law or daughter-in-law to the head of the household and subject to the sexual and marital prohibitions associated with unconsummated marriages (see above, p. 117). Sexual intercourse between the servant and any of these mahram kin would thus be considered incest and therefore, one must presume, far less likely to occur.

This arrangement permits the practising Moslem to carry out his devotions with a clear conscience. It permits the female servant to attend to her work without the necessity of being strictly veiled in the presence of the male members of the household, which would impede her efficiency. It also permits the women of the household to have a male servant in their presence without it affecting their devotions or behaviour. The servants themselves are protected from the same inconveniences as regards their prayers and also from accusations that they may be immoral because they are living with 'strangers'.

Sharing of space in a manner which conforms to religious rulings can be similarly arranged outside the home. Moslem women going on the pilgrimage to Mecca should be accompanied by a *mahram* relative. Since it is not always possible to arrange this with an existing *mahram* relative, the temporary marriage contract can be used to create a suitable *mahram* companion. A widowed lady and her sister-in-law's husband (her husband's sister's husband), both, therefore, *na-mahram* to each other, decided to make the pilgrimage in the same year. When they heard of each other's intentions, they thought it would be good if they could go together. Neither, being devout, could entertain travelling together until the *na-mahram* situation had been changed. This was done by the sister-in-law's husband contracting a nominal, temporary, marriage with the old lady's teenage granddaughter. The contract was stipulated to expire after their return from Mecca.

Something of a similar nature can take place, either through a temporary or permanent marriage contract, when a woman is a widow. Deprived of her married status by the death of her husband, she becomes a potentially available marriage partner for all *na-mahram* men. Although the celibate state is normally discouraged in Islam and widowed women in rural areas of Iran will often re-marry, amongst middle- and upper-class families it is common for widows to remain thus for the rest of their lives. Re-marriage in such cases is regarded as denoting a lack of affection and respect for their dead husband.[12] On the other hand, for the devout widow the celibate state in which she finds herself can cause ill-ease: if she is considered marriageable, her presence in *na-mahram* company invites attention from men who will think her available. The mere fact that she is potentially available, being without a husband, encourages others to scrutinise her behaviour and interpret it in the worst light given the slightest excuse.[13] From the religious point of view her presence in the same space as other practising Moslems of the opposite sex may cause both her and them discomfort.

By means of a marriage contract with a suitable partner who is agreeable to a nominal marriage with no consummation, such a widow is able to become forbidden in marriage to all men who are not already *mahram* to her, and, in addition, *mahram*, i.e. permanently forbidden, to the ascendants and descendants in the direct line of her 'nominal' husband. In effect she thereby changes what would have been the illegal act of fornication into one of adultery or incest if, by any chance, she were to succumb to sexual advances. This presumably makes it less likely to happen, as in the case of the servants mentioned above.

A widower may similarly contract a marriage of a nominal nature in order to have a housekeeper, if he chooses not to live with his children. Such a contract enables both parties, if practising Moslems, to live in the same house. The temporary nature of the contract, however, eases the tensions that often do occur within families when the father remarries on the death of his wife and the children fear the second wife will inherit part of his property. The *sigheh*, as mentioned above, according to Shi'ite Law as practised in Iran, does not inherit.

Temporary marriage contracts are sometimes insisted upon by more devout parents when their daughter becomes engaged to be married. Whereas most 'westernised' Iranian parents would consider the engagement (*nāmzad*) as sufficient proof of the boy's serious intentions and allow the couple to see each other alone, some religious parents insist either that they must conclude the permanent marriage contract (*aqd*) before they can enjoy this freedom, or arrange a temporary contract between them until the permanent one takes place. In this case, however, unlike the cases mentioned above where consummation of the marriage is neither intended nor occurs, the temporary marriage is a precaution just in case it *should* occur, so that it would then at least be legal. The girl is not likely to permit it to happen even so, since the status of temporary wife is not considered worth the loss of virginity.[14]

## Conclusion

Islamic laws relating to the forbidden degrees of consanguinity and affinity for marriage are similar to those laid down for the Jews in Leviticus (24: 6–18) which have been adopted by Christianity with certain modifications. Yet even here they constitute a considerable extension of the incest prohibition if they are compared to actual practice amongst Greeks, Egyptians, Persians and some groups of early Christians before the coming of Islam.[15] With the additional categories of person also included, whether explicitly stated in the Koran (as it is for fosterage, although not to the extent that it has been interpreted) or added later by Islamic jurists, they indicate a highly moral, if not puritanical, concern for all forms of sexuality to be confined to that between husband and wife. By seeking to remove all likelihood of illegal sexual behaviour, that is by making it a crime – at best fornication, at worst incest – which affects not only the partners in the crime but also their kin, Islamic Law, in effect, seeks to exclude all sexual connotation from between the sexes within the immediate environment in which men and women commonly find themselves.

One particularly tragic case illustrates the consequences incurred if these laws are infringed. It concerns a middle-aged Iranian man, living in a provincial city, who had been happily married for many years and had four teenage children. Like many Iranians as they get older, he started to take a more serious interest in his religion. In one of the books he studied he came across the impediment to marriage incurred as a result of the homosexual act. It happened that in his youth, prior to his marriage, he had had a homosexual relationship with his wife's brother. He was greatly disturbed by what he read and consulted his local religious leader. His marriage was pronounced null and void; his children were considered as worse than illegitimate – in itself a terrible stigma in Iran – since they were deemed to be the offspring of an incestuous union. The whole affair became public knowledge. The man's own family was completely destroyed from the point of view of their 'social' reputation; the wife's family were also shamed because of what had happened so many years previously. The man was obliged to leave his wife and children and move away from the area.

As I have suggested, Islamic law concerning the forbidden categories of kin for marriage corresponds very much to the actual composition of the household and its most frequent visitors. The situation may have been modified by the advent of dried milk and baby foods, by the unavailability of servants, and the lack of sufficient space to accommodate large numbers of people in places like Tehran where many families live in flats. But these are all of recent event. What *is* apparent in Iran is that just as *mahram* provides the idiom through which members of the opposite sex are permitted to share the same physical space, so also can it govern the patterns of social behaviour witnessed between 'real' *mahram* kin. Often, there is an affectionate and relaxed relationship between father-in-law and daughter-in-law, mother-in-law and son-in-law, uncles and nieces, aunts and nephews. The impediment of marriage enables them to share the same physical space *and* enjoy each other's company. Campbell (1964: 101 ff), in his study of a Greek community, comments on the easy, affectionate relationship between first cousins of the opposite sex who, in Greece, are forbidden to marry. In many areas of Greece there exist similar taboos over the mixing of men and women as seen in Moslem countries.[16]

The 'fictive' cases represent a manipulation of the *mahram* concept to make it possible for additional persons of the opposite sex to share the same physical space. As such they afford a striking example of what one can term 'marriage of convenience'. The marriage is fictive and so is the kinship that ensues. Consummation is never intended. There is no actual change in the status or role of the contracting partners: the servant remains a servant and is not treated like a son- or daughter-in-law. The widower and widow continue in their widowed state though ostensibly married. There is no change in patterns of behaviour between the old lady and her late husband's brother-in-law since they have come back from Mecca. The prepubescent child used as nominal husband or wife in the contract in all probability does not even know what has been contracted in his or her name. Yet the fiction, admitted as such by people involved in these contracts at one level, is seen at another level as fact. As the latter it satisfies the religious mores of many Shi'ite Moslems. This, in itself, attests to the strength of their belief that incestuous relationships are so abhorred that they could not occur. Their belief is perhaps more an ardent hope, which could be belied, if we accept the many stories told of a husband's infidelity with a female servant within his own home.

When we turn to Iran of the 1970s – in particular Tehran – where rapid modernisation appeared to have broken down the *mahram/na-mahram* categories of the past, especially amongst the educated elite, partly visible in the ground plan of Figure 6.3, we find that, as Soraya Tremayne so aptly remarked, 'The form has changed; the substance stays the same' (1980).

The dichotomy of the social environment into *mahram* and *na-mahram* categories of people, while in keeping with traditional ways of life in Iran, poses problems in periods of rapid social and economic change. In the past, and still in the provinces, most women spend their time within the house but this space is not a confining one from the point of view of social interaction: there is always someone with whom to talk and there are frequent visits received and returned. The constant companionship of relatives from early childhood, together with a limited experience of contact with people outside the extended family, makes most Iranian women heavily dependent emotionally and psychologically upon the continued presence of their family in adult life. As more women went out to work in modern Tehran and men pursued careers that gave them extra-familial contacts, the vast family parties of the past were replaced by large gatherings of friends. Public holidays that used to be spent visiting relatives now became holidays spent by the nuclear family outside the capital and abroad. For the older women and the younger ones who were obliged to stay at home to look after young children, and those without sufficient education to obtain 'suitable' employment outside the house, the passing of traditional ways of life represented social deprivation for which, given their traditional upbringing, they were ill-prepared.

For the emancipated Iranian woman who went out to work, the impoverishment of social life within the home, for which her absence from the household was a contributory factor, did not present the same problems: social interaction with friends and colleagues amply compensated. Yet her situation in public space, until comparatively recently the domain of men,[17] presented other difficulties. The reticent behaviour learned in earlier years as appropriate when in *na-mahram* company was ill-suited to mixed gatherings, the success of which depended upon more sociable qualities. At work, if she carried out her duties with brisk efficiency she ran the risk of being considered unfeminine; if she behaved in a more 'feminine' manner, she might be considered a whore.[18] If some Iranian men too readily equated the woman's presence outside the home as an indication of sexual availability, some Iranian women, likewise, equated their new-found 'emancipation' in the limited terms of sexual freedom.[19] In this, I would suggest, the *mahram* and *na-mahram* categories inculcated in childhood, while ostensibly rejected, were appearing in distorted form: the sharing of space with potential marriage partners was being construed, albeit unconsciously, according to strict Islamic principles where this was the behaviour deemed inevitable by Islamic jurists if *na-mahram* persons were permitted freedom of social interaction.

The present situation in revolutionary Iran affords striking examples of the application of such Islamic principles in everyday life. Men and women in each other's company outside the home can be stopped by Revolutionary Guards and questioned as to their relationship. In one case the man and woman were first cousins but this did not prevent their being taken before the nearest *komiteh* to have their relationship further investigated. The headmistress of a bilingual English-Persian school in Tehran was heavily censored for not segregating the three-to-five-year-olds in the kindergarten class and was given a long lecture on the immorality of the West where co-educational schools were permitted which, according to the school inspector, encouraged such vices as homosexuality.

One of the first pronouncements of Ayatollah Khomeini concerning women after the Revolution indicated that although women could hold high government office, their position as secretaries in the administration was considered as unworthy of the high status accorded to women in Islam. The new Islamic Constitution of the Republic of Iran states unequivocally that the woman's 'pioneering mission' is within the home raising her children. Many of the eventual consequences of the new legislation on the life of women are yet to emerge. Women are being retired from government service and educated women returning from studies abroad are having great difficulty in obtaining employment. However, one can envisage that if and when the political situation stabilises, there may well be increased opportunities for women in certain areas – in education, health and all matters pertaining to women – since the enforcement of strict segregation will preclude men from employment in services provided for women. On the other hand, if the Islamic authorities are successful in propagating the virtues of early marriage for girls – Ayatollah Khomeini advocates marriage before the first menses (1979: 135) – there may not be a sufficient number of suitably educated women in the future to fulfil these roles in the segregated area of women's public space.

## Postscript

It is now thirteen years since the Iranian Revolution and twelve years since I wrote the above chapter. The theme which I explored, and the situations I described, remain of the utmost relevance in Iran today. The mass withdrawal of women from public sector employment and higher education, envisioned by some revolutionary leaders in the early 1980s, did not materialise (see Moghadam, 1991a, 1991b, 1992). The Iran-Iraq War (1980–88) was undoubtedly a contributory factor to this situation: women were needed as doctors, nurses, teachers and in government offices and factories; several thousand women underwent military training in the volunteer *Baseej* force and were appointed to 'lower-level' posts such as guarding ministries and banks.

The continuing presence of women in public space and te Iran–Iraq War have also contributed to a marked increase in the incidence of temporary marriage (*sigheh*), the nominal or 'fictive' form of which was a central theme in my paper. Although not categorically outlawed under the previous regime, its practice as a means of having legal sexual intercourse was regarded amongst the educated elite as distasteful or 'backward', and frequently kept secret by the couple involved. In the 1979 Constitution it was officially reinstated and the authorities subsequently made every effort to educate the public in the desirability of its use because of the deaths of hundreds of thousands of men in the war which left widows and their children without male guardians. It was also advocated as a means to fulfil the human need for more than one sexual partner legally and as a suitably Islamic alternative to decadent Western practices of free love for young people studying and working together. Shahla Haeri (1989) documents this and much further relevant information in her book on the subject. (317)

## Appendix: Mahram and Na-Mahram Kin, with Persian Terms

**I** (a) *mahram* to ego if male:

| | |
|---|---|
| mother | *mādar* |
| daughter | *dokhtar* |
| sister | *khāhar* |
| half-sister | *khāhar nātani* |
| mother's sister | *khāleh* |
| father's sister | *ammeh* |
| brother's daughter | *dokhtar barādar* |
| | *dakhtar zadeh* |
| sister's daughter | *dokhtar khāhar* |
| | *khāhar zadeh* |
| grandmother | *mādar bozourg* |
| great grandmother | *jaddeh* |
| and anterior | |
| granddaughter | *naveh* |
| great granddaughter | *natijeh* |
| gt.gt. " | *nabireh* |
| gt.gt.gt. " | *nadideh* |
| (literally 'not seen') | |
| and successive | |
| wife | *zan* |
| (also means 'woman') | |
| daughter-in-law | *arus* |
| mother-in-law | *mādar shouhar* |

(b) *mahram* to ego if female:

| | |
|---|---|
| father | *pedar* |
| son | *pesar* |
| brother | *barādar* |
| half-brother | *barādar nātani* |
| mother's brother | *dāi* |
| father's brother | *amu* |
| brother's son | *pesar barādar* |
| | *barādar zadeh* |
| sister's son | *pesar khāhar* |
| | *khāhar zadeh* |

| | |
|---|---|
| grandfather | *pedar bozourg* |
| great grandfather | *jadd* |
| and anterior | |
| grandson etc. | *naveh* etc. |
| (as above in (a)) | |
| husband | *shouhar* |
| son-in-law | *dāmād* |
| father-in-law | *pedar showhar* |

(c) For milk relationship

| | |
|---|---|
| suffix | *shiri* or *rezā'i* |
| e.g. milk-mother | *mādar rezā'i/shiri* |
| milk-child | *farzand rezā'i/shiri* |

For step relationship prefix *nā*
e.g. step-father  *nā-pedar*

**II** *na-mahram* kin:

(i) For cousins prefix *pesar* or *dokhtar* or suffix *zadeh* (male and female)
e.g. father's brother's son *pesar amu/amu-zadeh*
mother's brother's daughter *dokhtar dāi/dāi-zadeh*

(ii) sister's husband   *shouhar khāhar*
wife's brother   *barādar zan*
brother's wife   *zan barādar*
wife's sister   *khāhar zan*
If their wives are sisters, brothers-in-law are *bājenāq* or *ham-rish* to each other. If their husbands are brothers, sisters-in-law are *jāri* to each other.

(iii) For husbands and wives of aunts and uncles prefix *zan* or *shouhar*
e.g. father's brother's wife *zan amu*
mother's sister's husband *shouhar khāleh*

## Notes

1. For a clear account of the main differences between Shi'a and Sunni Islam see Hollister, 1953, chs 1–4.
2. Informal visiting would be supplemented by various types of organised social gatherings such as *sofrehs* (meals given to fulfil a vow), *rouzehs* (religious gatherings where a mullah was invited to speak about the Shi'ite Imams and martyrs) and religious feast-days like *moludi*, the commemoration of the Prophet's daughter's marriage to Ali. Regular

weekly or monthly gatherings (*dourehs*) would be held by women in their own homes; visits to the public bath were also an important social occasion.

3. I am using 'incest' as defined in the *Oxford English Dictionary* and as used by Querry (1872) to denote sexual intercourse between persons considered too closely related for marriage. By extension the 'incestuous marriage' is one between such relations.

4. A nineteenth-century Persian letter shown to me by John Gurney (Lecturer in Persian in Oxford) contains fascinating details of such a household. See also Mrs Meer Hassan Ali's description (1917) of upper-class Shi'ite Moslem society in nineteenth-century India; many of her observations are of direct relevance to the present paper.

5. See Querry 1871: 469; Hughes 1885: 15, for age of maturity.

6. In Kerman two kinds of knocker are attached to some old doors. I was told the ring-shaped one was for women to use; the pendulous one for men. The sex of any caller was told by the sound of the knock. If a man, the women disappeared or adjusted their veils; if a woman the men withdrew.

7. Altorki (1980) cites the use made in Sunnite Saudi Arabia of breastfeeding to circumvent strict veiling *and* to prevent future marriage between certain potential marriage partners. See also J. Khatib-Chahidi in V. Maher (1992: 109–32).

8. See Querry 1871: 469; Hughes 1885: 314ff; Baillie 1805: 312.

9. Khomeini 1979: 129 includes the 'nominal' marriage.

10. Baillie 1805: 312.

11. Browne (1893: 505–6) gives a description of *mut'ah* marriage. He also describes how certain mullahs dispensed with the stipulated waiting-time. See also Donaldson (1933: 185–86), Daudpota (1932), Westermarck (1921).

12. This may also have something to do with the fact that the Prophet's wives were not permitted to re-marry. Imitation of what the Prophet and his family did figures large in Shi'ite Islam.

13. It is virtually impossible for a woman – single, divorced, or widowed – to live on her own in Iran. Cf. Hirschon's comments on Greek attitudes (1978: 74).

14. The bride does not necessarily go to her husband's house immediately after the *aqd* ceremony. If the couple decide they do not want to remain married before consummation, they will still need a divorce. There are, therefore, virgin divorcees in Iran.

15. I dealt with the subject of close-kin marriage in a paper given to the Women's Social Anthropology Seminar, Oxford, 1978. For Greek practice see Lane Fox (1975: 418, 483), and the other sources he cites: Cumont (1926), Davies (1971), Gernet (1968). Middleton (1962) gives Egyptian evidence. E. Herzfeld (1947), Benveniste (1938), Christensen (1936) and Gray (1931) are writing on the Iranian area. Chabot (1902) gives information about some Nestorian Christians.

16. In Mecca, where it is forbidden for men and women to have sexual intercourse during the pilgrimage period of *manasek, na-mahram* men and women pray side by side, the women with their faces uncovered. The prohibition on even legal sex during this time appears to afford a relaxation of customs of sexual segregation in public. Peter Lienhardt drew my attention to this point.

17. In 1965 it was rare to find women working amongst men except in prestigious occupations such as university teaching. By the mid-1970s women were working alongside men in offices, hotels, shops and in the army. In 1978 there were women in the police force.

18. Even western-educated men and women (the latter not often themselves employed) readily attributed sexual immorality to female secretaries.

19. Soraya Tremayne (1980) includes much material indicating such attitudes in a detailed study she made of Iranian students in England (1970–4).

# 7

# Place and Face: Of Women in Doshman Ziāri, Iran

*Susan Wright*

## Introduction

Unravelling assumptions about women in societies where stress is laid on the separate worlds of the sexes and the seclusion of women, is a recurrent theme of anthropological writings of the 1970s.[1] Nancy Tapper remarked on the fascination of Western reporters in the Iranian revolution with the visible sign that the seclusion of women did not mean exclusion from public life, as women swathed in black cotton cloaks took a prominent part in street demonstrations. Cynthia Nelson used ethnographic literature to show that emphasis on male control of political activity does not exclude women from influence. However, the proud poise, freer movement and expansive gestures of men in contrast to the demureness of women, gossiping together never far from the home, is an image which, although found in many forms, has often been taken by observers to mean that women in Middle Eastern societies are excluded from public and political life. This chapter looks at relations between sexual arenas in a village in Iran through aspects of the social and physical space of women which are not stressed by informants.

In the village of a partially settled section of Doshman Ziāri division of the Mamasani tribal group it was emphasised that women were physically and conceptually excluded from the male arena of discussion and decision-making, and should observe restraint in movement and behaviour. A woman, on meeting a man, averted her face, shielding it with a hand, and answered requests for information with a subdued voice and downward-cast eyes. She never showed signs of attraction by, for example, laughing or appearing at ease. This behaviour was not just towards non-kinsmen; she adopted this distancing stance towards her husband when in the view of others. Women guarded against moving around the village without good cause. Their daily tasks centred on the house, and a thin, printed cotton cloak (*chādor* – which also means tent in Farsi[2]) was worn when a woman moved beyond the seclusion of home. It was always worn on the rare trips women made outside the village, to seek medical treatment in town or visit a shrine. Within the village, the space a woman considered home shifted diurnally. During daylight, when men were outside the village working in isolation on agricultural or herding activities, and women were in contact with their neighbours, the *chādor* was only worn to visit a distant part of the village. After dark, when men met in each other's houses to discuss and decide village affairs, and women were in domestic isolation, a *chādor* was worn whenever an emergency forced them to call on a neighbour.

The women's arena, no less public than the men's, was during daylight; the men's was after dark. The stress laid in the received view on the distancing seclusion of women from the male arena separated the two public times and spaces; they were integrated when husband and wife met in the early evening in the house which became a private space. However, this period was brief because, just as women were aware of the wider connotations of 'wandering', men were conscious of the ridicule attendant on those who spent too much time at home with their wives. There was a parallel emphasis on women's seclusion and concealment and men's gregarious egression. Unstressed was the public gathering of women and their extensive networks of kin which reveal men's relative isolation and reliance on their wives.

This material derives from fieldwork conducted between 1974 and 1976[3], and it seems that the balancing contrasts of male and female movement and behaviour patterns had modified in the last generation as women became less involved in agricultural work. New factors were prompting further changes, and were a source of intense discussion at the time of fieldwork. The Iranian Revolution and the war with Iraq will also have influenced ideas and activities in the village, but it must be emphasised that this material predates even the start of the Revolution, and is therefore firmly couched in the ethnographic past tense.

## Male View of Kinship

It was commonly averred that each man was responsible for the production of an income and the protection of the people and possessions of his household, by which a livelihood was assured. Most men engaged in a variety of activities, including wheat and rice cultivation, the sale of grapes as a cash crop, herding sheep and goats, and involvement in the service sector of the wider economy. The individual male head of household was expected to provide for his family, but rarely could the overlapping seasonal tasks of the mixed economy be completed in isolation. Similarly, responsibility to protect the members of the household and ensure that their behaviour did not invite reproach rested with the individual male, but its fulfilment depended on his relations with other men. A reputation for successfully managing affairs and repelling any threat to self or family was a man's best protection against insult or theft. Yet maintaining a reputation depended not only on personal abilities of bravery and perspicacity but also on the support, verbal and physical, of other men attracted by these qualities and success. Security was as ephemeral as reputation: it could be lost in a single encounter. It was the prize of a man who achieved a balance between collaboration with others to defend, exploit and expand his resources, and the maintenance of an appearance of self-reliance. It was lost as soon as a relationship of co-operation was transformed into one of dependence. The equally impelling desires for independence and collaboration were a source of tension in relations between men.

Men considered that a relationship of mutual support and discretion was only possible among sons and brothers. Close agnates hoped to depend on each other to exercise secretiveness towards others about their affairs, and to collaborate when any of them was insulted or threatened. Brothers inherited land and resources in common, and depended on co-operation to exploit and defend them; but management of such holdings, the allocation of labour and division of income, could be a source of friction. Families of many brothers or sons had greater potential for strength, but could less easily maintain the mutual confidence and support upon which that influence rested. A relationship of discretion and trust was thought not to be possible with men who were not close agnates. It was said that sometimes a group of brothers could co-operate with the descendants of those with whom their father had formerly shared trust (that is, sons of their father's brothers), especially if the relationship was reinforced by a marriage between children of the brothers. Beyond that, more distant kin were viewed with increasing degrees of suspicion.

For those who attempted to expand their activities and widen their connections and potential support, negotiation, different forms of collaboration with a range of outsiders and alliances through marriage were necessary. Success in preventing a relationship from becoming one of subordination depended on the continued support of close kin. The balance between solidarity with close agnates and links with distant kin became especially important when activities of the male domain involved negotiation and co-operation between several groups of patrikin. This occurred, for example, when a number of men whose lands were adjacent tried to arrange the joint employment of one man to guard their crops and keep off stray animals; when the irrigation of the village's rice lands had to be organised; or if several men with small herds tried to co-operate in the employment of one shepherd, or to arrange the herding of their combined livestock on a daily rota. In 1976 there was a protracted debate over the manner in which nearly half the village, about eight lineages, might organise the joint purchase and operation of a tractor. In 1975, negotiations failed over a project which aimed to involve the whole village in the construction of a wash-house and piped water supply, and such suspicion had been aroused between different elements of the village, that it ended in fighting. In affairs pertaining to the male domain, then, the individual attempted to balance an appearance of independence with the maintenance of support and protection from others (see Wright 1985). This received view of society, with the need for solidarity among close patrilines, and the likelihood of distrust between more distantly related kin was reflected in the layout of the village.

## Space in the Village – Patrilocality

The village, viewed from an adjacent hill, seemed a maze of flat-roofed, co-joining, earth-coloured buildings, strewn across one of the steeply rising foothills of the mountains. In winter and spring, when melting snow and rain transformed the ground into thick, clinging mud, the easiest way to traverse sections of the village was across the roofs by clambering up and down the different levels. Such roof-top trips were only halted by reaching a disjunction caused by one of the pathways which wound through the village. The widest of these ground-level routeways was a deep ravine, carrying a river in spring and the occasional Jeep in dry seasons, which cut through the village, separating the houses of the two main clans. On either side of the ravine, narrower alleys (*kucheh*) divided the buildings into clusters,[4] each usually containing the houses and stables of a patrilineage with associated clients: the genealogical and spatial relationships between twenty-two households in one cluster in the village is shown in Figure 7.1.

Within the spaces defined by the alleys, a further pattern could be discerned: each cluster was composed of several contiguous enclosures. An enclosure (*hayāt*) usually contained the houses of a minimal patrilineage, that is a father and his married sons (as in Figure 7.1, numbers 17 and 18, or 1 and 2), or a set of married brothers (for example, numbers 3 and 4), depending on the stage reached in their life-cycle. The buildings in one enclosure backed onto neighbouring ones occupied by patrilateral cousins. These, in turn, adjoined further enclosures where more distant patrilineal relatives resided. Distance between patrilines approxi-

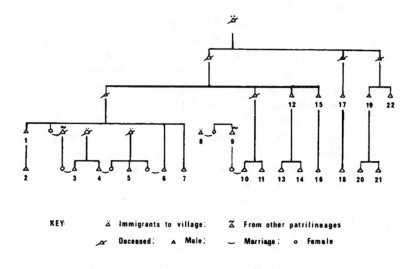

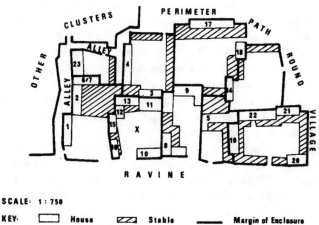

Enclosure X is detailed in figure 7.2

**Figure 7.1:** Relationship between Heads of Households in one Cluster in the Village

mately paralleled distance between enclosures within one cluster of buildings in the village.

Tucked against the outside of some of the enclosures were smaller houses belonging to relatives by marriage who associated with the patrilineage. Most of these were immigrants who had come to the village in the last sixty years and had built in proximity to the member of one of the established patrilineages who was their patron and employer (for example, numbers 3, 4, 5 and 8 in Figure 7.1). In several instances the male descendants of such an immigrant had become so numerous that they were able to establish themselves in independence of their former patron, and had found that there was not sufficient space around their original house for all the present households. The descendants of the immigrant then moved to the extremity of the area occupied by the clan of their patron, and built a new cluster of enclosures, divided from the others by the alley which had been the perimeter path around the village. The family of 9 in Figure 7.1 had developed in this way: while he occupied his father's house, his brothers had set up a new cluster. The patrilineage could also 'grow'; for example, numbers 6 and 7 and number 19 have left their crowded enclosures for new sites on the extremity of the village.

Each enclosure shared by close male kin was roughly square and edged with two, three or more rectangular houses. As with tents in their nomadic encampments, each house in the village commanded a different view of the enclosure, and each was situated alongside or on top of one of the stables. Gaps between the buildings were frequently walled, and the entrance sometimes gated, so that the layout gave the impression of a co-operative defensive unit. In this way they ensured that thefts of livestock, which always increased as tension rose in the village, might less easily be perpetrated.

When a son married he established his new household in his father's enclosures, either by refurbishing an existing house, or by building a new one in a vacant corner or on the site of a derelict stable. Through time the buildings within the enclosure changed, but the enclosure continued to be the focus of a minimal patrilineage. New households formed, and new patrilineages emerged, and the shape and size of the village modified accordingly. Yet this patrilocal residence pattern meant that whether a new house or a new cluster was built, the main design features of the village were continually replicated. Village geography mapped out the relationships between households in terms of the dominant patrilineal means of reckoning descent so that men who had the greatest obligation to co-operate and the greatest hope of mutual trust usually lived in proximity, and those who only held each other in suspicion were separated by distance, the alleys and the ravine.

## Men's Meetings

The importance of the residence pattern for the men was seen in 1976. When the fighting referred to earlier had died down, theft of livestock, the index of tension, remained prevalent. Relations between the clans, across the ravine, were tense, and between the constituent lineages on each side were wary. Yet attempts at co-operation were necessary for the organisation of the agricultural and herding activities and efforts were made to maintain contacts with geographically and genealogically distant men through the mediation of close kin of the enclosure.

Discussion always took place at night immediately after dinner, when the 'elder brother'[5] of one minimal lineage, wishing to test out an opinion or ask advice on an issue, called on the 'elder brother' of a set of his patrilateral cousins in a neighbouring enclosure. On subsequent nights there might be several further meetings between eldest members of neighbouring enclosures, and if initial contacts gathered momentum, one night several 'eldest brothers' would gather in the house of the most respected man in their part of the village. In debates such as those concerning the tractor and the water supply, ideas spread through many small meetings until eventually one of the most influential men invited others from many sections of the village to dinner.

As soon as a guest approaching a house shouted a greeting to announce his arrival, the host prepared the room, and his wife hurriedly picked up the meal tray, gathered her children, and moved out of the house. The husband laid out one of the best carpets on the side of the fire farthest from the door, and ushered in his guest, seating him there in the place called the high (bālā) position in the house (see Figure 7.2). As another arrived, the guest, recognising the newcomer to be more respected and influential than himself, vacated his high position and insisted the other should take it. On the arrival of each new guest, the seating order was reassessed, until the company formed an arc from the highest place, round in front of the fire, to the least respected men sitting with the draught from the door on their backs. The host watched the arrangement of his guests, anxious that none be offended, but limited in his ability to interfere, from his position on the opposite side of the fire where he brewed and served the tea (see server's position in Figure 7.2).

Both the arrangement of the seating and the drinking of tea which followed that order were the occasion for much formal etiquette. The discourse was similarly structured, with those in the highest positions accorded most leave to speak. Each laced his statements with elaborate sentiments about his unworthiness to speak, and tested out others' standpoints without irrevocably committing his own. Those accorded most influence tried to justify and enhance their position by displaying

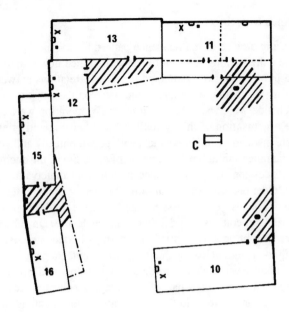

**SCALE:** 1:250

**KEY:**

—— House wall      ----- Interior wall      —— Party wall

—·— Stable - extending beneath house      /// Yard space

—◠— House fireplace      ● Yard fireplace

× 'High' position      ▪ Server's position

C Carpet loom - site of women's gatherings

**Figure 7.2:** Detail of Enclosure X (from Figure 7.1)

their sensitivity to the range of views, and by providing tactical poses through which different interests could be reconciled. The discourse was calm and measured, but this brought the tension into greater relief.

Sentiments expressed by each man were taken to be in accord with those of his close kin who were not present, and each 'elder brother' tried to balance the need to preserve the interests of those he spoke for, with the desire to reach an agreement to co-operate with the wider group. Neglect of the former would threaten the solidarity of his close kin; unwillingness to compromise would antagonise those present.

Overbalancing in either direction endangered his ability to gain a liveli-hood and protect his family and possessions, whereas success strength-ened his influence in future men's meetings.

Meanwhile the wife remained outside the house, finishing off the meal she was eating, clearing up the yard and servicing the men's meet-ing. The host rarely rose in the company of his guests, and if he needed some more sugar for his tea, if he could not find the cigarettes or when a meal was ready for the guests, the host's son, his younger brother, or an employee of his family was called upon to carry the required items from the wife outside the house to the husband by the fire. The wife rarely entered the house, and concealed by the darkness, stayed nearby but unseen by the guests. If a few men were gathered who were her own close kin, the wife would sometimes enter silently later on and sit, unac-knowledged, just inside the door. Very rarely a husband allowed or invited his wife to speak on such occasions.

## Women and Kinship

Women were not only excluded from men's discussions, but in the received view, only men had the right to become involved in matters affecting relations between households. Women were held to be innate-ly untrustworthy, and to be constantly endangering the reputation of close male kin who were responsible for their good behaviour and for their protection.[6] Until marriage, a girl was looked after by her father and brothers. On marriage, her behaviour and deportment bore on the reputation of her husband, but he shared with her brothers the obligation for her protection. A wife was the focus of the mingled responsibilities of two men and their close agnates who otherwise might hold each other in suspicion. Close agnates who shared the same enclosure and the obligations for mutual trust from boyhood to old age saw their sister, who was privy to their closest affairs, leave the enclosure and join another on marriage, while they were each joined by women from dif-ferent enclosures as wives. Women, the focus for ties between distant men, crossed the boundaries between groups of agnates which the men strove to maintain.

A marriage was achieved when the long-term strategies of two fami-lies coincided, when each considered that the link would be advanta-geous, and would extend their connections in a way which would increase their ability to protect their interests and expand their activities. The arrangement of a marriage was a saga of rising tension, as each stage, the initial overtures, the signing of the contract (*aghd*), the nego-tiation of the bridewealth (*bāshlogh*) and divorce penalty (*mariah*), and the agreement on the date for the start of the celebrations, was formalised at meetings between the men. Over the years it took to arrange a marriage, a family's perception of its interests might change, and other parties might intrigue against the match. The further negotiations advanced, the greater the danger, as one of the parties might use one of the formal meetings to inflict a severe loss of face on the other by refusing to reach agreement. There was no assurance that the negotiations would be successful until the end of the wedding, and tension increased with the approach of the final celebrations when the new bond of co-responsibility, with its potential for co-operation or friction, would be created between the two families.

On the third day of feasting and dancing, the wedding culminated in men and women, villagers and guests, flocking together round the house of the bride's father. Whilst they vied with the drummer and trumpeter, with shouts of 'Hey Congratulations', the groom's brother approached the house where the bride had been secluded for the duration of the celebrations. Against the resistance of the bride's mother, the groom's brother gained access, the items of the dowry were carried aloft for all to see, and the bride was led out, her head completely covered with a crimson silk scarf. Bride and dowry were installed in a Jeep (a recent innovation; previously she travelled on horseback) and were driven, followed by the shouting and waving crowd, to the enclosure of her husband's family. Once she had been led into her husband's new house, the celebrations were suddenly over.

The physical movement of the bride across the boundaries between men, from her natal to her affinal enclosure, was the climax of the wedding. Thereafter, whilst the men sought to maintain co-operation and unity within their enclosure, she was an ever-present link with the outside. In the days and months after a wedding, the position of a bride was often stressful. Until very recently, a bride was given a special haircut which was only allowed to grow into the married woman's style after the birth of a child. Although no longer distinguished in this way, the new bride's activities were a source of constant remark for other women. During the day, when the men were working outside the village, the new wife was closely supervised by her mother-in-law, who not only adjudged her ability to make bread, cook the evening meal, and fulfil other household tasks, but saw that the new member of the enclosure did not act indiscreetly, reveal information about her son's affairs, or behave in a way which would invite comment. The mother-in-law played an important part in reducing the threat a new wife posed to the concord within the enclosure. Meanwhile the bride's own mother tried to ensure that she was treated well, and her brother was similarly concerned. Even when a wife had gained respect, had several children, and her interests had become tied to those of her husband, she never severed links with her natal enclosure. She visited her mother, and her brothers might visit her. Moreover, she maintained close affective ties with her married sisters and her mother's relatives.

Space in the village takes on a different aspect when viewed from a woman's perspective. A woman moved from one enclosure to another on marriage and continued thereafter to pervade the boundaries men sought to maintain around close agnates. The patrilocal residence pattern in which men were physically grouped into clusters of close and distant kin, meant that their wives' closest relatives were scattered. A married woman's male kin were in two locations, in her husband's and her father's enclosures, and her female kin were dispersed over many enclosures. A woman maintained links with a wide range of physically distant kin, yet the accepted behaviour pattern kept her near her marital home, and her closest daily association was with her mother-in-law and sisters-in-law, who shared the space of their husbands' enclosure. These were rarely her own close kin: her link with her neighbours was through recognition of the ties and obligations pertaining between their husbands.

## Women in an Enclosure

In the previous generation, when families depended to a greater extent on an income from agriculture or nomadic herding, women used to join their husbands in the mountains to help with the work. As the local economy diversified, and as old methods of processing products gave way to selling grapes as a cash crop and to milling cereals mechanically, women rarely joined their husbands in the fields. The wife's domain centred on the house and enclosure, running the home and processing the products brought home by her husband.

Women, working near their homes, within sight and earshot of their sisters-in-law, did not, however, treat the enclosure as an undifferentiated space. The part of an enclosure immediately in front of a house door where the wife undertook most of her work was literally called 'the space of the house',[7] but will here be referred to as yard-space. This space was often shaped by the right angle obtaining between the front of a house and an adjacent stable, or other wall; in better houses it was built as a partially roofed extension to the house. The different types can be seen in Figure 7.2. Women from houses 10 and 12 had an open, right-angled yard-space, and the women from houses 11 and 15 had partially covered spaces. (The women of houses 12 and 15 had the use of all the space between their own and their son's houses, 13 and 16, as the latter worked in other parts of Iran for most of the year.) Each yard-space contained a fireplace a little distance from the house door where meals for guests and bread for the family were cooked. Cooking utensils were usually hung on a wall beside the house door, and the protruding roof beams of the adjacent wall were festooned with drying washing. The length of the walls used in these ways gave an indication of the dimensions of a yard-space but there was no physical boundary to divide this space from the rest of the enclosure, save where the packed ground, beaten down by continual use, shaded into the dusty and dirty no-woman's-land in the centre of the enclosure.

Women spent most of the morning working in their yard-spaces making milk products, preparing food, cleaning and tidying, and caring for the children who were too young to move with safety outside the enclosure. Most tasks could be completed by a woman working alone, but were more effectively managed by working in pairs. None required co-operation on the scale of the men's work and there were only two kinds of formal working arrangements between women. Two or three neighbours whose families had small herds would take it in turns to process the combined quantity of milk. They employed an elaborate means of recording their daily milk yield, and divided the products proportionately at regular intervals. The second form of co-operation was a partnership between two women to weave carpets. They set a loom near one of their houses (see Figure 7.2), and used their own wool when available, but more often received materials and a fixed payment for their work from another villager. In these arrangements, great care was taken that work and proceeds were equally shared. This was also the case with other, informal forms of co-operation between women; only a few poor women occasionally accepted payment from another to do a specific task for her.

The wafer-thin bread was baked every four or five days, and although each wife had her own utensils, flour and fireplace, often neighbours, or sisters if they lived nearby, saved fuel and time by working together. Sifting and cleaning rice and wheat would be done by an individual woman, but she might be joined and assisted by a neighbour or relative. Other tasks, like clothes washing, collecting drinking water, or taking wheat to the mill, required a woman to leave the enclosure and put her youngest children in the care of another woman. If a woman was married to her patrilateral cousin, her natal home was nearby, and she could call on her mother for help. Usually even this was too inconvenient. They looked to each other for help in many small ways through the morning, and depended on the other women with whom they shared the enclosure.

However, a woman could not automatically expect assistance; if one visited another's yard-space to offer help, she trusted that the visit and the offer would be freely reciprocated on a later occasion. If it was not, it seemed that the other woman was expecting to receive help, but did not view her neighbour as worthy of repayment. This was resented. The visiting patterns of women in an enclosure reflected the level of accord between them. Women who did not co-operate and visit each other's yard-spaces were either at odds themselves, or were reflecting in their own behaviour discord which had developed between their husbands or between the husband of one and the personal kin of another. The mother-in-law often played an important part in mediating relations between her daughters-in-law, which otherwise might create or exacerbate tensions between her sons.

Strained relations between sisters-in-law often found a vehicle for expression through the other creatures which frequented the enclosure through the day. There were special sounds to shoo away chickens, sheep, goats and dogs, and the village was filled with these sounds as women repeatedly tried to keep their own and other's animals away from their yard-spaces. Chickens, in particular, tended not to discriminate between yard-spaces within an enclosure, and even wandered into other enclosures. If one trespassed and refused to leave, a woman might send one of her children to the owner's house to inform her of her chicken's intransigence. Other times, seemingly suddenly, a quarrel blew up between two neighbouring women over this everyday occurrence. Comments were shouted across the enclosure which implied that the woman was unable to restrain and order other aspects of her life. In the most heated instances it was implied that she would not mind men wandering into her private domain. The quarrel subsided when one of the women left the public arena of her yard-space and disappeared into her house, as only infrequently would a woman intrude on another inside her house.

It was through such a medium as chickens that tensions between women were manifested. Clashes between women were overheard by their neighbours, and usually died down quickly. Repeated and vehement arguments came to the notice of their dispersed female kin and, later, to the men responsible for their protection. Heated and protracted arguments were between women confident that their husband or brother would be willing to take their part, and often were a reflection of tensions already developing between men. Close male kin had a clear priority to maintain relations of solidarity and trust, and this was eased by the fact that men spent most of the daytime in isolation outside the village, working on their lands. Tension between brothers, cousins or in-laws might be suppressed: it might be revealed in friction between their wives and sisters who were in face-to-face contact through the day and might spread through their embracing sets of female kin dispersed over several enclosures.

## Women's Gatherings

The wider links between women became evident in the afternoon when the pressing domestic tasks had been completed, and they took up other work like spinning. This is a portable task, and early in the afternoon some of the women would be seen carrying their children and their wool and spindle over the roof or along an alley. If a neighbour was in her yard-space she called out and invited the passing woman to enter. The hostess would carry out her house carpet and lay it in a sunny place, either on the edge of her yard, or in a neutral part of the enclosure. The two women sat in the sun spinning and chatting. Soon they were joined by other wives of that enclosure and from nearby, who, seeing a gathering, came and joined it. Small gatherings took place in most enclosures at different times but the largest groupings only assembled around a woman who was known to be in a relatively well-off family, who was respected for the standing of her father, brothers and husband, and was known for her own respectability and perspicacity.[8] Sometimes the gatherings had a formal aspect, when, for example, a woman donned her cotton cloak (*chādor*) and passed through several alleys to visit a sister married to a distant patrilineage. More often the gatherings were of women from nearby enclosures and clusters of houses.

These gatherings had less formal etiquette than the men's meetings. The seating pattern did not so obviously portray the ranking of the women. The hostess, as the focus of the gathering, often sat with the most respected of her guests on her carpet, with her daughters and sisters-in-law and other neighbours, with their children in a cluster around them, sitting in the dust. The women did not use the same deference in their discourse as the men, the only indication of rank was when some interrupted and interjected in the conversation, and others submitted. Although the gatherings did not have the same formalities as the men's, the discourse was highly structured. Women chatted about matters pertaining to their own domain, but even such apparently innocuous subjects as cures for children's ailments and the cleaning and milling of grain had to be handled with care. A comment about another's household, if negative, could be taken as criticism, or, if positive, could be seen as a sign of covetousness or jealousy. Remarks about another's child were prefaced with phrases like 'Thanks be to God' or 'What God wills', so that if the child suffered thereafter it could not be imputed to the woman having an evil eye. Such sentiments derive from Islamic concepts on the power of intentions, inner thoughts or even words to harm the bounty of another.

Embedded in the chatter of women was the feeling that whether complimentary or deprecatory, a comment could be taken to imply a sentiment towards the woman's household. Statements had to be guarded as each of the women present would have some link with all the others: any direct comment would be seen as an intended offence, and would divide the women gathered. If reference was made to one of the women who had quarrelled that morning over the chickens, it would be indirect, perhaps by remarking about her inability to make good bread or to keep her children out of danger. By such allusions, women hinted their views on the rights and wrongs of a situation and the present connections and sympathies between them became clear. As soon as the conversation moved on to events in a distant part of the village, or another settlement, matters which had less direct relevance to any of the women assembled, the statements became more direct, reference to names and events more specific, and although the discourse was still convoluted, the matter at issue and the opinions of the women present were easier to discern.

The women's arena brought together wives from neighbouring enclosures, most of whom shared at least one relationship through their husband, brothers, mother and married sisters with every other woman present. Together they had contact with and knowledge of enclosures in many of the clusters on their side of the ravine. In contrast to the men's discussions, where a man's views were taken to be agreeable to his close kin, each woman hinted her own assessment of situations and attitudes which she derived from information and opinion gathered from an idiosyncratic and expansive range of kin ties. The women's mode of discourse was as intricate and involved as the interrelations between them, and each participant, with her diverse ties with other women and her often contrasting obligations to her husband and her brothers, frequently had sympathies with both sides of any series of incidents.

## Meeting of the Two Domains – The House

Towards dusk the women's gathering dispersed, and each returned to her yard-space to receive the older children when they came home from school, and to prepare the evening meal. After the interaction of the women in the morning and their gatherings in the afternoon, their public arena faded with the light. At the same time, the men who had been working in isolation through the day returned from the mountains to their houses to finish the last of the day's work and eat, before their visits and meetings later on. The contrasting use of time and space reflected the separateness of the male from the female sphere of activity, but as the men moved from the day's isolation outside the village to the public arena in the village at night, and as the women moved from the public arena of the village in the day to isolation in their homes at night, the movement patterns and arenas coincided for the short period of intervening twilight.

In most seasons the husband returned home with some produce. In summer and autumn he arrived with his donkey loaded with wheat, rice or grapes, and in winter with firewood. On arriving in the enclosure, he dumped the load on the edge of the yard-space, and stabled his donkey. Briefly the two domains met as the husband, under the direction of his wife, spread the rice or grapes on the roof to dry, stored the corn in the house, or broke the firewood into usable lengths. From then on his wife took over the processing and use of the products.

The meeting of the two domains was further exemplified by the house itself, into which the husband then moved. The building belonged to the husband, who was responsible for its upkeep and repair, especially for keeping the flat mud roof clear of snow in winter, and compacted with a wooden roller to prevent leaks. The disposition of effects and use of produce inside the house were in the charge of the wife. She looked after the bedding and the best carpets stacked on a wooden structure along one of the short walls of the house, and made sure the woven bags of corn, can of paraffin and other products were kept dry and out of the way of thieves. All the items necessary to set up a household were included in the bride's dowry (Luri – *pashā arus*; Farsi – *jehāz*) which was carried with her to the new house on the wedding day. Some of the items were made by the bride's family; most were purchased by her father, mainly with money given by the groom. The groom's contribution (*bāshlogh*) was formally settled by the men of the two families, but the bride's father, if he was able, would add his own contribution, and in the richest households would match the sum of the *bāshlogh*. The furnishings and equipment of the house therefore derived from the two families of the husband and wife and rights to the household effects were not generally defined. For example, when the woven donkey bags, traditionally made by the wife's mother as part of the dowry, were no longer used because migration ceased, merchants came to purchase them. In some houses the husband claimed the right to dispose of them; in others the wife was confident she could sell them and keep the proceeds.

Similarly, the boundary between the male and female domains of providing and processing was variably drawn. For example, chickens, although primary products and the focus for many altercations between the women, lived in the enclosures and were always fed and reared by the wife. In some households, the wife, being responsible for ensuring that there was always adequate provision for unexpected guests, controlled the number of chickens, the meat used for that purpose, and decided the price and sold any extra hens. At the other extreme, some husbands would sell a chicken without reference to their wives. In general, women controlled the use of the products they processed, but sales to merchants were in the hands of the men as they made the trips to town. However, discretion over the use of surplus varied greatly. Usually a woman would give directions to her husband about food and household goods to be purchased in town and he would not question the need or expense, but would find a means of raising the necessary money. In the village, a woman decided whether to grant requests from neighbours for paraffin or items of food and she usually had small amounts of cash and would send her son to buy needed items from the village trading shop, without reference to her husband. However, some women had discretion over allocation of the wheat crop, how much to mill, how much to keep for the next year's seed, and how much to sell. Some husbands discussed with their wives whether to sell a sheep, and whether to sell the wool or make a carpet; others considered this no affair of their wives.

Appropriately, the usual occasion for settling such matters was in the evening, whilst the house was a private space, and the husband ate the meal he had provided and the wife had prepared. Reminiscent of the pattern of the men's meetings, the husband at this time sat on the high, warm side of the fire, and his wife sat opposite him. She started to break the sugar cone into lumps whilst the kettle boiled, so that she was ready to serve tea once he had eaten. Seated as host in relation to her husband, the wife was not ranking herself with the others present. This was in accord with her usual stance; she was distanced from, and did not appear to obtrude on the male domain.

Whilst preparing the tea she might comment that there was a shortage of bread, implying that her husband was remiss in not providing sufficient firewood, or she might mention that sugar or tea was very expensive in the trading shop, indicating that he had not bought the requested amount on his last trip to town and that another trip was necessary. In the same tone and manner she might mention the altercation between two of her neighbours over the chicken, or recite some incident through which she revealed a piece of information or hinted at an attitude relevant to an affair currently being discussed by the men. The husband would never solicit such information; he merely received and responded. If he found the information unacceptable to his own interpretation or point of view, he would angrily retort that she should not quarrel with other women or listen to gossip. If her ideas had greater impact, or if her view coincided with his own, the remark would be received without comment, and in a few households where the wife felt free to make her opinion nearly explicit, a conversation might result. Information the wife had gleaned and views she had generated from the women's gatherings were transmitted to the husband, or a version of them presented in such a way as to influence him towards her own point of view. A very able woman could influence her husband to accommodate the concerns of her other kin, or would forewarn him of the diversity of views he was likely to encounter in the men's meeting later. In these interchanges, the balance between the two domains and the two arenas, whose separateness was stressed in the received view of the society, was resolved by each husband and wife in the private space of the house, and in each case the boundary was established differently.

## Face

The degree to which a wife felt free to exercise discretion over the disposal of goods and products, and to use the information she had gleaned from the women's gatherings, was often referred to through expressions using the word 'face' (*roo*). A woman who had a more constricted domain and less freedom to express herself compared her position to that of another by saying 'Her husband gives her more face'. A husband would indicate that he maintained his authority by saying 'I don't give her face to do such a thing', and a woman who felt she could not do something, that it would be unseemly or shameful, would say 'My face won't let me do that'. Through these expressions the private resolution of the two domains was explained or defended in the context of the public arenas.

In private, a woman guarded against appearing to obtrude on her husband's domain; in public, her behaviour and deportment distanced her from the male arena and influenced her husband's success at appearing to have control over the household and its relations with others. Her conduct towards other women and her retiring stance towards men reflected on the reputation of the male kin who were responsible for her protection. If her behaviour gave rise to comments about her husband's ability to manage his affairs, or if her quarrels with other women provided a rival with the opportunity to diminish her husband's support, she affected her husband's standing and respect in the male arena, on which his ability to protect the people and possessions of his household depended.

A man's reputation, the esteem in which he was held by other men, was reflected in the word *ābroo*, a conjunction of the words 'sweat' and 'face', which alludes to the fear of being disgraced or outwitted. *Ābroo* was held by men who over many years had gathered repute for successfully managing their affairs and expanding their support and influence; it could not be gained from an isolated action, but could be lost in one encounter.[9] The more a man gained a reputation for his ability to protect himself by skilful negotiation and successful expansion of his supporters, the more complex his affairs and the wider his interests, the greater became his dependence on the skills of his wife to manage the household economy, mediate relations and reduce tension between the wives of his close kin, and assess and influence attitudes through gatherings with her personal kin and neighbours.

Whilst a man attempted to preserve the balance between an appearance of self-reliance and collaboration with others, through the support and solidarity of his close agnates, his wife balanced an appearance of reliance on her husband with the maintenance of her expansive links with other households. She threatened his balance and his *ābroo* by an appearance of independence, but her ties were often the source of contacts and information necessary for the protection of his interests and the expansion of his resources. The greater the reputation of the husband in the male sphere, the more he needed his wife to have 'face'.

## Conclusion

In the received view of society women were the responsibility of, and subordinate, to men; descriptions of everyday activity in this chapter indicate how women's behaviour reflected this. Accordingly, informants of both sexes did not emphasise the possibility of some women gaining secluded but significant influence in village affairs, and the means by which this was achieved.

As men left the village to women during the day, and as women's concealed presence at night distanced them from men's meetings, separate male and female arenas formed within the diurnally shifting use of village space. Contrasting male egression and female seclusion not only emphasised the separateness of arenas, but degrees of achievement of these ideals indicated the standing and influence of an individual in his or her social sphere. Although separated by time and space, the two arenas were not exclusive: women's influence within the female arena was related to the amount of protection male kin could afford her, and, conversely, men's standing was affected by the behaviour of women for whom they were responsible. It was therefore rare for a spouse, however able, to gain considerably greater respect in one arena than the partner maintained in the other.

A successful man who, through co-operation of close male kin and attraction of clients, diversified his holdings, was continually engaged in maintaining his position, thereby protecting his kin and clients, by exhibiting and defending his standing in men's meetings. The more complex his affairs, the more he became involved in negotiating relations with men outside his cluster, in distant parts of the village. However, a man's influence rested not only on his performance in these meetings, but on confident expectation of co-operation and trust between close kin of the enclosure. With increasing outward movement of a successful man from his enclosure, management of the domestic economy and of relations between members of the enclosure rested on his wife. The abilities of a wife who in the domestic arrangement of the border between sexual domains, was 'given face', were not only recognised by her husband, but by others. Her social space in the women's arena was reflected in her use of physical space during the day. Other women left their enclosures to fetch water or visit the mill; she despatched daughters-in-law on these errands. A woman wore a cotton cloak (*chādor*) on these trips, considering them far from home; she wore one on a rare visit outside her enclosure. An influential woman's view of home was more constrained but her contacts expansive. She was the focus for women's gatherings, and from visitors to her yard, she gathered information and influenced opinion among neighbours and scattered female kin, whose networks spread through many parts of the village. Links between the arenas were complete when she 'fed' information and views amassed in afternoon gatherings to her husband over the evening meal, in preparation for his movement into distant parts of the village, where his only connection with men was mutual suspicion.

Influence or standing (*ābroo*) of a man, instanced by repeated movement away from home, the 'face' given to his wife, and her achievement of seclusion were interlinked. Through a generation, if a family achieved domestic balance between the arenas in accordance with the influence each partner gained in their separate sphere, success took a physical form. Clients and families attracted by a man's reputation for successfully protecting his supporters, and linked to him through women (maternal kin or relatives by marriage), came and built their homes on the periphery of the cluster of enclosures where he and his male kin lived. In the case of the few most successful men, social standing was reflected in the physical space they occupied in the village; it was achieved through recognition of the wives' secluded influence over public affairs.

# Notes

1. Papanek (1973) provides a comparative study of purdah in societies to the east of Iran, and views veiling and female seclusion as integral to sex role and status allocation. Nelson (1973, 1974) discerns, from accounts of Islamic nomadic societies, the possibility of women exercising power, despite the male/public and female/private dichotomy used in most sources. Wright (1978) studies the cluster of ideas which portray women in Doshman Ziāri as unreliable dependants of male kin, and shows how women exercise influence in accordance with the obverse, but unexpressed, implications of these interrelated concepts. Tapper (1979) attacks several Western assumptions about women in Middle Eastern societies, and stresses the influence of the wider social environment on social relations involving women.

2. Mamasani is one of the southern-most groups in the Zagros Mountains considering themselves Lurs. Their language is Luri with a generous smattering of Farsi words. Most of their terms used in this paper are Farsi; where there are alternatives in current use, both the Farsi and Luri are given.

3. Fieldwork was conducted between September and November 1974 and from November 1975 to November 1976. I am grateful for financial assistance from the Social Science Research Council, the Emslie Horniman Anthropological Scholarship Fund, the British Institute for Persian Studies, the Henrietta Hutton Memorial Travel Award, and the Oxford University Committee for Middle Eastern Studies.

4. The word 'cluster' is employed to describe the arrangement of buildings. When there was not a term for such a segment of the village, a 'cluster' was denoted by the proper name of the lineage residing there.

5. 'Elder brother' (Luri) – (*kaka gaftar:* no equivalent Farsi term used) is literally 'bigger brother'. The term *gaftar* was also applied to the few most influential men in the village to whom a wide range of kin and clients looked for protection.

6. Ideas about the nature and position of women in Doshman Ziāri have been discussed more fully in Wright (1978).

7. 'Space of the house' is a literal translation of *fethā-ye too* (Luri) or *fezā-ye khāneh* (Farsi). Here it is referred to as yard-space to distinguish this area from the embracing enclosure *hayāt* (Farsi).

8. A respected man was given recognition through the title *gaftar*, but there was not a special term for these focal women. This is in contrast, for example, to the Shahsavan of Azerbaijan in north-west Iran, where Nancy Tapper found recognised women leaders to whom the term *aq birček* was applied (1968: 74–89).

9. To lose respect is literally a compound of 'sweat of the face' and 'to pour', *ābroo rikhtan*. This conjures up the tension experienced in an incident when each man tries to judge when to use wit or reasoned argument, when to speak slowly or frenziedly, and how to balance calmness with alert readiness to fight, in order to outmanoeuvre the other and avoid the disgrace of defeat.

# 8

# The Sexual Division of Domestic Space among Two Soviet Minorities: The Georgians and the Tadjiks

*Tamara Dragadze*

This (rather condensed)[1] chapter focuses first on the relationship between the sexual division of domestic space and the division of domestic labour, and secondly on the relationship between the division of domestic space and the position of women outside the home. The two ethnographic examples I shall use, the Georgians, whose land is wedged between Russia and Turkey and borders the Black Sea, and the Tadjiks, a Farsi-speaking people bordering on Afghanistan, both underwent fundamental and revolutionary upheavals when they were absorbed into the Soviet Union in the early 1920s.

This very choice of peoples inevitably compels us to be aware, at least peripherally, of a continuing debate in women's studies: to what extent does a change in political order – and the advent of Soviet power is a dramatic case – alter the position of women merely through the changes introduced in the economy? It has been argued that the abolition of capitalism, private property, small landholding, tenant farming and small-scale production of petty commodities (all of which have been associated with the subjugation of women to ruthless market forces) might in itself promote the establishing of equality between the sexes. Yet without a deliberate policy towards improving the position of women, do such revolutions pass them by? Lastly, does the pre-Revolutionary condition of the women involved, their previous position in their religion and culture, determine their subsequent position more than deliberate policies of change?

## The Case Studies

In both of the rural areas, in contrast to Soviet urban planning, housing is far from uniform and standardised, since each family plans a home for itself according to whatever supply of materials can be obtained in an irregular, scarce market. The layout of the houses which I shall sketch are therefore only basic types. Thus, although two rooms are the

156

minimum requirement for a house in the area studied in Georgia, there are frequently houses with four rooms. And although among the Tadjiks in the valley I visited, the rubric was to build houses round a rectangular courtyard, houses were sometimes built along one side only. (However, I never saw them built in a triangle.)

Finally, the comparative method used in this chapter attempts to look at an extremely limited set of features in two societies, without wresting these features from their background in what Professor Evans-Pritchard would call a 'scissors and paste' technique. In order to avoid the pitfall of biased selection of fact this approach necessitates an almost exclusive focus on ethnographic detail.[2]

## Georgians

I did my fieldwork in the province of Ratcha in north-western Georgia. The soil is poor and peasants practice, as in past centuries, a mixture of agriculture and dairy farming. Before the revolution, the majority of families were small landholders with a brother or two temporarily migrating to the towns to work as craftsmen or in catering and domestic service, leaving wife and children in the care of other brothers. Collectivisation did not change this pattern much. Today the domestic unit still consists of a group of brothers, the youngest living with the parents (see Figure 8.1) and their wives who are brought in from other villages and their children. Each member is employed in a different sphere, including the light industries developed in Ratcha in Soviet times. Although the villagers, both men and women, work on collective farms, and often spend some time in short-term employment in towns during their life, they still concentrate their energies as much as possible on their own plots. The main economic aim of the domestic unit is to achieve a balance between the availability of cash incomes from salaried employment and sufficient agricultural produce for home consumption (in this area there is no surplus to sell) and both sexes contribute towards this end.

Since time immemorial no woman has ever done heavy work in the fields, which is considered to be a man's job. She will, however, help in the harvest, shell beans or feed animals. If she works on the collective farm her share of labour is carried out by other family members when she has a babe-in-arms. She may take cattle to pasture in nearby meadows, but the men take them further afield. A woman who is qualified to work in the tertiary services, in nursing, accountancy, office work or teaching is considered to be a desirable wife and mother. Women in Georgia have been the guardians of literacy. It is they who learn to read

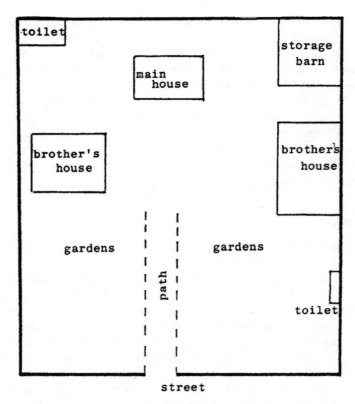

**Figure 8.1:** Georgian Village – Layout of Houses in Domestic Unit

*Gate and path*: The space between the gate and main house should ideally be enough for a guest, after announcing his arrival at the gate and walking slowly in, to allow his male host to put on his jacket and see that something will be ready to drink, and for the hostess to wipe her face and arrange her headdress and to see to it that nothing will burn if she is cooking.

*Brothers' houses*: These are built anywhere convenient on the land surrounding the main house. Next-door neighbours are often the father's brother and his sons. The father usually lives with the youngest brother (his son).

*Main house*: usually at far end of plot. Women go between the houses borrowing and lending odds and ends and contributing food and help whenever a guest arrives in whichever house.

and recite the epic poem 'Knight in the Panther's Skin', the book of which is a requisite of a bride's trousseau. Today it is they who teach their children to read and help them with their school homework. A good touch for handwriting in a woman is considered a virtue.

At home women care for poultry and pigs, and do light gardening in the plot by their courtyard, assisted by their menfolk. In the house, however, women have sole responsibility for all cleaning, cooking and caring for clothes. Men will play with children but women attend to all other childcare. Thus, in the house, the division of labour according to sex is sharply defined and adhered to. Yet the males and females are not confined to a particular space. Women are as much part of the 'outside' space – employment, village community life in the roads, hall and *kalo* (threshing place) – as in the intimacy of the house, where they move and work everywhere. When a guest arrives, women are present to meet him or her. Although they might then go to cook and prepare, they are called to the table to drink and be honoured by the first toast dedicated to the *diasakhlissi*, mother of the house. Women come and go throughout the meal; some sit at table while others serve in turn. Men come and go carrying flasks of wine from the cellar to the table. Even the cooking areas are not used exclusively by women since, especially in the 'lower cooking area', wine is kept there too (see Figure 8.2). When there are no guests, women may, for example, bring vegetables to wherever the rest of the family is gathered to peel in their company. Only when men antic-

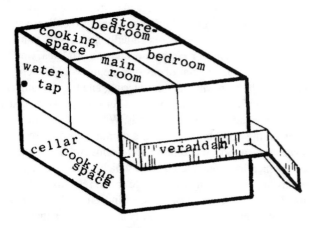

**Figure 8.2:** Ratcha (Georgian) Village House Plan

*Verandah*: for entertaining and overnight accommodation in summer months.

*'Main' room:* sometimes called 'guest room'. Entertaining in winter. Large table and many chairs. Cabinet for display.

*Bedrooms*: just beds and cupboards. Children until at least seven years of age sleep in parents' room. Usually single beds only.

*Cooking space*: water tap (used by men in their tasks as well as women) and kitchen table where family meals are eaten.

*Cellar/cooking space*: 'bulk cooking', i.e. baking, bottling, preserving. Food storage. Wine cellar.

ipate heavy drinking do they try to keep to themselves, perhaps in the shade of a tree in the courtyard or on the verandah, mainly to escape women's censure. It is, in this case, avoidance by men of women, not the other way round.

Georgians are still Orthodox Christians, and the Mother of God is identified with womanhood as a whole. Here, furthermore, women are associated with stability, the maintenance of order (a woman could throw her headscarf between men to stop them from fighting). Women hold the family and the village together. Men are conceived of as being unreliable, prone to fits of jealousy and irrational feelings. Men come and go but women stay put. Women are perceived by the community as agents of social control.

## Tadjiks

I did fieldwork in villages in the valley areas near Dushambe, in one Tadjik village near Samarkand, and in another near Pendjikent. In pre-revolutionary times land was owned by beys, mullahs and the emir of Bukhara. The poverty of the peasants is vividly remembered by the elders and reinforced by official propaganda. Most peasant women, like most men, then held no property, but they were further deprived, since their status was subordinate both conceptually and legally to men. The men of a village would meet near the mosque and drink tea, which each contributed in turn. On special occasions meals would be consumed there too. It was the men who did this catering, and the cleaning after it. Women were confined to their houses whenever possible and wore veils, even if they had to assist in the fields. With the advent of the Soviet government, the economic base of the dominant groups of beys and mullahs was broken. Social and political reforms for the villagers were thus accompanied by economic changes which, when they went in the peasants' favour, lessened their resistance to the reforms of their social traditions. But, nevertheless, many women in Central Asia were brutally martyred by traditionalists when they began discarding their veils and seeking education and employment outside the home, and their memory is kept alive by official propaganda, emphasising the wickedness of the old regime.

Education at school today is co-educational. Girls frequently marry on leaving school, with boys who after having finished their education have just completed their subsequent military service. Their first child will be cared for by relatives while the young mother learns a skill or acquires further education. She will then work sporadically in some profession, or continuously in crafts at home (as, perhaps, a jeweller, a gold-thread embroiderer or seamstress) to fit in with child-bearing. Tadjiks have one of the highest birth rates in the world (crude rate 49 per 1,000; cf. 34.6 per 1,000 in India). The preferred marriage is between cousins, maternal or paternal, who often live in the same village. So a woman has relatives on both her parents' sides, and on her husband's, with whom to share childcare. This enables women to pursue careers outside the home, as village administrators, nurses, clerks, teachers and farm workers, and as long as they dress modestly with a headscarf and the traditional long trousers under their calf-length dresses, they command respect at work from males and females alike. The elaborate and fascinating history of the changes in the position of these Central Asian women will be dealt with in detail in a further paper.

At home women cook, clean, care for children, and if a male visitor comes to the house they will hardly be visible. In good weather men are

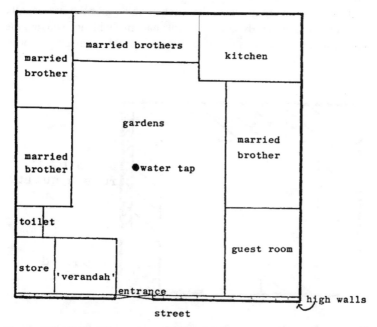

**Figure 8.3:** Tadjik Village: Layout of Domestic Unit

entertained by their male hosts on a shaded platform in the courtyard; in bad weather in a designated room inside. Female visitors are always entertained inside unless it is well established that no men will be around, in which case they will sit on the balcony, if there is one, outside the room in warm weather.

Whereas in the Georgian case, the entertainment of guests, of both sexes, and general companionship, takes place in the home, the Tadjik men where I did my fieldwork still like to gather outside whereas Tadjik women do not. Furthermore, women are not expected to loiter at work but to go home as soon as it ends. Tadjik men also tend to cluster in one area of the 'compound' (see Figure 8.3) and women stay in their own husband's room or in the kitchen. Yet men do cook, make tea and sweep in the company of other men to avoid a woman having to be present to do these tasks. In fact, they sometimes excel in these activities, unlike the Georgian case. In both societies the entertaining of guests occupies a large part of a household's time, so male assistance, even occasionally, is no mean contribution to women's work as a whole. Women are associated with 'home-making' less exclusively among the Tadjiks, although women make the rugs and cushions which furnish their rooms almost entirely (see Figure 8.4).

Unlike the Georgian case, the kitchen and water tap are usually shared by all households and the parents may live with any son, not the youngest only. Note also that the 'verandah' (that is, raised platform)

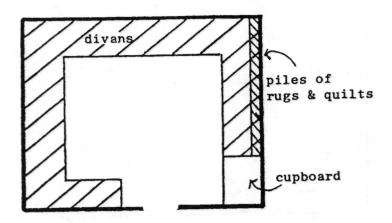

**Figure 8.4:** Tadjik Village – Room Interior

A house consists of one or two such rooms, or more, undifferentiated in contents and function. A man and his wife and children will sit and eat here. They will also sleep here, either with all their children or with the very youngest, the others going next door.

and the guest room are close to the door going into the street and are separate from the other buildings.

## Conclusion

It is important to remember in both cases that the patterns outlined above are only indicative of general trends since other factors, and in particular migration to the towns, have a strongly modifying action. Some tentative conclusions may nevertheless be drawn from this material which raise issues which will be developed in further discussions in another paper.

### The Domestic Division of Labour and of Space

The relationship between the domestic division of labour and space among the sexes is weaker than I had expected. Paradoxically the stronger, stricter division of domestic labour among the Georgians is accompanied by a lack of sexual division of space. Among the Tadjiks, on the contrary, the very division of space tends to lead to a weaker division of labour. Furthermore, in neither case are space patterns primarily generated by the 'practical' need of women's domestic work (e.g. labour saving). As for the important question of how the prestige status of women is affected when men perform the same tasks, we are again confronted with a paradox. In the Tadjik case, the art of cooking, which both men and women practise, for example, appears to be less prestigious than it is among the Georgians, where it is a mystery for the men which only the women can perform.

### The Division of Labour and Space and Kinship Patterns

The variation in the division of labour and space in the two cases could be accounted for in part by the differences in the kinship systems. Among the Georgians, cousins never marry. In the village they can never have sexual relations with the neighbours they are brought up with, their own age-cohort and others. In the Tadjik case, however, only siblings are excluded from being potential partners. In my opinion, a stricter division of the sexes, expressed in spatial patterns in particular, helps the older generation to maintain control over sexual and conjugal relations where eligibility for such is relatively open.

### The Division of Space and the Role of Women Outside the Home

The relationship between the division of space and the role of women outside the home is not very marked. In both cases women may hold positions of responsibility in their professional life, but this does not seem to affect their domestic responsibilities and how much the male members of the household will assist them, or they help the men (in fetching wine, for example, among the Ratcha villagers). Among the

Tadjiks, it must be conceded, a woman with high social standing outside the home, head of the village council or school, is more likely to mix with male guests than a dairy girl, but conceptually her role as a woman outside and inside the home are kept separate. Before Soviet times Tadjik women only had a place inside the home, and today their place here is spatially determined as then.

## The Domestic Division of Labour and Revolutions

In both ethnographies the domestic pattern of space has remained untouched. Houses and their layout have continued unchanged despite the marked transformations of Soviet rule. Likewise, the sexual division of labour in the house has also remained more or less untouched. The Revolution has, of course, affected the position of women outside the home and among the Tadjiks it has been remarkable. Yet in both cases it is the help of kinswomen (grandmother in Georgia; all women relatives in Tadjikistan) rather than increased labour-saving gadgets or state care which has permitted women to work outside the home successfully.

## Cognitive Maps and Domestic Space

The traditions developed before the Revolution, some religious, some national, have shaped the way people of both societies view the roles of men and women in the home. These are considered to be 'right' and have persisted tenaciously. These sex roles, moreover, are associated with ethnic identity by men and women alike. The outside world is where change is tolerated and indeed exploited to personal advantage. It is only there, as yet, that 'modern' architecture and design is destined to transform the rural horizons of the two peoples examined here.

# Notes

1. This is a version of the paper delivered at the seminar series in 1980 which forms the basis of this book. It forms a historical record of those parts of the Soviet Union at the time.

2. At the time of writing, I had done fieldwork in Georgia initially over a period of three years, from 1969 to 1972, with several return visits, the last in January 1979. My work on the Tadjiks was a continuing project; I did fieldwork in April and May 1979 and intended returning there when it became possible. Unfortunately, the subsequent invasion of Afghanistan by Soviet troops made this morally impossible.

# 9

# Spatial Domains and Women's Mobility in Yorubaland, Nigeria

*Helen Callaway*

## Constraints and Freedom

For this discussion of the particular constraints and the notable independence of women in Yoruba society, I have selected four frames of physical space (arranged from larger to smaller unit) for analysis:

1. The layout of the city
2. The traditional lineage compound
3. The more modern dwelling of a 'nuclear' family unit
4. Woman's inner space, her reproductive capacities

In order to interpret 'the position of women' in relation to these spatial domains, we must first, of course, turn to the meanings assigned within the particular Yoruba cultural context.

By 1981 the Yoruba-speaking peoples of south-western Nigeria[1] number from 12 million to 15 million. They live in densely-packed towns and cities, from which they commute outwards to a radius of 20 to 30 miles to their farmlands. Although Yoruba cities have grown rapidly in recent decades, they did not arise in response to modern industrialisation, but represent a unique and long-established Yoruba way of living (Mabogunje 1962; Krapf-Askari 1969). As early as 1505 the Portuguese mention Ijebu Ode as a large town; in the mid-nineteenth century the populations of Ibadan and Ilorin were estimated at 70,000 and Abeokuta at 60,000. These large cities with their rural networks encouraged a lively exchange of goods and fostered the early specialisation of craft industries. This urban way of life with its developed political and economic institutions shows itself in close relation to the Yoruba world view, which defines both the physical space and the social positions of women and men.

What do the layouts of cities, compounds and individual dwelling units tell us about female-male relations? This raises important theoretical issues. The Yoruba cosmology as articulated in the oral heritage of Ifa divination (Bascom 1969; Abimbola 1976) and in Yoruba writings (e.g. Johnson 1921; Biobaku 1957; Idowu 1962; Ojo 1966; Fadipe 1970) shows gender relations as hierarchical rather than egalitarian, not rigidly authoritarian but giving the impression of power radiating from a central source, male-oriented, male-dominated, with a distinct separation of spheres. We find in practice, however, that the instruments of power are finely tuned with checks and balances. We find that difference in gender roles does not necessarily mean the dominance of one and the subordination of the other, certainly not in any total way across the field of female-male interrelations. Historical studies show that in the pre-colonial society some Yoruba women held significant and independent positions in economic affairs, exhibiting considerable mobility in covering long distances for trading enterprises; other women became leaders of religious cults; a few outstanding women achieved responsible and powerful political roles (Beier 1955; Awe 1977). There would therefore seem to be an inconsistency (even possibly a contradiction) between the male-articulated ideology and female practice, between the prescribed cultural rules and the practical reality.

Peter Lloyd states:

> Many writers describe the African marriage payment as creating for the wife a status of near slavery, and literate Yoruba sometimes adopt the same usage. Yet the overt submissiveness of the Yoruba wife to her husband is perhaps the corollary of her great economic independence and her freedom to secure divorce. (1965: 566)

How are we to understand the scene of the Yoruba wife curtseying deferentially to her husband before going out to spend the day in the market-place as an energetic entrepreneur? This scene might be examined as an illustration, in Shirley Ardener's analysis (1975), of how the member of a subdominant group expresses herself in terms generated by the dominant group. Clearly the differentiation of female and male conceptual models of society in their manner of articulation and their content, as set out in the widely-known essay by Edwin Ardener (1972), is of key importance.

In the Yoruba context, this analytical framework might be usefully extended to include the distinction between ideology and practice, shifting the focus 'from the mechanics of the model to the dialectic of strategies' (Bourdieu 1977: 1–9). If ideology is taken to be the system of ideas or laws with accompanying social sanctions which maintain and reproduce the structure of power relations between groups and classes, then the articulated Yoruba model can be seen as a predominantly male cultural production. Yet these sets of unwritten rules which guide marriage arrangements, agricultural activities, market exchange, political interaction, religious observance, social ceremonies, dance, the entire spectrum of human affairs, are flexible enough in practical reality to allow females (and males, of course, as well) a wide range of strategies. A woman may adhere to the rules in ways which gain her the greatest advantage at each juncture. For example, by following the rules for divorce (meeting the time deadline in announcing her desertion, repaying the bridewealth, etc.), a wife may leave her husband for a preferable, perhaps wealthier, man without great difficulty. Thus, even if 'the rules of the game' appear to be written by men, women are clearly not just 'pawns in a men's game'.

It would seem that women in Yorubaland have developed a model of operation, complementary to the dominant male ideology, which has allowed them autonomous economic roles, the possibility of considerable political influence, freedom for independent mobility, and choice in the question of sexual partners. They learn sets of strategic improvisations. And because they exercise these options with spirit and imagination, the male image of Yoruba women is often projected as that of great power and great danger. Women personify both the highest values of womanhood (mothers with deep affective bonds, wives with reproductive capacities for continuing the patrilineage, economic managers achieving wealth) and the most malevolent evil (life-destroying witches).[2]

## The Analysis of Space: An Anthropological Approach

We turn next to the question of spatial domains. In his discussion of the ways in which different societies organise and use dwelling space, Rapoport (1969) reviews alternative theories by architects and cultural geographers of the determinants of building form. Of two principal types of explanation, one stresses the physical determinants of climate, the need for shelter, the available site, materials and technology, while the other places greater importance on such social determinants as economics, defence and religion. Rapoport criticises these determinist views, particularly since they are so often set out in terms of a single causal factor, and instead attributes house form to a whole range of socio-cultural factors against the background of possibilities within a particular environment.

An anthropological approach, of course, has its own specific concerns. In relation to spatial domains, three separate analytical levels might be set out.

(a) The first is *physical* space, 'what is on the ground', so to speak. Here we are concerned with physical things, human constructions within a particular ecology: the layouts of cities, the spatial ordering of family compounds, the divisions and allocation of space within individual domestic dwellings, the placing of various items of furniture and domestic tools. We note as well the constructions allowing for movements through space, such as streets and roads, bridges, and so on; and constructions arresting movement, demarcating boundaries, such as walls and fences, or ditches and trenches. There are also spaces deliberately left between physical constructions, which like the holes in a three-dimensional sculpture, may well have more 'meaning' than the physical forms which enclose and define these empty spaces.

(b) The second analytical level might be called *social* space. This has to do with traditional anthropological interests: the kinship structure; the social and economic organisation; the division of labour between the sexes and the generations; the domestic life-cycle; and so on. In relation to Yoruba culture, these are intimately associated with the yearly cycle based on agriculture, with its migrations from farm to city, where religious festivals mark the alternation between the seasons; then, the weekly cycle of four days in Yorubaland with the designated market days in different specified places; and the day-night cycle which predicates the movement of women and men through different areas of space.

(c) The third analytical level is *metaphysical* space. This refers to the cosmology or world-system, the moral and religious order, the belief structures which have developed through the historical and material conditions of a particular society and define its uniqueness. Metaphysical space presents the logical ordering of the visible and invisible universe, with its detailed classifications of knowledge and rules for moral action. From the viewpoint of an observer from a different culture, these classifications are seen to be arbitrary. But from within, they are seen as a transcendent order set apart in its sacredness and sometimes only partially revealed to lay-women and men.

Metaphysical space is the highest analytical level in the sense of being the most comprehensive and abstract, both prescribing the ordering of social and physical space and legitimating it. This symbolic ordering often overrules, or places restrictions on, utilitarian purposes. An excellent illustration was Renée Hirschon's description of the large items of furniture cluttering the limited dwelling space of Greek families in a poor urban settlement. What appeared as confusion in physical space in fact demonstrated the clarity and orderly perfection of metaphysical space.

## Yoruba Cultural Blueprints

The Yoruba case shows a particularly clear example of structural homologies between levels: its cosmology or religious world view, its social relations, its layouts of cities and family compounds. In a paper on 'Yoruba Metaphysical Thinking', Adesanya (1958) discusses the coherence of Yoruba thought, the compatibility among all the disciplines:

> Philosophy, theology, politics, social theory, land law, medicine, psychology, birth and burial, all find themselves logically concatenated in a system so tight that to subtract one item from the whole is to paralyse the structure of the whole. (1958: 40)

He calls this an 'architectonic of knowledge' and the insight is a significant one: the wholeness of a logically interconnected system, the isomorphic relations perceived between structure and event.

How has this knowledge been maintained in a pre-literate society? While it spreads to the whole of the populace through myths, folktales, praise songs, proverbs, the enactment of rituals, the observation of everyday etiquette, and so on, as an extensive and esoteric body of knowledge it has been transmitted from one generation to the next through the ritual chants of the Ifa oracle. This extended corpus of oral poetry has been called 'the Yoruba encyclopaedia',[3] including as it does the whole cycle of Yoruba arts and sciences – religion and philosophy, codes of law and morality, history, medicine and natural sciences. Training for this divination with its required art of memory may take as long as ten years. Ifa priests, it should be added, are always male, although I found one exception, a woman who claimed to have been taught Ifa by her husband after she had passed through menopause. 'Ifa is too strong for child-bearing', she explained. This secret, comprehensive, and powerful system of Yoruba knowledge is thus designated and maintained as a male domain.

The Yoruba cosmology is far too complex to be set out adequately in a few paragraphs here (see, e.g. Morton-Williams 1960, 1964; Idowu 1962; Bascom 1969; Kamau 1976). In its main outlines, the natural world, *ile aiye*, the world in which humans live, is believed to be homologous with the heavens, *ile orun*. The earth and the sky are of the same size, each with four sides, the number four being 'the sign of completion and perfection' (Morton-Williams 1960: 372). Ifa symbolism shows four cardinal points in the world, each guarded by a god (*orisha*); the Yoruba town has four (or multiples of four) gates.

In one version of the creation myth, Oduduwa the creator god descended the chain from heaven to Ile Ife, threw a handful of sand on the waters, and placed on it a cock and a palm nut. The chicken scratched the sand, creating hills and valleys, while the palm nut grew into a tree with sixteen branches. The sixteen branches are said to represent the sixteen parts of the world, and the nuts form the origin of the Ifa divination system, which uses sixteen palm nuts as counters. After creating the world, Oduduwa became the first Oni of Ife and the ancestor of all the Yoruba, thus forming a direct link between the gods and humans, between mythical time and historical time. In its ideal form, the human world is organised according to the pattern originally created at Ile Ife. Aside from this myth of common origin, the Yoruba have no collective reference to a time when they were united in a centralised political unit. Some fifty kingdoms or city-states exist (or have existed) with considerable differences among them in social structure and political processes. Despite these variations, however, it is evident that a set of cultural blueprints exists and that in the construction of human living space in Yorubaland an attempt is made to recreate the design of the cosmos. It is often said, for example, that the city of Ibadan once had sixteen gates.

## Places of Power in the Yoruba City

In her description of the layout of the Yoruba town, Krapf-Askari writes,

> The *oba*'s palace is the converging focus of all interests; each road passes through a quarter under a quarter-chief, and all the quarters, as well as the compounds of their chiefs, look towards the palace. Similarly, within each quarter, the various compounds are as far as possible grouped around that of the quarter-chief. (1969: 39)

The geographer Ojo states that this form of town plan derives from the socio-political structure of each Yoruba kingdom, which 'imposes on Yoruba towns a more or less identical morphology' (1966: 132).[4] As the town replicates the design of the cosmos, he notes, so does the layout of the *oba*'s palace (ibid.: 132–40). The palace is rectangular and, like the town, surrounded by a thick wall. Facing the main gate is the *oba*'s public throne. The courtyards nearest the gate are for public use, while the inner ones are private. The first courtyard is the location for public ceremonies presided over by the *oba*. Each successive courtyard leading into the centre is occupied by persons closer to him. The inner ones are occupied only by the *oba*'s intimate wives, and it is here that they cook his food. The innermost courtyard is reserved for the *oba* himself. Besides being his private quarters, this courtyard represents a shrine, for it is the centre and thus the most holy place in the kingdom. Crowned in a sacred ritual, the oba has supreme responsibility for the defence of his kingdom against invaders, its internal political stability, its food supply through the fertility of the soil, and its continuity of lineages through the fertility of women.

At each level, the pattern is repeated with the place of highest authority and importance at the centre. As Kamau notes (1976: 347), the centre of the earth is located at Ile Ife; the centre of each kingdom is its capital town; the centre of the town is the palace representing sacred political institutions; the centre of the ward is the residence of the ward chief; and finally, the centre of the compound is the dwelling space of the head of the patrilineage. The spatial design of the cosmology is thus replicated at each level from the universe to the person in this male-oriented vision of power structures.

We have already had a glimpse of women in the palace, as wives, some no doubt wielding indirect political influence. While oral history reveals that at certain times women have actually held the throne, these cases would seem to be anomalous, as for example the regent Queen Ida of Ketu (Parrinder 1956: 64). But there have been formal institutional places of power for women within the palace. Writing of the royal household in Oyo, the Yoruba historian Samuel Johnson (1921: 63) lists eight titled ladies of the highest rank, eight priestesses, and other ladies of rank aside from the king's wives. These ladies hold special powers, the greatest being wielded by the *Iya kere* who has charge of all the king's treasures and royal insignia. Should she be offended, she is able to prevent a state reception from proceeding by withholding the royal insignia. She is the person entitled to place the crown on the king's head at the coronation. The interesting point about these royal attendants and priestesses is that with the assumption of office, they are from that time on (and Johnson states an emphatic 'of course') to remain celibate. They are thus marked off as non-sexual, non-child-bearing women; in a sense, set apart as non-women. The *Iyamode*, the highest official in one of the outhouses of the palace, is not only required to be celibate for life, but she is known as *Baba*, or father. The king kneels for no one else but her, looking upon her as his father, for she represents the spirits of his ancestors (ibid.: 65). In this case, a reclassification process has explicitly transposed a 'natural' female into a 'supernatural' male (cf. Silvia Rodgers's account of the reclassification of women in the British House of Commons, this volume).

In his paper on the Yoruba Ogboni cult, Morton-Williams (1960) tells us that the Alafin of Oyo does not attend the meetings of this secret society which has important religious and political powers. Instead, he hears about the transactions from a certain woman of the palace whose duty it is to attend all meetings of the secret society on his behalf (ibid.: 365). While most of the elders of the society are men, and it is these who are termed *ogboni*, a small number, usually six, are women, termed *erelu*, who represent the interests of the women of the town. These members have reached the stage of *agbalagba* – 'adult having adult' – meaning those old enough for the eldest of their children to have become adults (ibid.: 368). They have reached a specified stage in women's life-cycle, considered to be beyond child-bearing and sexual activity, a state (familiar in other societies) which confers responsibilities and powers not open to women during their reproductive years.

Another institutional place for a female leader is that of *Iyalode*. A description of the *Iyalode* of Ibadan in 1854 is given in the diary of Anna Hinderer, the wife of the first CMS missionary in Ibadan.

> These Yoruba people have some very nice arrangements about their form of government. I found out that there was an *Iyalode* or mother of the town, to whom all the women's palavers (disputes) are brought before they are taken to the king. She is, in fact, a sort of Queen, a person of much influence, and looked up to with much respect . . . . I went with the children, and we found a most respectable motherly looking person, surrounded by her attendants and people, in great order, and some measure of state. (Hinderer 1873: 110)

At about the same period the famous *Iyalode* of Abeokuta, Madame Tinubu, traded in palm oil and ivory and supplied the whole Abeokuta army with guns in the defence against Dahomey.

The difficulty in assessing the political role of *Iyalode*, as Bolanle Awe states (1977: 145-6), is that Yoruba political systems were not uniform from one kingdom to the next, the powers of the *Iyalode* were strongly curtailed during the colonial period, and while the nineteenth century is fairly well documented, the annals of oral history before that time are fragmentary. Awe describes the *Iyalode* as a co-ordinator of women's activities, including settling their quarrels in her court. She represented 'the voice of the women in government', meeting with them to determine the women's stand on such questions as the declaration of war, the opening of new markets, or the administration of women at the local level. 'As a spokesman she was given access to all positions of power and authority within the state, exercising legislative, judicial, and executive powers with the chiefs in their council' (ibid.: 147–48). Yet, as Awe adds, she suffered from the big disadvantage of being always outnumbered as the only female among male chiefs in the decision-making body.

If the palace represents the symbolic centre of political authority, primarily a male domain with certain limited positions of power for women, directly outside the palace stands the main market of the city. It is here that women flourish in independent economic activity (Mabogunje 1959; Sudarkasa 1973; Karanja-Diejomaoh 1979). This is an arena both of women's solidarity and of self-achievement. Some women gain considerable wealth and status. In this sphere of economic exchange, which includes both women and men, women operate unambiguously as independent women. Pregnancy is considered normal, carried proudly by the prospective mother, and admired by others. Babies are portable, tied on their mothers' backs and accompany them everywhere until they are weaned at between eighteen months and three years.

In Ibadan the most outstanding marketwoman I met was Alhaja Humuani Alaga. In 1932 she was the first woman in the city with enough capital, and courage for risk-taking, to open a textile shop. Although she had no formal schooling, she was able to keep accounts in her head. She gave out on credit to her agents hundreds of pounds worth of cloth and, even during the depression, she managed to extend her sales network further and further into outlying districts. As she became wealthy, she became prominent in public affairs. She led various women's groups in getting through improvements for marketwomen and in providing scholarships for Moslem girls at secondary schools and at the University of Ibadan. She educated her own daughters in universities in Britain and the US, as well as her sons (five surviving children). Alhaja Alaga is self-made and greatly respected. She, of course, represents the highest possibilities of women's achievement in the market. Many other women operate in the economic sphere with far less flair, some gaining only bare subsistence.

## The Patrilineal Compound

Bascom writes, 'As in many other African societies the lineage is a self-perpetuating group that includes the departed ancestors, the living, and those yet to be born . . . a cyclical and endless character' (1969: 115). Certainly in Yorubaland strong emphasis is placed on the continuity of generations and on the invisible presence both of deceased ancestors and of children yet to be born. The spatial location for this conceptual lineage is the family compound. Lloyd observes how the large rambling compounds are being replaced by modern houses built on the land of the owner's lineage. 'Thus, although the buildings continually change, the compound still remains as a territorial and social unit' (1965: 560). This section will examine 'women's space' in such a compound through the life history of a particular woman in the indigenous section of Ibadan.

The entry of this rectangular mud-walled compound was once guarded by wooden gates which no longer exist. Directly opposite the entry is a building with a verandah and imposing pillars, the chief's house, and beyond that, the mosque. Here the men of the compound congregate every morning in answer to the prescribed call for prayer, while the women carry out their prayers separately, each within her own domestic quarters. Along the inner wall of the compound the sons of the lineage have their dwelling units, some of crumbling mud-brick, others faced with cement. Each has a principal room for the male and smaller ones for his wives. Water is carried from a public tap some distance from the compound and stored in earthen jars. Cooking takes place on open fires outdoors or on small charcoal burners within.

Oriatu (a fictional name, one typical in Yoruba Muslim families) lived here in 1969, when she told me her life story during a series of meetings. (Ten years later when I inquired about her, she was no longer there and it proved impossible to trace her in the brief time available.) She was in her early thirties when I met her, with a baby daughter not yet weaned. She had a room in the house of her husband, a goldsmith some fifteen to twenty years her senior. She was his fourth wife. The other wives were no longer in residence. One had gone to Kano, another had divorced and remarried, and the third had her own house elsewhere in Ibadan.

Oriatu earned her living on a piece-work basis at home, making the designs for batik. This she did by dipping a chicken feather into a paste of cassava starch and deftly sketching the traditional patterns onto a white cloth. (When the cloth is dyed, the indigo does not penetrate through the starch and the motif stands out in a lighter shade.) If Oriatu worked steadily at her job from morning until dark, she was able to earn about five shillings a day, enough at that time to buy food. Her husband has been unable to contribute anything to the household expenses for herself and their child.

Her own father, Alhaji Amadu, was a successful farmer, then in his late sixties and still in vigorous health. He had had three wives, each producing families of children. We visited him in Ibadan at his spacious house, faced with cement, and with a balcony on the upper storey – a visible indication of prosperity and prestige. Without any formal schooling himself, he had sent two of his three sons to universities and the third to a technical school. His nine daughters had *no* schooling.

In her early childhood Oriatu had lived with her mother at the farm hamlet, some twenty miles outside Ibadan. When her mother died, she was sent to her eldest sister's household in Ibadan for training. At the age of six, Oriatu was expected to help sweep the house and the compound, care for small children, carry water, and help with chores of grinding foodstuffs and cooking. Later she began to learn the skills of making *adire*, the Yoruba batik. This was a Moslem compound where the women in purdah (rare among Yoruba Moslems) carried out the complete process of *adire*-making, working in a quadrangle open to the sky but enclosed from the outside world. They drew the designs, then stirred the cloth in large vats of indigo dye and, after the allotted number of days, hung the cloth on lines to drip streams of blue onto the packed earth.

Oriatu left this compound at her first marriage, when she was about eighteen. Her first husband was some ten years older, a clerk in the agricultural department with a monthly salary. His first wife was pregnant, and he was looking for a second wife. For a while Oriatu was happy in his household, she said. Her husband provided for her and the senior wife treated her well. Later there were two junior wives. She never told me directly what went wrong, but it became obvious that she was referring to witchcraft. Her first two babies had each died suddenly from convulsions. Other children in the household had died. Fearing for the life of her third child, Oriatu decided to go to her father's house. She went to the divorce court where judges assessed her repayment to her husband as £10, a comparatively low figure because she had lived in his compound for seven years and had borne him three children, although only one had survived. She paid this amount out of her own savings from making batik. Although the husband had the right to keep their small daughter, he had many other children and did not want to take care of her. Oriatu took the child with her to her father's house. Here tension developed between herself and her father's third wife. 'Even now', Oriatu explained, 'my father's third wife does not like me or any of my sisters to visit him. She is afraid he will share some of his wealth with us.'

It was not long before Oriatu accepted an offer for marriage. This was the goldsmith from the compound in Oje. Oriatu thought he was a wealthy man who would take care of her and the children they would have. But he had never given her any money. Still he was a kind man, she said, not harsh as her first husband had been. The daughter from her first marriage was sent to live with her eldest sister because her first husband did not want the child to go to the compound of her new husband. When I came to see her, Oriatu had lived in Oje for six years. She had had two more children. One died soon after weaning and the second, a frail girl nearly a year old (weighing only 11 lb), was considered by Oriatu to be an *abiku*, meaning a spirit child who wants to return to the spirit world. Oriatu said she would like to have another child, perhaps two more, but particularly a son to support her in her old age.

Let us now trace Oriatu's history in relation to physical space: first her early childhood with her mother at her father's farm hamlet, then as a girl in her sister's strict Moslem household in Ibadan, then a young married woman in her first husband's house, next a divorcee in her father's relatively prosperous house in Ibadan made unwelcome by his present wife, and finally as the fourth wife of a senior man in the Oje compound. She was a 'stranger' here, getting along with the wives of other men of the lineage and showing the appropriate courtesies, but her closest alliances were with her own sisters, who lived in households elsewhere in Ibadan. Only a woman with sons belonging to the patrilineage or one who has gained economic independence has a secure old age. Her daughters would marry into other lineages and move away. A poor old woman without a son to protect her is likely to be accused of witchcraft. This is an unusual way of looking at 'women's space' in the patrilineal compound: from the perspective of a woman whose social space in terms of the male model is peripheral and even her physical space uncertain.

In her lack of economic achievement and her failure to raise any male children, Oriatu may not be typical. At our last meeting she hinted that evil spirits had prevented the fulfilment of her preordained destiny, an explanation for misfortune derived from Yoruba indigenous religion (see Idowu 1962: 169–85; Bascom 1969: 116–19). Yet for every woman who marries successfully, raises a large family of surviving children, and accumulates wealth through trade or craft production, there are others at the opposite end of the scale like Oriatu.

## The Individual Family Dwelling

How does 'women's space' differ in the household of an individual family dwelling? This discussion is based on the 'modern' cement-faced rectangular house of a Christian primary school teacher, Mr Ajayi (again a fictional name). Designed by himself, the house was built on family land in the heart of old Ibadan, next door to the dilapidated and now uninhabited mud dwelling of his father, who had been a worshipper of Shango and was buried beneath the mud floor of his house according to traditional custom.

Mr Ajayi's first wife had died of 'fever'. His second wife was a Christian like himself and also a primary school teacher, although with low qualifications she was only able to get a job in a village outside Ibadan. She took her youngest child (still suckling) with her on Monday morning, stayed in a room in the village, and returned to Ibadan on Friday evening. She was hoping to continue her teacher training in order to get a higher certification and thus a job within the city.

This might be called a 'nuclear' family, with one man and one wife, but there were numerous adult relatives visiting from the family farm hamlet some twenty miles away, and six children cared for permanently. Two of these were orphans of relatives, one a daughter from Mr Ajayi's first marriage, and three were children of the present marriage.

The front room of this house is a parlour with louvred window shutters to keep out the bright sunlight and let in fresh air. The modern-style furniture was bought from local carpenters. This is Mr Ajayi's space for entertaining his friends, listening to the wireless, and reading the daily newspaper. His wife enters only to serve his food or on his invitation. He also has a separate bedroom at the front of the house. The other rooms are bedrooms, one for his wife and their infant children, others for older children and relatives. At the back of the house is a walled-in open space with a hearth for cooking, a storage room for foodstuffs, a space for bathing, and a pit latrine.

What follows is a generalised account of female and male space within a domestic dwelling, outlining traditional customs in the polygynous society and their continuity today in modified forms. The first point is the separation of female and male activities in both physical and social space. The traditional Yoruba domestic life was hierarchical. Mabogunje writes,

> The father is the object of great respect, often verging towards reverence both by the children and even the wives . . . . On a social survey of many villages around Ibadan, for instance, we discovered that apart from the oldest wife, the other wives felt it was beyond them to mention the name of their husband to us. The father, on his part, has to keep a dignified distance from most of his junior wives and often from his children who grow up more to revere, respect, and even fear him than develop filial affection for him. (1958: 29).

With the exception of some elite families who have high educational backgrounds and experience abroad, this distance is maintained to a varied extent even in Christian families of one man and one wife.[5] Although Christians may attend church services together, the wife will have her own women's church association and the husband his. Many families do not eat together as a unit, but follow the tradition of the male having his food brought to him in his own living quarters. In a polygynous family, his evening meal may be served by the wife whose turn it is to be sexually available. The wife, or wives, eat in their own part of the house, where the children are also fed.

Sleeping quarters are usually separate. A man has his bedroom, and his wife or wives will sleep each with her own youngest children. In relation to women's menstruation, a male informant said, 'The monthly period can spoil good medicine. No strong warrior would ever spend the whole night until daybreak with a woman. Women are anti-strength.' The same belief was expressed about pregnancy. But even when a woman is not pregnant and not having her period, it is still not a custom for a wife and husband to sleep together through the night. This infor-

mant continued, 'The best thing for a woman is to have her own room
and the man to keep to his room. Men who are strong do not sleep with
women. They won't have time to think.'

Notes taken from interviews with men during my fieldwork reveal
male attitudes:

> The husband is the master of the house. He keeps the house for the wife to
> live in. The wife will say 'the owner of my house' (*baale mi*) referring to the
> husband. In Yoruba custom, your wife is not your equal. When a woman
> begins to feel equal, she will become unpopular. Divorce may occur. In
> Yorubaland we don't take a woman as an equal.

> When you own the house, the front of the house belongs to you. Nobody can
> do anything without your permission. You own the whole thing totally. This
> is the belief of a man about a wife. When a woman is given you, she will
> obey. If she doesn't do what you like, she's in trouble.

This harsh proprietary view may be the outward expression concealing
unconscious jealousy of women's independent economic capacities and
also fear of women's recourse to excessive male dominance – adultery
and/or divorce. Factors relating to marital instability and the very high
divorce rate among the Yoruba have been analysed (Okediji and Okediji 1966; Lloyd 1968).

## Women's Inner Space

So far, we have been concerned with building constructions and spatial
layouts in the conventional sense, the external world of cultural arte-
facts. There is one further important link in this spatial code of information. This relates the external to the internal, women's inner space. The
key to the continuity of patrilineages is the reproductive capacities of
wives who are brought in from other lineages. The male owns the house.
He also 'owns the pregnancy' (a commonly-used phrase) of his wife,
gaining sole sexual and genetricial rights through marriage and the payment of bridewealth. A Yoruba geographer characterises his own people
as having 'always been preoccupied with the problems of fertility of
human beings as well as crops' (Ojo 1966: 185). The agricultural
metaphor is further extended in some parts of Yorubaland where the
sperm is considered a seed, the miniature of the fully-formed child.[6]
This makes explicit the idea of the physical determinancy of the foetus
from the father and the space for its growth being the mother's womb.
Again, the centre marks the significant space, providing for the reproduction of the next generation, the sons to carry on the line of men
traced from the mythical past to the infinite future.

It is often said in Yorubaland that a man's wealth is measured by the number of his children (before recent years, that is, when high food prices and educational costs have changed the picture). In the earlier economy based mainly on agriculture, more sons meant a larger united labour force to clear land and maintain its production. This would generate wealth, which would then allow the bridewealth payments for more wives, thus creating further alliances and affording the possibility of more children. Strength of numbers, the wealth this made possible, the clients thus attracted, gained its further dimension in political power. If this represents a male point of view, the desire for many children is also expressed by women. Not only are children the means for security in old age and for higher esteem from the husband and the wider society, but also they provide women with strong emotional bonds, considered to be closer and more lasting than that of husband and wife. In her delightful study of the meanings of Yoruba names, Oduyoye (1972) lists many names expressing sentiments about children, e.g. Ayòdélé ('Joy reaches our home'), Ọmọniyi ('Children are the glory of their parents'), Ọmọléye ('Children are the real status symbols'), Titilayò ('Endless is my joy'). As Lloyd writes:

> The Yoruba passionately desire children, sons above all. Childlessness is the worst plight which can afflict both men and, especially, women, for other forms of achievement – wealth or political office for instance – cannot compensate for it. (1974: 163)

Both traditional medical practitioners (*babalawo*) and the prayer healers of the evangelist churches (*aladura*) give much of their attention to women for problems of infertility or barrenness, for healthy pregnancy and safe delivery, and for protection of infant children against disease and malevolent forces (Callaway 1980). Even with the rapid social and economic change of recent years, this preference for large families has shown few signs of lessening. Demographic studies in 1975 show

> . . . most wives were still polygynously married, completed fertility averaged around seven live births per woman with little clear evidence of change or of the emergence of significant differentials, and long periods of postnatal lactation and abstinence were still prevalent. (Caldwell and Caldwell 1977: 195)

In native law and custom, the child always belonged to the legal husband of the wife. This is expressed in a proverb: 'He who owns the tree owns the fruit on it.' Even if the wife is known to have been 'wayward', the husband would still claim the child, as stated in another proverb: 'The king does not reject any child born within wedlock.' This refers to the situation of a king who may have as many as 20 or 30 or more wives and not have time for all of them. Even if he knew that he could not be the genitor of a child of one of his wives, he would claim the child as his own. Since 1925, this custom has been changing. At that time the colonial government enacted the Judicature Act which ruled that principles of equity must prevail against the rigour of any law. When a paternity case reached the higher courts, the colonial judge ruled against the legal husband, who did not profess to be the genitor of the child, in favour of the proven natural father. From that precedent, many paternity suits have come to the courts and the trend has been for the genitor to be recognised.

An outsider, and particularly a feminist, might ask, 'What are the mother's rights over her child?' She has *no* legal rights. But, as noted earlier, there is a difference between the harsh legal formal rights and what actually happens in practice. No child is taken from a mother who is breastfeeding her child, even when she divorces her husband. Usually in such cases the mother keeps young children until the age of seven or so, although sometimes the paternal grandmother takes over a child for her son. Even though the father claims 'ownership' of a child for his lineage, it is the mother who usually has the intimate care of children and the closest affective bonds.

## Women's Mobility

Although the traditional society had its class divisions of royal families, chiefs, commoners and domestic slaves, Yoruba history (e.g. the classic study of Johnson, 1921) shows how individual men used strength in war and skill in negotiation to gain political power and wealth. This history shows only fleeting glimpses of women. As in so many parts of the world, the history of Yoruba women has yet to be written, and indeed will be difficult to reconstruct (Awe 1977). It is clear that the spreading influence of both the Moslem and Christian religions and the establishment of colonial government strongly reinforced the male-oriented ideology of the indigenous society. In modern education, the advantage was heavily weighted for males, first in gaining basic literacy and later in achieving higher education with professional degrees in law, medicine, engineering. The development of cash crops in agriculture, the stimulation of commerce, all favoured men. Even so, the construction of transport systems and the expansion of markets during this period also benefited women. Yoruba women, like those from other ethnic groups throughout West Africa (Leis 1976: 129), were quick to take advantage of new products for exchange and the possibilities of trading over greater distances. During the colonial period a few Yoruba women rose to prominence as important political figures (the late Mrs Olufunmilayo Ransome-Kuti might be cited), as heads of schools, as wealthy traders.

In terms of spatial structures, the indigenous Yoruba cosmology would seem to have designated a world of male domains as shown in the layouts of cities and palaces, agnatic family compounds, individual dwelling units, even women's reproductive space. According to this cultural model, men for the most part control areas of external space and women are expected to move from the place of their birth in their father's house (metaphorically, if not literally) to the locations of their (successive) husbands. Men also 'own' women's internal space, the child in her womb. This analysis focusing on spatial domains suggests both the subordination and dependence of women. A wider view, however, reveals other tenets of Yoruba social organisation which serve as countervailing forces, promoting women's autonomy and self-defined development.

Women's mobility itself presents them with key choices. It allows them strategies not only to improve their economic activities but to select (or entice) a man for marriage and to divorce freely if difficulties come and alternatives arise. While marriage arrangements appear to give males full control over their wife or wives, polygyny and the relative ease in divorce discourage enduring social intimacy and thus the psychological dependence of a woman on her husband. Related to this is the expectation that women maintain independent economic activities throughout their adult lives. While the concept of preordained individual destiny – for women as well as men – comes across in one sense as deterministic and fatalistic, in practice it has the paradoxical effect of motivating individual achievement and legitimating independent ventures. A successful person's manoeuvres are validated by calling her success the achievement of her destiny, while an unsuccessful person is considered to have been held back by evil, mystical forces. All these factors promote women's individual and collective enterprise. If from one view, then, women are characterised as moving between and within the spatial domains controlled by men, from another perspective they can be seen taking personal risk and exercising considerable freedom in fulfilling their destinies.

## Acknowledgements

For lively anthropological discussions on Yoruba women, I wish to thank Professor Constance Sutton, Wambui Karanja-Diejomaoh and the Reverend Emmanuel Babatunde. I should like as well to express my gratitude to all the members of the Oxford Women's Anthropology Seminar for their continuing flow of ideas and friendly support. There is space here to name only one: Shirley Ardener, for her perceptive critical help in shaping this and other work.

# Notes

1. Studies of the Yoruba-speaking peoples comprise a vast and growing literature. Selected sources for this summary include: Johnson 1921; Lloyd 1965; Ojo 1966; Bascom 1969; Fadipe 1970.

2. Studies of Yoruba women as sources of mystical evil include: Morton-Williams 1956; Prince 1961; Harper 1970; Hoch-Smith 1978.

3. Called this by Professor Robert G. Armstrong in personal discussion.

4. While this classical model is found in the northern Yoruba kingdoms with agnatic lineages, Lloyd (1966) notes a grid-type layout for Ijebu and Ondo with cognatic descent groups.

5. On the basis of a demographic survey, Caldwell and Caldwell write, 'By the measures which may be quite inappropriately used by outsiders, conjugal relationships are not particularly close. Only 31 per cent of wives usually eat with their husbands (and 48 per cent never do so), 30 per cent join each other at festivities or parties, and 26 per cent visit friends together. Only 27 per cent sleep in the same room as their husbands and a very small number in the same bed' (1977: 203).

6. A view held by the Egbado Yoruba, according to the Revd. Emmanuel Babatunde. For a similar view in other societies, see my discussion of 'the denial of physiological maternity' (Callaway 1978: 167–8).

# 10

# Where Women Must Dominate: Response to Oppression in a South African Urban Community

*Rosemary Ridd*

The 'ethnographic present' in this chapter is the late 1970s. On the face of it, the women described appear to contradict the model of women as a *muted group* whose view of life has to be adapted to a *dominant* male system.[1] However, it will become evident that first, it is only special circumstances which produce this effect and secondly, that it is a temporary phenomenon. In the inner city area adjacent to the central business district of Cape Town where, as in comparable cities the world over, the inhabitants represent a kaleidoscopic amalgam of many social and ethnic backgrounds. In Cape Town, under South African apartheid legislation, this community is deemed to be *non-White* and its members are nearly all classified (as though of one homogeneous group) as 'Coloured'.[2]

## Social Space and Race Classification

The South African population is officially divided into three 'race' groups, namely: *Black, White* and *Coloured*.[3] The *Coloured* group is further divided into seven sub-groups: *Cape Coloured, Cape Malay, Griqua, Indian, Chinese, other Asiatic* and *other Coloured*.[4] For some purposes, however, the government differentiates *Asian* (presumably meaning the *Indian* and *other Asiatic* sub-groups of *Coloured*) as a fourth major 'race' group.[5] While the term 'Coloured' was in common usage before apartheid was introduced,[6] its rigid definition for purposes of discriminatory legislation has made people very much opposed to accepting it to describe themselves.

Of the 'Coloured' members of the community with which we are specifically concerned, the majority Christian section is 'Cape Coloured' and a substantial minority, 'Cape Malay'. The Christians resent being called 'Cape Coloured' and argue that the government has created an arbitrary dividing line between 'White' and 'Colour' where in reality there is a continuum of colour gradations with no absolute cut-off point in social space. Some claim that they should have been classified 'White', and some have been reclassified from 'Coloured' to 'White'. During the 1960s, the area was full of stories of families torn apart by race classification. There were cases of old school friends, cousins and even siblings who ceased to recognise each other publicly, the 'White' for fear that his race classification might be brought into question, the 'Coloured' in defence of his own dignity.

The Moslems likewise object to being called 'Cape Malay' because it has become an 'apartheid term' and conflates their identity with that of being 'Coloured'. They argue that, though like the 'Cape Coloured' they are of mixed ancestry, as Moslems they occupy a social space separate from 'Coloured'. Christian and Moslem have been pitted against one another through apartheid and each derides the other as 'Coloured'.

## Geographical Space and Group Areas Legislation

Our area of study may be divided into three contiguous sections, namely *District Six, Woodstock* and *Walmer Estate*. Though each is different in character from the others, together they occupy a picturesque setting, just East of the city centre, where the land stretches up from Table Bay towards the lower slopes of Table Mountain, or more specifically, Devil's Peak. Seen at close quarters, however, the area loses some of its glamour, for it is located in what geographers describe as the 'twilight zone' of the city. Much of it was built at the turn of the last century to meet pressing demands for cheap housing in Cape Town at a time of industrial boom and to cope with the influx of immigrants from up-country and overseas.

*District Six,* quintessentially a cosmopolitan community, symbolises defiance of the residential segregation of 'race' groups enforced by Group Areas policy. Despite the appalling poverty and squalid accommodation, it possessed a liveliness and sense of excitement as a place where people from all walks of life might jostle together in the streets. The character of this area and its people is summed up in Afrikaans as *deurmekaar*[7] (mixed up). District Six was said to possess 'the soul of the Coloured people' because of the heterogeneity of its residents in terms of their race, colour and economic background.

District Six could not be allowed to remain. In February 1966 the government announced plans to remove residents to 'Coloured townships' and for the demolition of their old homes in preparation for the redevelopment of the area exclusively for Whites.[8] While this news brought public outcry from liberal Whites as well as the local inhabitants, nothing could be done to reverse the decision. The storm of protest did arrest the demolition process, however, because White businessmen were fearful of public opinion against them and were reluctant to buy this building land. As a result, the area remained half demolished, half standing for more than a decade, with 10,000 people still to be moved away, overlooking the wreckage (Cf. Franck *et al.* 1967).

*Woodstock* was once the first suburb of Cape Town on the main road leading out through District Six to more salubrious (and now exclusively White) residential areas like Rondebosch, Claremont and Constantia. Rapid urbanisation, some sixty to eighty years ago, has left it today a forlorn and shabby 'Cinderella suburb', as local newspapers call it. Woodstock people are known for their dubious claims to 'White' identity, for their preoccupation with symbols of 'respectability' and for their openly expressed prejudices against those 'of colour'. The term 'Woodstock White' is commonly applied to 'poor Whites' and 'pass Whites' who are struggling to be accepted by those whom *they* would describe as 'real Whites'.[9]

*Walmer Estate*, the newest of the three sections of this area, was built up the slope towards Devil's Peak. It borders on District Six (which separates it from the city centre) to the west, and on Woodstock (which separates it from the coast) to the north. It provides good housing for a 'Coloured' social elite and commands a magnificent view down over the harbour. Its residents look down their noses at both the 'Coloured' slum-dwellers of District Six and the 'poor Whites' of Woodstock.

In June 1975 Walmer Estate and part of Woodstock were officially proclaimed together as a 'Coloured area'.[10] This long-delayed decision was seen as small compensation to the 'Coloured' population for the loss of District Six. The remainder of Woodstock was left in the hands of the 'Woodstock Whites'.[11]

This inner city area as a whole has a special interest for us here because its very social diversity sums up the irony of 'Coloured identity'. Here is a place, adjacent to the centre of a major South African city, where people who are themselves of mixed racial and cultural backgrounds are subject to apartheid policy which demands the strict segregation of one racial and cultural group from another. Moreover, this area has been a thorn in the flesh for government planners because it demonstrates vividly the arbitrariness of 'Coloured' as an official 'race' category and because many of its residents who are of 'lighter complexion' are poorer than their darker-skinned relatives. It represents a topsy-turvy world, the antithesis of the order that apartheid contrives to establish. Its future has been problematic, even when compared with other 'Coloured' residential areas which have been purpose-built as segregated townships.

On the other hand, when viewed by the rest of Cape Town's 'Coloured' population, those living in this area are essentially 'non-White' like themselves, but represent a staid, tradition-bound community which is generally unsympathetic to progressive ideas, especially those of Black Consciousness. During the school boycotts and protest marches of 1976 (in the wake of Soweto) and 1980, it was in the 'Coloured townships' on the Cape Flats like Manenberg, Bonteheuwel and Elsies River, that the police intervened and where the ensuing violence brought these events to the headlines of the international press. The inner city area remained relatively quiet.[12]

## A Corollary to Muted Group Theory

### The Model of Women as Muted

Interest in women among social anthropologists developed with the awareness that the bulk of field research, while purporting to reflect the character of a society as a whole, really depended on its male informants. It rested on the assumption that women, whose views were often more difficult to ascertain, shared the same outlook as their husbands, fathers and brothers. Women remained in the background, out of focus or *muted*, sometimes treated as the object of attention through men but rarely the subject in their own right of anthropological study. To remedy these defects of male bias it has been necessary for anthropologists to direct their attention specifically towards women in order to ascertain whether they do in fact share common perspectives with their male counterparts.

### Corollary – Where Women are Dominant

On the basis of 'muted group theory' it would be reasonable to suppose that the 'Coloured' women of this inner city area form a muted group (in relation to men in this community) within a muted group ('Coloured' in relation to dominant White society).[13] The mutedness of 'Coloured' people in relation to White political and economic dominance, however, has produced circumstantial change in the male/female relationship within the community. It may be contended that men feel the discrimination against them as 'Coloured' more directly because their frame of reference is more specifically in the public sector controlled by Whites. In consequence, for the 'Coloured' the home has been elevated as a place of refuge and women thrust into the vital endeavour of preserving the dignity of the family against the humiliation of apartheid.[14] The exclusion of the 'Coloured' men from the White man's *social* and *geographical space* has produced a situation where, for the 'Coloured', the home is paramount as the *physical space* controlled by women.

In this chapter we must consider *why* women are dominant and look at the traditional values which they have transformed. Then we will consider *how* women maintain their position of dominance through the control of the home as the woman's 'enterprise'. Lastly, we will consider female dominance as an inherently unstable phenomenon. The community is *matrifocal* rather than *matriarchal*: the latter implies an entrenched kinship system which is independent of external pressure.[15] The matrifocal situation described here is a response to oppressive conditions, both political and economic, and is subject to social change. In this community there are definite signs of social change (resulting partly from improving economic conditions and partly from developing awareness of political oppression) which indicate the diminishing of the dominance of women in the future.

## Traditional Value-systems

Two traditional value-systems have had an important influence on this community. First, European (mostly British) missionaries and social workers who came to live in District Six during the first half of this century gave the people hope that by acquiring the cultural attributes of the European they would gradually become assimilated into White South African society. Secondly, a strong Islamic influence has been maintained through the Moslem members of the community. Though both these systems have dictated a clear pattern of male dominance, their values have been actively promoted by women and, as a result, the male/female position has been reversed to fit the community's own requirements.

### European Influence

The view in District Six of the Afrikaner contrasts markedly with that of the English-speaking White for historical reasons. The Afrikaner is seen as one who genealogically shares a common social space with the 'Coloured' but has *built up* barriers between them. The image of the Afrikaner is based on an acute sense of alienation by kinsmen sharing a common symbolic ancestry in the union of the early Dutch settlers with Hottentot women.[16] Feelings are typified in the following extract from field notes where a District Six woman explains the Afrikaner/ 'Coloured' relationship:

> When Jan van Riebeek[17] came to South Africa 300 years ago he didn't bring a wife. He was a man and a man can't stay away from a woman for a long

period of time. It's not like now when you can hop back in two ticks: it took
weeks to travel from Europe, so he took his Hottentot and Bushman women.
It was the natural thing to do and their children became 'Coloureds'. You
know, they now teach in the schools that van Riebeek brought his wife with
him; but I went to Zonnebloem [an elite 'Coloured' school on the edge of
District Six] and I know that he had no wife when he came. And the Afrikaner too; he came from them. We are all mixed up; we say 'deurmekaar' . . . .
The Afrikaner is white and we are brown; that's the difference. And the
'Coloured' and Afrikaner will always hate each other, we have been cut off.
The Afrikaner hates the 'Coloured' because he knows where he came from.
It's the British who gave us over to the Afrikaner, a good couple of years
ago. When the British were here we could go where we liked and marry who
we liked. That's how we married the British and other foreigners, but we
can't do that any more.

The English, however, are seen as foreigners and are associated with
attempts to *break down* the social and geographical space division
between White and 'Coloured'. They have been idealised as bearers of
culture and, as a result, local standards of respectability have been
derived from them. Women in particular hold firmly to what they
believe to be English values, based on observation of Europeans a generation earlier. Apart from the missionaries domiciled in District Six,
there were also English factory supervisors in Woodstock up to thirty or
forty years ago who took pains to instruct their girls on good posture,
hair grooming and manners. For a 'Coloured' girl to be accepted for factory work in those days was considered an achievement and those who
recall their teenage years in the factory as though it were a finishing
school.

Symbols of respectability are still apparent in the use of the English
language in preference to Afrikaans.[18] The latter is spoken colloquially
and considered to be uncouth, especially in the form used by gangsters.
English, by contrast, is perceived as a standardised language, spoken
internationally, and is used for polite conversation by women in the
home. English is also the language of the Anglican and Roman Catholic
Churches, which are accorded high status in this area, in contrast with
the Dutch Reformed and Moravian denominations which hold their services in Afrikaans.[19]

Much social status is afforded by having personal connections with
Europe and people take pride in having relatives who have emigrated
away from South Africa. When they return for a holiday they come with
the panache of having lived outside the apartheid system. There is great
excitement for their Cape Town relatives at the prestige their visit will
bestow on them. One Woodstock family bought a new living room suite
and carpet to celebrate the arrival of two English teenage relatives who

had never known South Africa. Ironically, the latter created considerable disappointment by falling short of the idealised standards of behaviour expected of them.

Though European values are still very important to respectability, attitudes are gradually changing. Three factors may account for this. First, there is the growing awareness among women that however long they espouse European culture they will never be assimilated into the White South African population. Secondly, there is the sense of being let down by the British who, it is commonly said, 'have left us to our fate', have not put up an effective resistance to apartheid and have lost their former prestige in world affairs. Thirdly, there is a sense of disillusionment with current standards of behaviour among Whites (as illustrated above) which contrast with those of the upper-middle-class missionaries a generation ago. While Black Consciousness is still fended off in this area, the efforts of women to instil traditional European values into their children are diminishing.

## The Islamic Component

The second influence on this community has come from its own Moslem minority. These people, described by Whites as 'Cape Malay', seem to non-Moslem members of the community to offer an exotic alternative to Western culture. While the non-Moslems are generally antagonistic towards the religion and life-style of the 'Cape Malay', there has always been a steady stream of converts, mainly women who have married Moslem men to acquire a new self-respect as something other than just 'Coloured'.

Among the Moslems themselves, the sense of separate identity has been greatly promoted by the women. They have done this by maintaining three types of practice. First, the women have been largely responsible for keeping up the cultural traditions associated with the 'Cape Malay'.[20] While the *khalifa* (sword dance) displays and 'Malay' choirs are exclusively male preserves, it is the women who organise the grand 'Malay' wedding receptions, who take the major part in celebrating *māwlid* (the Prophet Mohammed's birthday) and who delight in wearing glittering robes on their return from *Haj* (pilgrimage) and on other festive occasions.

Secondly, it is the women who steadfastly uphold their religious devotions, notably prayer five times daily and the month-long fast of *Ramaḍān*, by their own example. While these are incumbent on all Moslems, women are often tolerant of the shortcomings of the men. The women ensure that the rules of the religion which affect daily living are maintained. Pork and alcohol are forbidden, and though no woman likes to hear reports of her husband or sons being seen drinking in the street, she will not always remonstrate with them except during *Rama̱dān* when such stories bring much greater shame. Women pay attention to social decorum and teach their children to resist what is *makrūh* (distasteful) in Islamic life. If a child behaves badly he may be told he is like the *Christe mense* (Christian people).

In a religion which is associated in Western minds with male dominance, the symbols of this control have been adapted and even used in a positive way by the women in their effort to secure for the Moslem a separate space. For example, the *burka'* (a prayer garment covering the woman from head to waist but leaving the face open) is associated in some countries with the suppression of Moslem women and their exclusion from public life. Here it is treated in a positive way as a symbol of the religion. It is worn for prayer but usually taken off before going out into the street. It is frequently made from fashionable material and I have often heard women declare that it makes them look sexy. Similarly, menstruation (in the practice of Islam often associated with uncleanness, a time when women may not touch the *Qur'ān*, enter a mosque, fast or pray) is seen in positive terms as a period for cleansing the body after which a woman can start life refreshed with a ritual bath.

Here, too, there are signs of social change, but, unlike the European influence which is diminishing, Islamic values are intensifying and men are assuming more responsibility for them. The practice of religion is becoming more puritanical as the more socially-based traditions (now derived as 'Cape Malay') are discarded. Moreover, with increasing numbers who can afford to make the pilgrimage to Mecca, Moslems are becoming more interested in the practice of Islam in the Arab world and women are giving way to male authority.

## The Home as Women's Physical Space

Marriage is often tenuous and often short-lived, but it is a vital *rite de passage* for a young girl to establish her home, her own *physical space*. Hypergamy (marrying upwards) is the means by which she seeks her social position in the community, and a home or space of her own as an autonomous unit which she can control.

Among well-to-do Walmer Estate families, the virginity of daughters is an essential prerequisite for an advantageous match; among the poor, District Six, families it may be sufficient that they are not evidently pregnant on the wedding day. On their first visit to a home, guests are frequently shown a wedding album produced from the top of a wardrobe so the housewife can boast a respectable marriage. What she doesn't point out is that she has conformed with the general pattern of marrying a man from a family deemed to be of slightly higher status in terms of colour, money or religion. This would not be immediately apparent from the marital relationship, for though the marriage is normally virilocal, the wife is quick to assert herself in her own home, or if necessary in a room in her mother-in-law's home. Having established this as *her* space, she uses it to assert dominance through the control of the household budget, household organisation and decision-making, socialisation of children, attitudes towards men and through hospitality.

Around puberty the physical space of male and female is divided; the former remains in the street; the latter stays inside where she learns to keep house exactly according to her mother's system and to give orders by practising on her brothers and younger sisters. Girls in their early teens may be heard bullying their elder brothers who meekly resign themselves to reprimands which they would never accept from other boys, even senior in age.

A daughter at home will contribute by working either under her mother's supervision, or in her place if she is out at work. Every teenage girl acquires some responsibilities and receives the respect of her younger siblings like a second mother. In many families the eldest daughter is respectfully addressed as 'Tittie', rather than by her name.

Teenage sons are shooed out of the house into the street. Unsocial behaviour is generally tolerated by women as though it is in boys' nature, and complaints are mild. No effort is made to socialise them into the household routine. Outside the house the respect of a son for his mother does not diminish, even amongst the toughest of gangsters. The greatest offence one man can give another is to swear by his mother, to insult or even mildly criticise her. 'Jou ma se moer', or simply, 'Jou moer', is highly abusive, even by District Six standards, and a just cause for violence. Though they could translate it as 'your mother's womb', people claimed that it had such emotional connotations that it defied verbal interpretation. It implied the very essence of a man's being; his identity as well as his honour rested in his mother from whose womb he entered this world. *Moer*, in standard Afrikaans, is the womb or uterus of an animal. Relegation of a man's mother to a state of nature has deep significance, implying that he is less than human.[21] To insult a man's wife, girl-friend or sister may attack his honour but this is by no means as powerful as insulting his mother. Throughout his married life he is expected to visit her every day, to see that she has all she needs and to comply with her requests.

The wages of a working child are considered the rightful property of the mother, who has already sacrificed so much, and who will continue to feed, clothe and protect her child until marriage and who still has responsibility for any younger ones. A youngster will say, 'I work for my mother', in recognition of her vicarious power through her children. Very often a good proportion of this money is reserved for the daughter's wedding or for the furniture her son is expected to provide his bride. Where a youngster 'grew up in front of his granny' while mother went out to work, his wages go to his grandmother.

## Husbands

A wife does not have the overt control over her husband that she has over her children. Rather than issue him with orders, she is more inclined to disregard or even ignore. By monopolising the running of the house and the affection of the children, she effectively precludes him from any function in the home. She may threaten the children by saying, 'Daddy will beat you', but she rarely gives him a positive role.[22] It is a woman's duty to see that her husband is looked after. She risks being criticised by other women if she does not have his food ready on demand. While in other societies this may be interpreted as female submission, here it is a very positive performance on the part of the woman and represents the man's dependence on her for his biological needs.[23]

In general the husband-wife relationship is that of antagonism, the wife as the aggressor, the husband defending himself. The common pattern in courtship is for the younger woman and her mother to secure a favourable match. Much less pressure is placed on a man to select a suitable bride. Yet once the marriage is contracted, the wife has secured her position in the community and sees no further achievement to be obtained through her husband. Parents emphasise that it is essential for their daughters to remain virgins until marriage (although this is not always achieved). A son's sex drive is considered natural and cannot be controlled. In marriage the wife typically maintains a puritanical outlook, regarding sex as a male biological need which she may withhold at her discretion.

In disputes, if a man uses violence to control his wife, it reinforces the association of the male with the *deurmekaar*. If a wife complains to someone in authority, perhaps a priest or social worker, about her husband's failure to bring home his wages or spending his money on alcohol, she can be sure of a favourable hearing. More commonly she copes on her own by sending him 'to Coventry', refusing him sexual relations or, in the last resort, turning him out of the home.

In one household I knew well, a small boy of three began his life with his mother, his mother's mother, and his mother's mother's mother. His mother's mother's mother's mother had also lived in the same house but had died shortly before his birth. His mother later married his father but his maternal relatives continued to exert a powerful influence over the marital home. His mother's mother had thrown her own husband out of the house, asserting that he was spineless and drank too much. His mother's mother's mother, a domineering woman even by District Six standards, lost her husband to another woman a few years after her marriage and brought her children up single-handed.

At the time of my fieldwork, he lived with his parents and his mother's mother's mother, with his mother's mother just down the road. His father was a quiet reflective person who, ever since childhood, had made his living by helping in his father's hawking business. He was forced to leave his father's employ by his wife, who was anxious to exercise more control over him. After a while as a driver, he found temporary and very heavy work as a dock labourer. His half-hearted attempts to become literate were foiled by his wife, who knew it would reduce his dependence on her. On many occasions he considered leaving home, especially when his wife and her grandmother nagged or screamed at him simultaneously. Once he went to live with his own mother, but returned to his wife after a few weeks, much against the will of his own mother and sisters. In spite of his affection for his two children, they will grow up very much dependent on their mother for social stability. His son still bears his wife's maiden name.

## Hospitality

Social prestige is strongly associated with giving, and hospitality extends the woman's sphere of influence to those outside her nuclear family who enter her physical space. This is clearly seen in her relationship with any person who eats regularly in her home. Whether she charges him or not she puts him in her debt. By eating in another household he acknowledges his own lack of self-sufficiency and his dependence on the woman of the house.

Hospitality offered to more casual guests would appear, in Western terms, informal. In fact, it has its own form: a woman does not invite another person into her physical space at a specified time and date because she would be committing herself to an obligation to entertain. The visitor who arrives 'on spec', however, is beholden to the hostess, whose routine has been interrupted and who may continue with household chores while talking to her guest.

## Women in Men's Space

The street is essentially a male domain where men and boys identify their own territory, not as individuals (as women do in the home) but in groups, whether as organised gangs or less structured clusters of friends. Though in District Six some unmarried girls stand on street corners with their male age-group, such behaviour would be considered far beneath the dignity of a married woman because she derives respect as one who controls the home.

Women associate street life with disorder (the *deurmekaar*), which is contrary to their aspirations to respectability. Yet if a local woman should venture into the street at night she does so with a measure of safety because she commands status as a woman, mother and homemaker and a respect which extends beyond a mere display of chivalry towards her.

## Conceptual Space: Sexual Roles and Social Change

From the foregoing data, a pattern emerges of the underlying, unconscious social structure and the trends of social change at the level of *conceptual* or *meta-space*. Two paradigms may be presented, the first *synchronic*, based on a male/female dichotomy, the second, *diachronic*, based on social change.

### The Male/Female Dichotomy

For women, life is a continuous struggle against a hostile social environment and against falling into the *deurmakaar* state of disorder and aimlessness. It entails reaching out for some basis of self-respect, a cultural identity other than 'Coloured'. In assuming this responsibility, women have held fast to the symbols of respectability: the use of the English language, membership of the Anglican or Roman Catholic Churches, a well-ordered home which conforms to standards recognised in the neighbourhood. They do this through their control of the home as their own physical space and control of those who enter this space.

The men, in contrast, occupy an amorphous physical space outside the home and are more inclined to resign themselves to the hopelessness of the *deurmekaar* state. This state is sometimes expressed with a shrug of the shoulders when a man says, '*ons is Gam: ons is net so*'[24] ('we are outcast: that's how we are').

The nature/culture dichotomy, so useful to structuralists in the past and often applied to male (culture)/female (nature) relationships, is reversed here, viz:

| *female* | *male* |
|---|---|
| culture | nature |
| the home | the street |
| circumscribed physical space | amorphous physical space |

| order | the *deurmekaar* |
|---|---|
| respectability | the outcast or *Gam* |
| the English language | colloquial Afrikaans |

## Social Change: Present, Past and Future

*The present*: The current situation is essentially ephemeral and must be viewed in relation to social change. Strictly speaking, 'the present' refers to the period of fieldwork, 1976–8, though the picture which unfolds may be broadly described as belonging to the whole era following the Second World War when apartheid policy was brought into operation. The female paradigm is now dominant and those features associated with it hold sway. It is a period of transition when, though poverty is being alleviated, the way forward is blocked by political oppression. The community is being thwarted in its natural progression into the broader social and geographical space of the public world dominated by the Whites.

As a result, the community is thrown back on itself, forced into fierce competition among its own members for scarce resources within a restricted geographical space, and strait-jacketed by a legally prescribed social space. Colour, class and religion become launching pads for conflict. Among 'pass Whites' in Woodstock there is tension and mistrust among neighbours where, it is said, even a best friend may betray you by revealing your 'Coloured' family background. The growth of affluence in Walmer Estate brings class consciousness and contempt for the poor. Mutual prejudices between Moslem and Christian illustrate incisively how competition (notably for houses, jobs and women) may lead to mistrust of the Moslem and even accusations of witchcraft, on the one hand, and high-mindedness towards Christians on the other. It is a situation where families must look after themselves and women take responsibility for this by holding firmly to symbols of respectability.

*The past*: Looking back to the hey-day of District Six with its vibrant cosmopolitan community, people remember their struggle for day-to-day survival. Economic pressures often blotted out political considerations. The household was matrifocal because it depended on the women for stability but there was less intense social pressure to be respectable. People were more prepared to accept their lot, and the *deurmekaar* state of mixed-up-ness in the community as a whole had more positive connotations than it does today. The street was a place of vigorous social interactions, whether casual encounters, public meetings or carnivals. The home was important for family life but the street had its place in the life of the community. Social problems were faced with a sense of optimism that *alles wil reg kom* (all will come right).

*The future*: Some indicators of change in the position of women have been pointed out in the course of this chapter and others left implicit. These are both economic and political.

In the economic sphere the signs of social change are clearest in Walmer Estate where relative affluence is associated with higher education, professional employment and international travel. Where the weekly wage-packet is replaced by a monthly salary cheque, the latter is retained by the salary-earner and only a portion paid to the wife or mother for housekeeping. There is also less pressure on a woman to supplement the family income by her own efforts. Furthermore, a change from rented accommodation (often in the name of the wife who takes responsibility for monthly payments) to home ownership usually means a transfer of the control of property to the male householder. While the woman's control of the home is diminishing, the home itself is becoming relatively less important as members of the community claim a greater share in the public space, which has hitherto been monopolised by the White man.

International travel has enabled members of the community to gain a more global perspective on their situation. It has already been indicated, for example, that people are forming new, less idealised, impressions of the English. Even the poor who have not had the means to travel, often point to the inadequacies of White women in the domestic and personal sphere. They say that Whites do not know how to eat properly: they eat small portions of very plain food which would never pass for a proper meal in District Six. Whites do not show enough love for their children when they are young, so that as teenagers they abandon the parental home and live independently in flats. Whites do not know how to express their emotions: they cannot accept death but crack up and sometimes even commit suicide after the loss of a loved one.

Among Moslems, it has been stated that there is a movement towards closer identification with the Arab world as an alternative to the West and a closer conformity with the daily practices of Arab life on a basis of male dominance.[25] Moreover, among well-to-do 'Malay' Moslems there is an incentive to find a good match for their daughters among the Indian Moslem community in and around Cape Town where the ultimate authority of the man as head of the household has never been in question.

Secondly, there are the factors relating to political change. The political future of the 'Coloured' people stands in limbo; here there is the irony that the effects of apartheid policy in the long term will run counter to its own design. Segregation of White from *non-White* and disillusionment with modern European culture are gradually leading the 'Coloured' people into a new social space based on consciousness of being *Black*. This process is developing more rapidly in 'Coloured townships' where there is no history of blurring the line between White and *non-White*, but people in these areas are gradually influencing those who remain in the inner city area on which we have been concentrating.

This political consciousness will contribute to the breakdown of dependence on old standards of respectability which represent an *ancien régime* and which women have used as a stopgap since the old days of penury. It will also produce a sense of a new public space within the *Coloured Group Areas* as an alternative to that of the White man.

## Culture of Poverty: A Postscript

Reference has been made to matrifocus in a *culture of poverty* situation. Much interest has been taken in the matrifocal household, especially among American sociologists over the last two decades where attention has been directed towards the plight of the poorer Black American family. The case has been made that the matrifocal household is a response to economic deprivation which has 'robbed the man of any basis of authority . . . as economic provider, a leader in his own community, and a spokesman for his family in dealing with the world outside'.[26]

Sociologists are inclined to see the matrifocal family as a problem family where the position of the woman is used as an indicator of malaise in the community, which must be understood and remedied by better planning on the part of local authorities.[27] It is seen as a problem entrenched in the *culture of poverty* syndrome in which women are pathetically struggling with broken families and a splintered community.

In this chapter women have been shown to take a more positive and indeed militant approach to their situation, determined to confront their difficulties and make something constructive out of them. They possess a clear understanding of how to deal with them and where their responsibilities lie. These Cape Town women have been thrust into a position of vital authority in the home as a result of economic and political oppression which curbs expression in the public sphere. It is a situation where women *must* dominate for the sake of the family and community rather than one of challenge to male authority. It is also a situation where women have been forced to conserve traditional notions of respectability until such time as they can be replaced by other sources of human dignity. The matrifocal household, however, is an ephemeral phenomenon established in response to special conditions, a transitional phase in the struggle against oppression. The aim has been to show how and why women may not always be *muted* and how the home may be used as a base for dominance.

Since this article was first written, much has changed in South Africa. First, *District Six* has gone, demolished, leaving only a few mosques and churches. But, though District Six has gone in terms of bricks and mortar, it remains very much a reality in symbolism.

Second, as we all know, the *political situation* has been transformed since the late 1970s. My chapter was written with an awareness of the language and mood of Black Consciousness. The hesitant protest politics of the 1970s, inspired by the Black Consciousness Movement, gave way to a more organised and confident form in the 1980s, especially after the launch of the United Democratic Front in 1983 (the UDF, of course, being part of the Congress movement), and now we see the fruit of this in a well-developed range of organisations preparing themselves for a share in power.

Third, on *the position of women*, I have been shown to have been correct in my analysis of women's dominance in District Six as a domestic-centred control in conditions where men were stifled by apartheid in their aspirations (or from having aspirations) in the public sphere, and I have been correct in my prediction that this situation would change as economic conditions improved and the political situation became more radicalised. During my stay in District Six, from 1976 to 1978, women spoke for men. When I went back to Cape Town in 1983–4, men spoke for women.

## Acknowledgement

I wish to thank Professor M.G.Whisson, formerly acting head of the Department of Anthropology at the University of Cape Town, for reading and commenting on this chapter in manuscript.

# Notes

1. For a model of 'mutedness' see Introduction and subsequent chapters in *Perceiving Women* (1975) and in *Defining Females* (1978; Berg edition 1993), both S. Ardener (ed.).
2. 'Coloured' is used in inverted commas in this chapter to denote an apartheid term which is generally unacceptable to those so classified. These people usually avoid the term though it may be used derogatorily. When they find it necessary to describe themselves collectively, and 'we' or 'us' is insufficient to convey meaning, *non-White* is sometimes employed to denote a negative collectivity and a sense of rejection by Whites. *Black* is used by some of the more politically conscious but it is not yet widely accepted in this area.
3. The first Population Registration Act (1950) used the terms 'white', 'coloured' and 'native'. In subsequent legislation 'native' was changed to 'Bantu' and then to 'Black'. In general 'Coloured' is spelt with a capital 'C', however, and this practice is followed here.
4. See Proclamation no. 46 in the *Government Gazette*, vol. CXCV, No. 6191 (6 March 1959).

5. For example, Group Areas legislation makes provision for 'Asians' and 'Coloureds' to live in separate areas.

6. The Nationalist Government came to power in 1948 with a manifesto proclaiming apartheid policy.

7. This Afrikaans term is used in English to express a sense of disorder. While today it tends to have very negative connotations, especially among women for whom social order is necessary for respectability, in the past it was associated with a more happy-go-lucky attitude to life.

8. See Proclamation no. 43 in the South African *Government Gazette*, vol. 16, no. 1137 (11 February 1966).

9. See Graham Watson (1970) for the 'pass White' perspective. In this chapter we are mainly concerned with the viewpoint of those classified 'Coloured'.

10. See Proclamation no. 135 in the *Government Gazette*, vol. 120, no. 4740 (13 June 1975).

11. This part of Woodstock was proclaimed 'White' as early as 1958 and remained an essentially mixed 'Woodstock White' area. Despite the 1958 Proclamation, its future has been uncertain and in 1979 a large section of it was reproclaimed 'Coloured'.

12. For observations on the events of 1976 and 1980, see Ridd (1980a, 1980b, 1980c).

13. See Okely on gypsy women as a muted group within a muted group, in S. Ardener (1975).

14. See Angela Davis (1971) for a comparable example of slave women in North America.

15. See Wendy James on matrifocality, in S. Ardener (1978; Berg edition 1993).

16. Marais (1939) states that very few Hottentot women had sexual relations with European men. Nevertheless, the unions that did take place have symbolic significance to the 'Coloured' person's sense of identity.

17. Commander of the Dutch East Indies Company fleet which brought the first European settlers to the Cape in 1652. Symbolically, he is the forefather of the Afrikaner people.

18. Afrikaans as a symbol of oppression for many Black South Africans was manifested in the Soweto outcry and its aftermath in 1976. See Hirschon (1979), especially chap. 10.

19. The fact that the Dutch Reformed Church (*Nederduits Gereformeerde Kerk*) has separate divisions for White, 'Coloured' and African reinforces its low status as an apartheid institution. The 'Coloured' division is known as the *Nederduits Gereformeerde Sending* (Mission) *Kerk*.

20. For a description of 'Cape Malay' traditions, see du Plessis (1972).

21. See S. Ardener's 'Sexual Insult and Female Militancy' and C.Ifeka-Moller on 'Female Militancy and Colonial Rule' in S. Ardener (1975).

22. Where there is little opportunity or expectation for a man to improve his position in life there can be no aspirations on the part of his wife to gain anything more from him than she has already achieved through her hypergamous marriage.

23. There is little tradition of eating out in restaurants among 'Coloured' people as they would not be served along with Whites. For District Six men there is the alternative between a good meal at home or a snack in the gutter.

24. Pronounced with the gutteral 'g', *Gam* is probably the Afrikaanerisation of Ham, the son of Noah cast into the wilderness.

25. 'They think they are Arabs', or 'they try to be Arab', are criticisms commonly heard expressed by Christians of their Moslem neighbours.

26. Safa (1971).

27. For example, Rainwater (1966, 1971), Scanzoni and Scanzoni (1976), Schulz (1969).

# 11

# Private Parts in Public Places: The Case of Actresses

*Juliet Blair*

## Introduction

The title is a precis compressing numerous themes related to concepts of physical, geographical, architectural, social and psychological space which will be examined in connection with the vocation of the actress. Her situation is unique in our culture in that it reverses the usual associations of women and their labour with private domains: she works in a public place where she is seen acting in ways that most women reserve for a private context. Further, her own private life and opinions often receive as much exposure to the public, through the media, as those of the *dramatis persona* she portrays. The contention is that the normal distinctions between 'private' and 'public' are neither incumbent upon nor possible for the actress, and that she may be structurally located in a 'private' relationship to society at large. One result of this is that although she is aware of the dominant rules governing the society of which her small dramatic world is a part, her experience permits her to fuse the value-systems, and to bring the naturally secluded private interpersonal sphere of women in the home into the light of public scrutiny. But her role in this may not be a neutral one. For this reason the concepts revealed by her behaviour are of specific interest to an anthropologist wishing to find out the social, political, economic and domestic organisations created by women.

Acting and role-playing have been associated with feminine duplicity, and it will be argued that the skills required for acting are those human characteristics polarised as female in our culture. Fieldwork and historical research are used to show how the actress has transformed the theatre, stage and drama to convey her perception of the world from a female point of view. A more detailed study of the conceptual world of the actress will be presented in another publication. The analysis attempted here maps out some salient features which indicate her social role as 'Public Woman'.

## Minds in Bodies

The social anthropologist's concern with the worlds of other peoples once seemed to suggest that it might be possible to make an atlas in which every social system and philosophy could be marked in and the boundaries more or less indicated. The picture of each small area being researched and jigsawed into the social map of the whole world now seems untenable. Efforts towards an anthropology of women have made such a cartographic exercise seem doubly daunting. The silence of sisters, mothers and daughters, which was interpreted as tacit confirmation of the male models of the worlds they lived in, can no longer be seen as a gesture of affirmation. It might hide a secret or muted language like the Bakweri *liengu* one,[1] through which another conceptual order of society may be approached. Nearer home, in France, Lacan's re-reading of Freud has emphasised the role that the phallus – the physical symbol of difference – plays in the acquisition of language.[2] If male and female differences are seen as the product of symbolic structures encoded in the language of the pre-existing culture into which one is born, it can then be argued that all women have suffered some degree of speech impediment brought about by trying to communicate female experience with a phallocentric tongue.[3]

In our society female traits, such as emotionality, subjectivism, hysteria, irrationality, have been devalued. Even empathy can be given negative connotations of passive suggestibility, and introspection regarded as narcissism or duplicity. Men (characterised by rationality, self-control, etc.)[4] have been thought to have a duty to control women for their own good and the sake of civilisation, lest they fall prey to their emotions. It seemed that the only women I could discover who have not only been able to indulge their emotional natures down the centuries, but have even turned their 'feminine handicaps' to advantage by earning a certain economic independence of men, were actresses.

To focus on the different physiological construction of men's and women's bodies (at the level of chromosomes and hormones, affecting organs such as the positioning of brain cells) is to look at the *physical interior* of the body in order to explain possible 'experiential' differences. Nowadays committees of scientists decide whether a person 'is' a man or woman by detecting steroids (rather than looking at the outward physical shape, or assessing the *feeling* of being a woman, a hairy woman, or a man). We have also reached a stage when operations on the *exterior* can be done so that others will perceive the physical structure as reflecting the *interior* state. The mutilation of a normal body because one has made the wrong identification with the *symbols* of the culture in which the meaning of sexual difference is invested, is obviously more drastic than merely shaving. On the other hand, perhaps it is no worse to amputate the female sexual parts to ensure that a woman cannot disrupt the social order than to structure her self-perception, her identity, with the meanings imposed by phallocentric culture. To experience oneself only in relation to men works like surgery on the mind, dividing the whole woman: virgin/whore, intellect/body, reproduction/decoration.

The chapters in *Defining Females* (1978, repr. 1993) illustrate how culture-specific the experience of being female is. The complexity of analysis required to understand the meaning of the category 'western women' has been indicated by Kristeva in her discussion *About Chinese Women* ([1976] 1977). Since de Beauvoir's *The Second Sex* (1949), Western woman has been aware that her experience is not just shaped by being born into a body that is female, and since Margaret Mead's cross-cultural study *Males and Females* (1950) the psychoanalytic anthropological perspective has been included in discussion of the cultural patterning of male and female behaviour. To find out whether there is a separate world of values invented by those 'bodies as lived in by the subject' (de Beauvoir, 1949, p. 65 of 1972 ed.) who are called women, and who learn to see themselves as representatives of 'nature', 'sexuality', 'love', 'chaos' and irrationality' outside the confines of the 'human' world of patriarchal order and law (Mitchell 1976: 405), only *they* can be consulted.

Two separate starting points are evident. First an approach to an understanding of the culture through an inspection of the divisions and oppositions associated with 'male' and 'female' as made manifest in a structural analysis. Secondly, an empirical approach – collecting information on how women order and evaluate this 'chaotic natural' sphere allocated to them. The experiential criteria of 'feeling' and 'emotion' which de Beauvoir mention remain the only ones by which the female can test the fit between how she is seen and the insights from her introspection.[5]

In considering minds in bodies in relation to the actress, several points may be noted. Her job in life is to appear to be many different women from classes, nationalities and historical periods different from her own. To accomplish this she may change her costume, shape, age, features, posture and so on – the appearance of the *external* body. She also attempts to portray character through understanding their actions, motives, emotions or their *interior* life, in relation to their specific environment. Her own body thus becomes the vehicle through which she experiences characters in plays, and the reactions of audiences, interviewers and others to her. She becomes an expert on 'women', but the only outlet for this expertise is to portray more women. One actress, therefore, is a host of informants on women. She has formulated her insights on the 'nature' of women 'as lived in by the subject' from a life of experience on the inside, accumulated in her own person. The heritage of recorded drama is her laboratory, and herself the guinea-pig. Traditionally excluded from the male sphere of making, inventing, achieving and shaping culture, woman's preoccupation has been with herself and those close to her (cf. de Beauvoir 1972: 362). Similarly, in the world of artistic culture, the actress has not encroached on the male sphere of *creating art objects*, plays, music, which live on for posterity, but has been occupied with *herself* as her art object.[6] The actress does not need a 'masculine' education or qualifications, and may thus remain outside the space defined as 'male'. She is seen as giving flesh to the writer's creations, his muse, malleable to the director, interpreting his will as his puppet, rather than a competitor with him in a male world.

## Public and Private: Geographical and Psychological Areas

### Geographical Space

Moving on from the concepts of physical interiors and exteriors to the social division of geographical space into 'male' and 'female' areas, it becomes evident that the 'natural' functions of men performed in private have played their part in the association of women with an 'instinctive' mentality. The idea of women as private property to be contained, more or less, in private areas demarcated by men, would seem an inevitable corollary of the empirical fact that men exchange women in marriage,[7] and not vice versa. The history of the complex of religious, social and legal sanctions which accompany this in our own culture will be entered, for the purposes of this chapter, at the period before women were first permitted to portray women in the English theatre.

According to Dusinberre, the two most important factors which contributed to changes in the theatrical depiction of the nature of women during the Shakespearean period were, the Puritan elevation of the middle-class woman, and the establishment of a public theatre not tied to court patronage (1975: 1–19). The new class of playwrights, writing for all classes of the public, rejected the literary stereotypes of women as symbols of lust or icons for courtly devotion (which the Humanists had also eschewed before them). From 1590 to 1625 those like Shakespeare and the majority of his contemporary dramatists who did not pander to the elite court taste, created a drama that was feminist in sympathy. They found 'that the old Pauline orthodoxies about women and about marriage must give way to the treatment of women as individuals' (Dusinberre 1975: 5).

With boy-actresses the idea that clothes make the man could be drawn into the dramatists' argument:

> They claimed that all clothes are a form of disguise and that theatrical disguise could be a revelation of truth about men and women. Secondly, they suggested that society's modes of identifying sexual behaviour required from its members not moral stability but good acting. If femininity and masculinity have any permanent validity, it exists independent of the clothes society ordains for men and women to wear. Thirdly, a woman in disguise – or the masculine woman in breeches – is changed by her male dress only because it allows her to express a part of her nature which society represses in the interests of that narrow femininity which Moore had attacked. Disguise makes a woman not a man but a more developed woman. (Ibid.: 233).

These lessons from the sixteenth century have been the workaday experience of the actresses performing these parts, as Jane Lapotaire described when playing Viola in 1974:

> It is impossible not to question all your attitudes to sex-roles, mental and physical attributes assigned to the sexes, and even homosexuality, when you are acting in *Twelfth Night*. The actor playing my twin Sebastian has narrower shoulders, smaller hands and feet than me. I can't see physical differences in the same way as I used to, nor think of myself as weak and feminine, in need of protection. Viola is a practical woman of action . . . . This production has made me think again about myself as a person, and a woman. (Personal communication)

Shakespeare's heroines have provided actresses down the years with their basic education, and perhaps even a hierarchy of roles against which they can assess their development both professionally and as a person. However, the Shakespearean dramatists' deviation from stereotyped images was a transient movement. Moreover, since then, the actress herself has entered the scene, and been able to speak and act for her own interests. But the conditions for her entry on the stage involved a resuscitation of the old conventional stereotypes, and these have remained dominant despite her continuous efforts to change them in drama and in her public private life. The Puritans had closed the theatres between 1642 and 1660 as dens of 'theft and whoredom, pride and prodigality, villainy and blasphemy' (Gilder 1931: 132).

The Restoration Court, however, accustomed to the spectacle of French and Italian actresses during their period of exile on the Continent, took advantage of the outcry against the abomination of seeing men in women's clothing, and combined this with the courtly ideal of womanhood as a moral and civilising influence, to swing public opinion in favour of the reformed theatre. Conveniently forgetting the part which Queen Henrietta Maria's predilection for Cavalier masques had

played in this – one could cost £3,000 then, and she would act in it herself – the new theatres were presented as places where the public could
see Moral Representations. The Royal patents granted to Thomas Killi-
grew and Sir William D'Avenant on 21 August 1660 accepted women
into the profession, and the patent of 1662 explained the changes this
promised:

> Forasmuch as many plays formerly acted do contain several prophane,
> obscene and scurrilous passages, and the women's parts therein have been
> acted by men in the habits of women, at which some have taken offence; for
> the preventing of these abuses for the future we do strictly charge, command
> and enjoin that from henceforth no new play shall be acted by either of the
> said companies, containing any passages offensive to piety and good man-
> ners . . . . And we do likewise permit and give leave that all the women's
> parts be acted in either of the said two companies from this time to come
> may be performed by women, so long as these recreations, which by reason
> of the abuses aforesaid were scandalous and offensive, may by such refor-
> mation be esteemed not only harmless delights, but useful and instructive
> representations of human life, by such of our good subjects as shall resort to
> see the same. (Gilder 1931: 142–3)

The puritan conscience was encouraged to reassess the theatre and
find it 'useful and instructive'. The moralists who had objected to the
harmful effects of seeing such beautiful boys as Nokes, Betterton and
Kynaston – whom Pepys described as 'the loveliest lady that I ever saw
in my life' – not only on stage, but also in the private coaches of ladies
of fashion still dressed in their women's attire, were placated by the
'harmless delights' of seeing women as women. However, this opti-
mistic effort at public relations conceals a set of hidden attitudes to
women which are so firmly entrenched in our culture that the word
'actress' still doubles for 'prostitute' in a press wary of libel. (It is Nell
Gwyn, rather than the virtuous Mary Betterton, who remains most
famous from among the first women players.)

To separate out the various implications in the Royal patent I shall
begin with the idea of 'seeing women'. A woman who can be observed
in public, or by men who are not related to her by ties of kinship or marriage, is considered in many cultures to be provoking attention to her
sexuality. The image of women is so bound up with the idea of stimulation to the heterosexual act that a man who fails to respond to a psychiatrist's picture of a woman (perhaps on the grounds that he only associ-
ates sexual intercourse with 'a deep meaningful relationship') is in danger of being considered abnormal. The visual stimulation of men is
thought to be such a basic biological fact that it is hardly questioned.
The requirement that women, in contrast, respond primarily to charac-

ter, moral and mental qualities in men, continues a romantic chivalric code through which women are seen as agents for controlling, civilising and rewarding the wayward energies of the man of action. The Royal patent exemplifies this code of gallantry. The puritan mind, on the other hand, knew full well from biblical teachings that woman was the source of evil. Even in the public place of the Church she must cover her head and remain mute. To focus the mind on the spiritual she must not draw attention to potential sin. Plainly covered and bare faced, the puritan woman could qualify as a candidate for equality, in much the same way as a latter-day feminist. Middle-class wealth enmeshed women even more. Females as chattel belonged in the private sphere of the home. If unprotected, the precious jewel of virginity could be stolen and ruin the value of a daughter on the marriage market; a mother might lose her son his legitimacy and inheritance. A wife exposing herself to the gaze of men could cause them to fall into the sin of covetousness. She could forfeit her husband's prestige by making him a cuckold, undermine his concentration on money-making, or disrupt his business relationships. Religion and law, therefore, gave women into the guardianship of their menfolk.

The actress, by appearing and speaking in public, exposed her male relatives to ignominy, and the male audience to temptation. She forfeited the status her male kin had given her, and as prey to the male spectator's view, she was fair game for his sport. One option for those early actresses was to succumb to a protector, and support her friends and children from that elevated position. But the actress also had the asset of a public platform from which to make her voice heard, and often the wit to use it. She could choose to avoid the domination of one man, and taste the power and safety of appeal to many. She could be her own woman, and speak her mind. What was in that feminine mind that society wished to hear from it, leads me back to the division of psychological characteristics between the sexes.

## Psychological Space

The association of women with the private domestic area of the home, rather than the social arena of public life, marked a division between the way men and women were seen as individual persons. A man whose public life involved the performance of certain social roles, as a lawyer, undertaker or magistrate, experienced a set of codes and conventions which ruled his behaviour as a public figure. In the privacy of his own home, the proverbial Englishman's castle, his private life was his own affair.

A man's life had a private side and a public side (cf. Lukes 1973:

59–66). Men could legitimately be two-faced. The sociological use of social role theory relies on the premiss that, to paraphrase Parsons, man does not act in his social relations as a total 'psychological' behaving entity, but only with a 'sector' of his total personality (1951: 34–35). The real personality of a king, to take an example which fascinated the early dramatists, could not be judged from the correct performance of kingly acts. His real personality would emerge in his private relationships. The most private of relationships was that between man and woman: a man and his other half – and, with the need for the 'angel of the house' to counter the hellish nature of the industrialist's machinations: his better half.[8] The whole male personality is perceived as requiring an amalgam of the private and public side.

Women, on the other hand, are perceived as acquiring their social identity *and* personal individuality solely in the sphere of the private. They are defined in relation to men, as daughters, wives, mothers and so on, and they perform for them, as housewives, servants, nannies, mistresses and so on. Women have functioned as men's private life, secreted in the attic, displayed in the reception room. There is room for her at every level, but not a room of her own.

Within this area of 'psychological space' in which an individual can experience the integrity of his or her total personality, the situation of men and women may thus be seen to be different. To seek a dimension comparable to the private side of masculine identity, a woman must look ever deeper into the privacy and secrecy of her mind, emotions, thoughts and feelings. Her body, the physical object, has belonged to her man (evidenced, for example, by the fact that new laws have had to be debated to protect women from violent husbands, and to define domestic rape). Woman's concept of herself, apart from this possession, involves a self-consciousness which we acknowledge in various ways, most usually by reference to the metaphorical space alluded to as 'the soul'.

In the case of the actress, the notion of a private identity, or even a soul that is separate from the body, is forced on them. A typical use of the metaphor of the soul to convey this elusive private identity was quoted by Kenneth Tynan in his article on Louise Brooks. She personified in her life and her roles the 'girl who gives her body, but retains her soul'[9] (Jean-Luc Godard, quoted by Kenneth Tynan in the *Observer Magazine*, 11 November 1979, p. 46). There is here a conceptual space for a woman which may be called the 'interior' as opposed to the 'exterior' body. Unlike a man's, this private interior cannot be expressed in private relationships, because her body has been born into a world in which its value and significance is as an object for exchange between men, and she has lost control of it. As an object given to men, her choice is between giving herself or *acting* as if she gives herself. John Berger explained this split within woman in *Ways of Seeing*:

> To be born a woman has been to be born, within an allotted and confined space, into the keeping of men. The social presence of women has developed as a result of their ingenuity in living under such tutelage within such a limited space. But this has been at the cost of a woman's self being split in two. A woman must continually watch herself . . . .Whilst she is walking across a room or whilst she is weeping at the death of a father, she can scarcely avoid envisaging herself walking or weeping . . . .
>
> One might simplify this by saying: men act and women appear. Men look at women. Women watch themselves being looked at. This determines not only most relations between men and women but also the relation of women to themselves. The surveyor of woman in herself is male: the surveyed female. Thus she turns herself into an object. ([1972] 1977: 46–7)

Physically vulnerable, economically dependent, seldom has she been free to make her actions reflect her mind. Only in a fantasy world, like the mad housewife in *Up the Sandbox*,[10] can she create a new order: one that would require a revolution of the concepts which form our social 'reality'.

With his superior strength, man can – metaphorically – lift a woman onto a pedestal, or rape her in the gutter. The physical circumference limiting the position of women remains, so to speak, determined by the radius provided by the length and strength of man's arm. But what he cannot reach, and what he does not have access to, is this interior region.

## Woman's Interior

In my title I used the phrase 'private parts' (which, as I heard from a policewoman, is the polite name to be used for the genital area) which conveys the *triple entendres* of soul, genitals and roles. In cinematographic language the word 'inserts' refers to the 'pornographic' bits, which focus on the genitalia. The film entitled *Inserts* (1977) thus combines the idea of sexual intrusion with the film-making practice of inserting into the cutting of the film the close-ups of copulation which had been performed by an *inferior* 'actress' (sometimes a prostitute), who simply provided the image of female pudenda to save the 'serious' *superior* actress from the embarrassment of exposing hers. The graduation from 'sexploitation' to 'straight', is the popular notion of the female actor's progress.[11] However, what was in my mind when I used the terms 'private parts' was this notion of the interior region: woman's unknown soul. Here again I can use the title of a film by way of explanation. *Interiors*, the 'serious' film made by Woody Allen (1978), is about the damage done to a family of girls who are raised by their mother, who cannot provide the structure of this interior dimension of life. She is portrayed as a beautiful, intellectual and cultured woman, whose profession is pointedly that of an Interior Decorator – designing interiors according to externally imposed rules. She is replaced by an uncouth, uneducated step-mother who lives by her own lights, not according to social and conventional wisdom, relying on 'instinct' and insights inspired from within.

It may be argued that Allen, or any other *auteur*, projects onto the women whom he directs in his films, the meanings and significance he requires to contain extensions of himself. But these are not entirely personal or idiosyncratic since they reflect the sex or gender-linked classifications of human nature inherited in our culture. The ideal of the rational, logical, objective, dispassionate, honest and just, civilised man, which the male child must *internalise*, requires that he must portion out the opposing qualities to the savage, or the female of the species. The unknown, unexplored 'dark continent' – as Freud described it – of woman's interiority, is a useful space for man to populate with beings who reverse the civilised order. But is this attempt to colonise the uncharted domain with dissenters and deviants the same picture that woman recognises as her real inner self?

By choosing the actress as the subject of my study I was looking for an answer to this question.

## The Actress Outside Society

The actress may be regarded as in a unique situation in society. In some respects she might be thought of as an 'ideal' or 'perfect' woman. As a 'Screen Idol', 'Dream Woman' or 'Love Goddess' she may be seen to possess those *external* qualities of beauty which women are supposed to cultivate to win economic security, status and legitimate offspring. In her case she may gain economic security with the licence to perform for *mankind*, not just one *man*. But she forfeits respectability because of this. Like the prostitute she is an object to be used for man's sexual fantasy, if not the reality. Her role as a public woman has traditionally denied the actress her social status within polite society. The boundaries of this were marked by the doors of that private domestic space inhabited by proper women who were the custodians of civilised mores. Frequently shut out from the sanctuary of the church, and the sacraments which mark the spiritual transitions through life and death, her soul was similarly *non grata*. With little incentive to obey the customs, rules and ethics of the dominant culture to which she was liminally connected, she could, however, invent her own standards, and live by her own directives. The actress has thus acquired a certain moral and economic independence.

This raises interesting questions. If continuities could be traced historically, and consistencies be found in the way the actress organises and conceptualises the rules she invents, would this indicate a pattern of life-choices and values which suggest an alternative female culture? Would this give clues to the state of her interior world?

My reasons for wondering about this were not, however, just prompted by her situation as an ostracised woman. They also arose from looking at the nature of her work: her profession. The actress may be thought to have professionalised the behaviour of all women.

## Making Private Interiors Public

When women have been given equal opportunity to compete with men for their job, they have been required to qualify themselves through an education whose rules and standards have been set by men,[12] whom they may try to ape. The actress, on the other hand, professionalises her ability to play the roles of all women, on which she has become her own authority. Plays have largely been written and directed by men, and so reproduce the roles designed for women by men in 'outside' society. A woman's education to perform her roles, and the actress's skill in appearing to perform women's roles, are learnt in the same way.

There is an inevitable duplicity involved in the ideal that all women should strive to act, or pretend to be, perfect wives, mothers, daughters or lovers. If they achieve the semblance of perfecting their roles, the man who judges them entirely according to their ability to role-play the parts he wants, can still wonder if they *are* really what they seem, or if they *really* feel what he thinks. For even the most personal private experience regarded as 'natural' may be learned from 'culture', as a young actress pointed out when congratulated on her simulation of an orgasm: 'I have never had one, I don't know what it feels like, or what you do, so I went to the cinema to learn how to fake it. For all I know all women have had to learn how to fake it, and its a complete myth!' If she looks and acts the part of a woman as defined in our culture, this is all that is necessary for her to do as a background figure to the main action of a man's life, lived out in the public world. As long as he is serviced, and she keeps his dirty linen private, her minor supporting role does not detract from his.

The actress, however, may see herself as a woman who has chosen her profession as an escape from the restrictions of role-playing in real life, as Susan Fleetwood explained: 'Because real life does not allow me to express all parts of myself, all those thoughts and emotions that people won't take because it somehow disturbs them'. . . (1977). To act women's parts in drama that are rewarding, the actress must win, or even create roles that go beyond the limits permitted in ordinary life. Better parts for the actress, through which she can express the range of her experience as a woman and her skill have, paradoxically, often meant that Good Roles were Bad Women. Several factors have contributed to the actress winning a larger part in the dialogue. Her box-office appeal has given her the power to demand roles which reflect her ability. Writers and managers have had to provide her with adequate vehicles to capitalise on her talent. When she could not get the parts she wanted she could form new companies, build theatres, conquer new countries as did Rachel, Duse and Bernhardt. She therefore created a life-style which fed her livelihood. Her personality furnished her art, her art gave financial support to her way of life, and these provided the experience reflected in her personality. To see the end-product of this vocational economy as providing the actress with a means of expressing herself through her art, or through her life-style, however, would be to miss the point. To see 'art' or 'money' as an end-product, instead of 'life', merely illustrates the way of thinking which is dominant in our culture.

To explain this I shall present a schematised social history as it has been mirrored in the history of drama, and the changes of scene. This attempts to show how the actress has grown in significance as women have been increasingly apportioned the 'private' part of man's life which is concealed behind his public facade.

## The Change of Scene to Domestic Interiors

The descriptions of plays as 'representations of *human life*' (my italics) in the Royal patent, shows how far they had come from the early mystery and morality plays concerned to instruct man's *spiritual life*. In the static feudal order (as documented, for instance, by Leoni di Somi, 1565) every man and woman knew his or her place, and the correct scenic background was instantly suggested when the characters stated their role.[13] *Everyman*'s life (c. 1495) was a series of predictable encounters and dialogues. His private life and thoughts were soliloquies in which his good side wrestled with his bad.

Renaissance humanism in the sixteenth century put man at the centre of his cosmology. Palaces, parliaments and battlefields were settings for the historical fight between man born into a divine order, and man achieving a new one. In the unsocial wild of the Heath, outside the palace, for example, Lear could find that kingship made him no better a man than the lunatic and the fool. Inherited roles gave way to achieved roles. It was here that women as background figures came to have more importance in revealing the sterling qualities, or dishonourable imperfections, hidden inside the prescribed manly apparel. The play provided a peep-hole for men to see other men in private. In secret dialogue with his woman he opened his mind to her, certain that the intimacies of the boudoir would go no further, until the 'sleepwalking scene' presaged the presence of the conscience in the unconscious.

Once female actors had moved their distracting admirers off the stage and into the audience they had a space, like Millamant, from which to lecture them on the rules of conscience dictated by the heart rather than by property interests. Women in their home territory gave as good as they got in the sex battles of Restoration Comedy, even when transplanted like *The Country Wife* (W.Wycherley, 1675). They lost that ground, however, with the industrial revolution when women were left at home while men went out to construct the self-made man. The shop-floor alternated with the drawing-room as background for individualism, leading eventually to *A Place in the Sun* (1951) and *Room at the Top* (1958). However, the rigidity of the rules which define social identity through work turned men once more to two-dimensional cardboard puppets, only of theatrical interest when they fall down. The role of 'lawyer', for example, has no fascination without *Inadmissible Evidence* (1968). The scene has moved from living-room dramas to kitchen sink, and by way of bedroom farce, with lavatory humour thrown in, into the most intimate areas of his behaviour through which his real and secret individuality may be distinguished from others. The modern man's dramatic search for himself begins at the moment when the incentives of the self-made man are questioned. It is in relation to woman, and the 'otherness' of her interiority (where he has dumped all those qualities and characteristics antithetical to his public career) that he seeks the lost parts of himself. Having searched for himself in every room of the house, he looks to her for what is missing in himself. The physical object of her body can now be divided into various parts for closer inspection.

## Her Features

### Externals

The pure innocent face of beauty – as reward for the man whose features have been weathered and wisened with experience – has, from time to time, been superimposed by the misty, far-off look of an unattainable enigma like Garbo. In reaction, the long legs and baby face of a Lolita like Bardot have reassured men of their superiority. High heels and a wobbly walk confirm the insecurity of women and their need for a strong arm.

The level of a man's virile self-esteem can be measured in reverse proportion to the size of her bust, the importance of which reflects, apparently, the sins of maternal deprivation. The real worth of a man, on the other hand, is reflected by the prostitute's heart of gold, when she loves him for free, without ring or fee. The actress, as a woman, comes to see herself as face and body, divided and assessed, and *herself* ignored, as Monroe complained (in a letter to N. Rosten) by quoting Yeats (Rosten 1974: 77):

> . . . only God, my dear,
> Could love you for yourself alone
> And not your yellow hair.

At her most vilified the whole woman is reduced to the crudest four-letter word, the close-up, blown-up image of *Inserts*. But even that image of the anatomical hole serves as a symbol of difference, the essence of the unknown world of *Interiors*, in which all the inexplicable and mystical parts are to be found, and man receives a fleeting experience of his own wholeness through the *Other*. The more society polarised 'human' characteristics into sex-linked ones, the more the *individual* needed a woman to be a whole human being, and the more the play became necessary as a 'reflection of human life' for man to be able to transcend his self-imposed limitations. The actress was not needed as a rival *individualist*, but as a woman through whom they could affirm or console themselves, as George Bernard Shaw described Ellen Terry:

> . . . every famous man of the nineteenth century – provided he were a playgoer – has been in love with Ellen Terry . . . [and many of them, he added] found in her friendship the utmost consolation one can hope for from a wise, witty and beautiful woman. (Quoted in Prideaux 1976: 1)

Through the play, or more intimately, through her friendship, she revealed the Interior relegated as the female province.

## Internals

It has been mentioned that the skills required of actors have been regarded as 'feminine'. In our culture it is unmanly to show grief, depression, or even the delights of victory, and it is narcissistic to practise these expressions in front of a mirror. It is duplicitous to pretend to be a doctor or prime minister when *real* men achieve these social roles through years of labour. This, perhaps, accounts for the emphasis that has been laid by the male actor on technique schools of acting, like the Coquelin school. The mastery of sets of movements qualifies them, eventually, not only to rise up the hierarchy of roles from spear-carrier to hero, but to become real peers of the realm.

The abilities of an actress, on the other hand, are more frequently associated with her instincts, and she has been more inclined to align herself to the Stanislavsky method of acting. Helen Mirren, for example (who was herself criticised by Benedict Nightingale in 1970 for being too intelligent and '*thinking* more than she is *feeling*'), made clear her partisanship with the Method and women by alluding to the battle between Olivier and Monroe during the making of *The Prince and the Showgirl*, when he humiliated her as a 'sex-object' unable to 'act': 'The audience may not notice the difference, but I'd describe my style now as more Marilyn Monroe than Laurence Olivier' (personal communication, 1977). The Method requires that the actor match up the internal feelings drawn from personal experience with the external manifestations of appearance. In this the actress's training as a woman in our society, habituated to conceiving of herself as an observed object, with a deeper mass or mess or sensitivity within, comes into its own. She is accustomed to think of herself as a duality – the superficial exterior behaving as prescribed by men.

My suggestion here is not that of Jung, that both men and women inherently possess male and female elements in which *animus* or *anima* predominate. Western polarisation of human characteristics has allocated man the mind, the intellect and rationality, allowing women to be the specialists in emotions.[14] It is therefore hardly surprising that the great actresses of the past could speak of their 'role' in society as Helena Faucit did:

> I have ever found my art a most purifying and ennobling one, and the aim of all my life has been to educate and elevate myself up to it . . . .Whatever gifts I had as an actress were ever regarded by me as a sacred trust to be used for widening and refining the sympathies of my audience. (Letter published in 1878, quoted in Findlater 1976: 124)

To educate people about their emotions, and through making them *feel*, make them change their opinions and behaviour, is a subversive activity. It undermines the validity of received wisdom, and forces people to accept the touchstone of feeling – a decried and denied area of life – as a test of truth.[15]

As women whose profession is to empathise, understand and identify with a whole range of female roles, from princess to prostitute, the stereotypes and deviants, actresses have to develop and rely upon their own codes to evaluate their fellow-women. The ultimate test of authenticity was not whether a role appeared right to the author, director or audience, but if 'it *felt* right to them'. As Eleanore Duse, among many, tried to convey, this put them at variance with the moral rules of the dominant society:

> Acting – what an ugly word! If it were merely a question of acting I feel that I could never have done it, and could never do it again. But the poor women in the plays I have acted so got into my *heart and mind* that I had to think of the best way of making them understood by my audience, as if I were trying to comfort them . . . . But in the end it is generally they who comfort me. How and why and when this *inexplicable reciprocity of feeling* between these women and myself began: that story would be far too wearisome – and difficult as well – if I were to tell it fully. But this I can say: though everybody else may distrust women I understand them perfectly. I do not bother whether they have lied, betrayed, sinned, once I *feel* that they have wept and suffered while lying and betraying and sinning, I stand by them. I stand for them. (Knepler 1968: 194, my italics)

In understanding her inner self through others, and others through herself, the actress tries to extend, develop and explore the area of the private, both for herself, and, because this is her public usefulness for others.[16] Since she is her own art object – mind, face, body, voice – it is the same instrument that serves for her private life and her public work. When her public theatrical roles have not provided her with fresh experience to grow through, and the stereotypes offered hold her back, they at least earn her enough money to spend her free time doing this. The importance of 'resting' as a private time to re-integrate, re-create, invent and explore herself was emphasised in remarks made by some two dozen actresses, who in their mid-thirties are household faces; for instance:

> I need my own adventures, travelling, relationships, even having my own baby, and doing my own house, for my own development as a person. Resting is only bad when you don't feel you are growing and learning at the same rate as when you are getting into a good role; or if no part is on offer which would give you a chance to communicate your new knowledge of yourself as a person. That sounds rather grand. What I mean is that acting gives you a way of communicating many parts of yourself to others, like any relationship. Only that way can you make them see themselves through the parts you play.

It is evident that the ideal of 'finding', 'creating' and 'inventing' their own lives is assumed automatically by them to be a necessary ideal for their audience as well as for themselves. For women whose roles have been directed by men, but who have power to convey new images of women through the media, the conflict between personal autonomy and political organisation is experienced as a personal conflict, as Jane Fonda said to *Newsweek*:

You can be a privileged movie star, or you can commit yourself to the idea that people can change their lives and can change history. I want to make films that will make people feel stronger, understand more clearly, and make them move forward – women and men. That's what I'm interested in. (*Newsweek*, 10 October 1977, p. 46)

Constant growth and change, development and understanding right up to death are represented:

The actress playing Gertie in The Old Wives Tale was obviously dying, and you knew that she knew it. But she used that play in such a way that she was passing on to the audience her humour and courage in the face of death. How to live and how to die. She was passing on her own experience of how to die! It was the most inspiring and moving gift to everyone who saw her. (Audience comment, 1977)

The freedom to 'be', and the communication to and recognition by others, of 'the person I am inside', was described by Liv Ullman; in acting, these 'unknown secrets within' herself come forward, 'adding to oneself as an instrument' so that others can recognise themselves (Ullman 1977: 208; 1975: 23).

From these quotations I want to draw attention to two main points. First, that the emphasis placed by the actress on expressing her 'real' self through interpersonal relationships – with an individual or an audience – may be thought of as an effort to translate her knowledge of the hidden interior life, and to gain public recognition of its existence and importance. Secondly, that the consciousness of the misfit between the roles allows the actress and the self she feels frustrated from portraying has involved her perpetually in trying to create contexts where all human interaction may be inter*personal*; that is, without the masks determined by social role-playing. This has been reflected in the history of the changes the actress as manager, designer, architect and technician has made, which may be characterised as 'domesticating' public space.

## Making the Theatre Intimate

It is not surprising that women should set about managing their own theatres. They were small worlds they could shape their own way. Typical examples, like Monsantier in pre- and post-revolutionary France, Neuber in Germany, and Vestris in England, are most famous for their innovations in audience seating, stage design and theatre decoration. New scene-changing devices and lighting techniques gave the effect of realism, including the outside and inside environment of the public and private world – which symbolically they formed into one under their own control. Their theatres were designed to be 'inhabited'. Debarred from the mansions of society women, their public salons became a home away from home where the artist and the elite met as equals. The society that had cast out the actress vied for invitations to her banquets, which were held in the specially designed ballrooms, greenrooms or on the stage. Her friends – politicians of opposing factions, prelates of different persuasions, and rivals for love and preferment – obeyed the etiquette of guests. In turn she was often a go-between, peace-maker, diplomat and adviser. Bernhardt, Rachel, Duse, Ristori, Langtry and Terry left their theatres as envoys to the world. Not only were they peers for royalty (as Isabella Adrienni, for example, had been before them) but ambassadors of the new self-made woman who rose from her 'fallen' position to create her own life (Knepler 1968: 6).

As managers they were similarly concerned to change the taste of their audience. They pioneered plays on contemporary issues and characters who spoke the language of the period: but were ahead of their times. In different respects their efforts towards a cultural revolution find parallels in the work of Bayliss, Littlewood, Thorndike or Ashcroft – turning museums of culture into soup-kitchens, delivering daily bread for the mind.

Two factors, the growth of population and technology, have contributed to impeding the actress's direct interpersonal relationship with her public. Large theatres, built with industrial wealth to enhance the prestige of towns, distanced her so that her world behind the proscenium arch was filled with larger gestures and emotions than theirs. Built in town centres, accessible to the whole community by road and rail, they served as places to meet, to see and be seen. The advent of television created another new situation. The box in the darkened living-room may unite people in a heterogeneous culture in the same way as a play on tour or a film on general release, but the individual is not united with the group in the process. It does not have that extra dimension created by a communal atmosphere and live communication.

The rewards of direct contact are lost to the actress in film and television work. Many successful actresses have therefore opted out of wealth and fame for long periods. They described the incentives for doing this as complex. Commercial theatre, which had given them a good training and income as well as the feed-back from a live audience, nevertheless often relied on old clichés and classics to be economically viable. They said that their personal need to develop as actresses made them search for new parts in new plays, and these were most usually put on by low-budget, subsidised fringe-groups in community centres, schools, old churches and other public buildings. Proximity to the audience improved acting skills. More rewarding roles, relevant to the lives of the people for whom the work of the actress was their leisure, could be found. A two-way involvement in issues and interests common to those used to acting out the 'life' that others stayed in to watch, transformed theatre into a more pertinent medium for changing the conditions which made a soap opera or match-of-the-day a substitute for family and community life. As one retired film star described this,

> The needs of society and my own feel the same. The woman who is so isolated that she stays in to watch Coronation Street, because that community seems more real and accessible than her own, is trying to live vicariously. I see my wish to be an actress as the result of finding no context, no community in which I could be who I want. In the film world you can only be yourself with the assistants, make-up artists, dressers – people who know you and you really know, oases of 'real' relationships.
>
> In community theatre you can express yourself through the part you play, then you can be your real self in the bar with them afterwards. Both sides fit together. They criticise, discuss, argue, and what is more they don't only talk to you but husbands talk to wives and neighbours. People start to communicate.
>
> Then things really start to change. Tabooed subjects come out, especially in feminist theatre, then self-help groups start, or crèches, medical lobbies – when we think and write and act about our own real innermost problems as individuals, the audience and the group discover that they are not isolated individuals, and this gives us the strength to actually do things *en masse* to change ideas and institutions.

Over the last ten years the Arts Council and local authorities have subsidised successful fringe and community theatre groups and writers, on the grounds that 'minority arts' which speak to the actual condition of the potential audience are of great importance to the majority.[17] There was a consensus of opinion at the 1977 national meeting of fringe-theatre workers that the feminist theatres had been the most successful. One direct result of the interest in women over the last few years has been the new film, television and national theatres' productions (and revivals) with women as the main protagonists. An indirect result has been that actors in prestigious national theatres like the Royal Shakespeare Company have encouraged their managements to allow them to form small touring companies performing in schools and villages. In this way the barriers created by technology are avoided; the gap between 'real life' and the 'arts' is diminished; and the actress finds the context she wants to strip away in the stereotyped images which oppress her as an individual and as an actress, which she is otherwise doomed to perpetuate for her audience.

## Communicating the Interior World

The theatre as a place set apart from normal life, where beautifully painted people disguised in pretty costumes, or conversely exposing bodies normally hidden, divert the public from their everyday worries, has continuously been adapted by the actress as writer, director and manager for her own ends – communications of that 'interior' world created by 'everyday worries' which have been categorised as personal ones. The ideal, my informants suggested, can best be described as a 'change or exchange' of perceptions about the 'real nature of this personal experience'. To illustrate this I shall use some notes from my fieldwork. In this final section I try to draw together the most central areas of private and public which link the spheres of 'inside' and 'outside' worlds discussed in the chapter.

The following analysis arose from my trying to answer the question of a male colleague who is an anthropologist and psychiatrist. He asked – of course – 'How can a lovely, intelligent, nice girl like 'E' take her clothes off in public?' The act of appearing nude is traditionally justified to the nosey reporter as acceptable to the actress 'if the integrity of the script demands it'. Who judges whether or not it is worth it, after the economic necessity of paying the bills has been eliminated, is the actress herself. 'E' was then appearing in a modern play about a man's search for himself – the writer's – in which she was supposed to reveal her body during the course of a 'one-night stand'. She could not blatantly refuse to do this and earn a *bad* reputation, which would jeopardise her chance to get more work. Instead she inveigled the lighting technician into blacking out the stage before she had finished fumbling with her bra.

The reason she refused to expose herself was not that she felt a socially induced prudery, but her dislike of the play: 'All the female characters are unreal – just there as stereotyped peripheral wife and whore – while the hero and his brother go through their mid-life crisis. I won't be used for this.' Later that year she was again asked to undress in a play for the RSC. This time she described the reason for nakedness as 'worthwhile':

> Because the play is about apartheid, racism, sexism and classism. Both of us have to be naked, and that helps to avoid making it the usual sexploitation. If we can make the audience experience real concern for the couple – their hope and vulnerability – it will work.

She compared what she was trying to achieve to her friends' experience performing Athol Fugard's *Statements*:

In this production there was no furniture, scenery – a bare stage. No make-up, no clothes to hide behind. Very little movement – only the relationship between the two people to interest the audience. Throughout the play the couple are cornered animals daring the punishment society inflicts because their relationship is the expression of their utmost humanity: a real under-standing care and love for another. That's what sexual love is about for me, risking everything because you really love and understand the person, and have your real self acknowledged and 'seen'. It's not to do with macho ideals of owning, possessing, conquering a body, but the ultimate consummation between minds expressed through bodies.

The naked stage and bodies worked like the film technique of the close-up, focusing attention on the faces expressing the minds through the dialogue. After a short time the audience did not notice the nudity of the actors or their colour.

From the unsolicited comments of the audiences from the ethnic groups characterised in these plays, and who had previously 'believed' in apartheid, it appeared that they had 'changed their mind' because of what they experienced through the play. This was explained by one high-caste Indian woman:

I have never imagined the possibility of marrying anyone who is not the right group for me. I haven't even seen a man naked, and I felt terrible when I saw them like that. But later I didn't mind, or see the bodies – it was impossible to see those two people loving each other like that and to think it is wrong. It makes me think that perhaps arranged marriages are wrong; and marriage is really something between two people – that comes out of their relationship, if you see what I mean.

When I reported this comment to the actress she said: 'Then it has been worth it. I could not bear to have gone through all that without someone seeing it from my point of view!'

The actress had the personal and private reward of feeling that her own perceptions, which she had clothed with the character she was act-ing, had been recognised and affirmed. The reality and truth of her own concepts had somehow been verified. She had communicated *herself* through a part. In the unreal context of a theatre she had been able to make public a private reality. The fact that one other person, at least, accepted this, confirmed her subjective interpretation and its objective existence. Thus the experience from one 'interior' found its way out into the public world and transformed another's perception of it.

By contrasting notions of private and public areas of physical and conceptual space, I have tried to suggest that the actress, through her professional and feminine preoccupation with the interpersonal, has been concerned to undermine the way she is 'seen'. This has involved altering those concepts which dictate her life through role-playing for men and trying to have the values she has learned in this way accepted in the larger world. In other words, she has been engaged in a critique of dominant social values informed according to a 'private' world in which woman's perceptions are central.

# Notes

1. E. Ardener, 'Belief and the Problem of Women', ([1972] 1975: 9).

2. See Lacan, *Ecrits*. For an exposition of the implications for feminism see Coward 1978.

3. See the discussion of 'muting' in S. Ardener, 1975 and 1978.

4. See Broverman *et al.* for the coincidence of socially valued human characteristics with 'male' ones, 1968.

5. S. Ardener has used 'femineity' in contrast to femininity to differentiate between these two levels of abstraction and articulation, 1975: 46.

6. The acceptable transient nature of her art was described by Rachel (Richardson 1957: 187), and recently T. Keane as 'to do with the whole NOW and LIVING' (Morgan, *Spare Rib*, vol. 65, 1977, p. 27).

7. See Fox 1967. Mitchell uses Lévi-Strauss, *Structural Anthropology* (1968), p. 50, to make this point (Mitchell 1976: 374).

8. This simplification derives from the complex analysis of the effects of the industrial revolution on the liberal notion of individualism, made by A. Foreman (1977: 93–94).

10. P. Zindel's adaptation of Anne Richardson Roiphe's novel, directed by I. Iersher. See Joan Mellen (1974: 244–54), 'Counter-Revolt: Up the Sandbox'.

11. M. Rosen noted the way in which well-known actresses have redefined the notion of intimacy by their willingness to appear nude; see 'Clinicians of Decadence' (1975: 331–32).

12. See Okely 1978, for some of the contradictions in such education, and Delamont 1978, for contrary ideals of female education held by pioneers in the neneteenth century.

13. See A. Nichol (1961: 237–62).

14. Kristeva, for example, analyses reasons for this (1978: 34–35).

15. The actress Sara Boyes, a graduate in philosophy and logic, brought this home to me in 1977. Eight years of acting had separated her so far from the logical parameters of the academic world that, quite unself-consciously, when discussing the two scientific explanations put forward to explain some feature of human behaviour, she said: 'Wait a few moments and I'll feel whether either of them is true'. After a long pause she ventured that she thought neither were, according to her memory and experience.

16. Several informants described this function as the way they could use their gifts, as they had no talent, for example to do social work, teaching or medicine.

17. See the thirty-second annual report and accounts of the Arts Council, 1976/77, p. 8.

# Bibliography

Abbot, E. (1877) *Flatland. A Romance of Many Dimensions*, reprinted Oxford, Blackwell, 1962.

Abdela, L. (1989) *Sex Appeal*, London, Macdonald.

Abimbola, W. (1976) *Ifa. An Exposition of the Ifa Literary Corpus*, Ibadan, Oxford University Press, Nigeria.

Adesanya, A. (1958) 'Yoruba Metaphysical Thinking', *Odu. Journal of Yoruba and Related Studies*, Vol. 5, pp. 36–41.

Allen, P. (1978) *The Cambridge Apostles – The Early Years*, Cambridge University Press.

Altorki, S. (1980) 'Milk-kinship in Arab Society: an unexplored problem in the ethnography of marriage', *Ethnology*, Vol. XIX, No. 2.

Ameer Ali, S. (1965) *Mohammedan Law*, Vol. II, Lahore, Law Publishing Co.

Annan, N. (1955) 'The Intellectual Aristocracy' in J. H. Plumb (ed.), *Studies in Social History*, London, Longmans, Green, & Co., 1955.

Ardener, E. (1959) 'Lineage and Locality Among the Mba-Ise Ibo', *Africa*, Vol. XXIX, No. 2.

—— (1971) 'Introductory Essay' in E. W. Ardener (ed.), *Social Anthropology and Language*, London, Tavistock Press.

—— (1972) 'Belief and the Problem of Women' in J. La Fontaine (ed.), *The Interpretation of Ritual*, London, Tavistock Press. Reprinted in S. Ardener 1975.

—— (1975a) 'The Problem Revisited' in S. Ardener 1975, pp. 19–27.

—— (1975b) 'The Voice of Prophecy', The Munro Lecture, delivered in Edinburgh.

—— (1975c) 'The Cosmological Irishman', *New Society*, 14 August.

—— (1975d) 'Some Outstanding Problems in the Analysis of Events' in E. Schwimmer (ed.), *Yearbook of Symbolic Anthropology*, London, Hurst, 1975.

—— (1987) '"Remote Areas": Some Theoretical Considerations' in A. Jackson (ed.) *Anthropology at Home*, London, Tavistock, 1987.

——(1989) *The Voice of Prophesy* (edited by Malcolm Chapman). Oxford, Blackwell.

Ardener, S.(ed.) (1975) *Perceiving Women*. London, Dent; New York, Halsted.

—— (ed.) (1978) *Defining Females*. London, Croom Helm; New York, Halsted. Reprint, Berg, 1993.

—— (ed.) (1992) *Persons and Powers of Women in Diverse Cultures*, Oxford and Providence, Berg.

Arts Council (1976/77) *Annual Report*.

Awe, B. (1977) 'The Iyalode in the Traditional Yoruba Political System' in A. Schlegel (ed.), *Sexual Stratification. A Cross-Cultural View*, New York, Columbia University Press, 1977.

Bailey, F. (1971) *Gifts and Poison*, Oxford, Blackwell.

Baillie, J. (1805) *A Digest of Mohammedan Law according to the tenets of the twelve Imams*, Calcutta, The Honourable Company Press.

Barette, C. (1972) 'Aspects de l'ethno-ecologie d'un village andin', *Canadian Review of Sociology and Anthropology*, Vol. 9, No. 3, pp. 255–67.

Bascom, W. (1969) *Ifa Divination. Communication between Gods and Men in West Africa*, Bloomington, Indiana University Press.

Bateson, G. (1967) *Naven*, Stanford, California, Stanford University Press. Original edition 1936.

Beier, H. U. (1955) 'The Position of Yoruba Women', *Presence Africaine*, Vol. 1, No. 2, pp. 39–46.

Benveniste, E. (1938) *Les Mages dans l'Ancien Iran*, Paris, Librarie Orientale et Americaine.

Berger, J. (1977) *Ways of Seeing*, Harmondsworth, Pelican. First published 1972.

Biobaku, W. O. (1957) *The Egbas and their Neighbours, 1842–1872*, Oxford, Clarendon Press.

Bolgar, R. R. (1977) *The Classical Heritage*, Cambridge University Press.

Bourdieu, P. (1977) *Outline of a Theory of Practice*, Cambridge University Press.

Brain, J. L. (1976) 'Less than Second-Class: Women in Rural Settlement Schemes in Tanzania', in N. Hafkin and E. Bay (eds.), *Women in Africa*. California, Stanford University Press.

Browne, E. G. (1893) *A Year Amongst the Persians*, London, Black.

Brownmiller, S. (1975) *Against our Will*, New York, Secker & Warburg.

Broverman, D. *et al.* (1968) 'Roles of Activation and Inhibition in Sex Differences in Cognitive Abilities', *Psychol. Rev.*, Vol.75, pp. 23–50.

Caldwell, J. C. and Caldwell, P. (1977) 'The Role of Marital Sexual Abstinence in Determining Fertility: A Study of the Yoruba in Nigeria', *Population Studies*, Vol. XXXI, No. 2, pp. 193–213.

Callan, H. (1975) 'The Premiss of Dedication: Notes Towards an Ethnography of Diplomats' Wives', in S. Ardener 1975, pp. 87–104.

—— (1978) 'Harems and Overlords: Biosocial Models and the Female' in S. Ardener 1978, pp. 200–14; 1993 ed., pp. 168–86.

Callan, H. and S. Ardener (1984) *The Incorporated Wife*, London, Croom Helm (Routledge).

Callaway, H. (1978) '"The Most Essentially Female Function of All": Giving Birth', in S. Ardener 1978, pp. 163–85; 1993 ed., pp. 146–67.

—— (1980) 'Women in Yoruba Tradition and in the Cherubim and Seraphim Society' in O. U. Kalu (ed.), *The History of Christianity in West Africa*, Harlow, Essex, Longman Group.

Campbell, J. K. (1964) *Honour, Family and Patronage*, Oxford University Press.

Campbell-Jones, S. (1979) *In Habit: An Anthropological Study of Working Nuns*, London, Faber and Faber.

Carrithers, M. and S. Collins (eds.) (1980) Wolfson College Seminars on 'The Notion of the Person' (publication forthcoming).

Carrithers, M., S. Collins. and S. Lukes (eds.) (1985) *The Category of the Person*, Cambridge University Press.

Chabot, J. B. (1902) *Synodes Nestoriens (Synodicon Orientale)*, Paris, Imprimerie Nationale.

Channon, Sir H. (1967) Chips: *The Diaries of Sir Henry Channon* (ed. R. R. James), London, Weidenfeld and Nicolson.

Christensen, A. E. (1936) *L'Iran Sous les Sassanides*, Copenhagen, Ejnar Munskgaard.

Collis, M. S. (1960) *Nancy Astor*, London, Faber and Faber.

Corneliesen, A. (1977) *Women of the Shadows*, New York, Vintage Books.

Coward, H. (1978) 'Rereading Freud' in *Spare Rib*, Issue 70, pp. 43–6.

Cumont, F. (1926) *Fouilles de Doura*, Paris, Europos.

Currell, M. E. (1974) *Political Woman*, London, Croom Helm; New Jersey, Rowman & Littlefield.

Daudpota, U. M. (1932) 'A Brief History of Mut'a', *JBBRAS*, N. S. VIII.

Davidoff, L. (1979) 'The Separation of Home and Work? Landladies and Lodgers in Nineteenth and Twentieth Century England'. In Burman, S. (ed.) *Fit Work for Women*, London, Croom Helm.

Davies, J. K. (1971) *Athenian Propertied Families*, Oxford, Clarendon Press.

Davis, A. (1971) *The Black Woman's Role in the Community of Slaves*, The Black Scholar, December.

de Beauvoir, S. (1972) *The Second Sex*, Harmondsworth, Penguin. Originally published in French, 1949.

Delamont, S. and L. Duffin (eds.) (1978) *The Nineteenth-Century Woman. Her Cultural and Physical World*, London, Croom Helm.

Donaldson, D. M. (1933) *The Shi'ite Religion*, London, Luzac.

Donley, L. W. (1980) 'House Power: Swahili Space and Symbolic Capital', paper delivered at the Conference on Structuralism and Symbolism in Archaeology, Cambridge, England, in March.

Doughty, P. L. (1970) 'Behind the Back of the City: "Provincial" Life in Lima, Peru', in William Mangin (ed.), *Peasants in Cities*. Boston, Houghton Mifflin Company.

Douglas, M. (1966) *Purity and Danger: an Analysis of Concepts of Pollution and Taboo*, London, Routledge & Kegan Paul.

—— (1968) 'Social Control of Cognition, Factors in Joke Perception', *Man*, N. S. Vol. 3, No. 3, pp. 361–7.

—— (1970) 'Heathen Darkness, Modern Piety', *New Society*, 12.

—— (1973) *Natural Symbols*, London, Barrie and Rockcliffe, Harmondsworth, Penguin.

Downs, R. M. and R. Stea (1977) *Maps in Minds,* New York, Harper & Row.

Dubison, Jill (ed.) (1986) 'Gender and Power in Rural Greece', Princeton, Princeton University Press.

du Boulay, J. (1974) *Portrait of a Greek Mountain Village*, Oxford University Press.

—— (1976) 'Lies, Mockery and Family Integrity' in J. G. Peristiany (ed.), *Mediterranean Family Structures*. Cambridge University Press.

du Plessis, L. D. (1972) *The Cape Malays*, Cape Town, A. A. Balkema.

Durkheim, E. (1976) *Elementary Forms of Religious Life,* trans. J. W. Swain, 1915. New Introduction by Robert Nisbet. London, Allen & Unwin.

Durkheim, E. and M. Mauss (1903) *Primitive Classification*, trans. R. Needham. London, Cohen & West, 1963; first published in France 1901–2.

Dusinberre, J. (1975) *Shakespeare and the Nature of Women*, Basingstoke, Macmillan.

Eco, U. (1973) 'Semiotics of Architecture: Function and Sign' in I. Bryan and R. Saner (eds.), VIA Publications of the Graduate School of Fine Arts. Philadelphia, University of Pennsylvania Press.

—— (1976) *Theory of Semiotics*. Indiana University Press.

Eichler, M. (1980) *The Double Standard: A Feminist Critique of Feminist Social Science*, London, Croom Helm.

*Encyclopaedia of Islam*. Leiden, Brill, 1936. New Edition, London, Luzac; Leiden, Brill 1971.

Engels, F. (1972) *The Origin of the Family, Private Property and the State (1884)*, New York. Also ed. E. Burke Leacock. London, International Publishers.

Evans-Pritchard, E. E. (1940) *The Nuer*, Oxford, Clarendon Press.

Fadipe, N. A. (1970) *The Sociology of the Yoruba*, Ibadan, University Press.

Findlater, R. (1976) *The Player Queens*, London, Weidenfeld & Nicolson.

Foreman, A. (1977) *Feminity as Alienation: Woman and the Family in Marxism and Psychoanalysis*, London, Pluto Press.

Forster, E. M. (1978) *The Longest Journey*, London edition, Penguin.

Fox, R. (1967) *Kinship and Marriage*, Harmondsworth, Penguin.

Franck, B., G. Manuel, and D. Hatfield (1967) *District Six*, Cape Town, Longman.

Friedl, E. (1989) *Women of Deh Koh*, Washington and London, Smithsonian Institution Press.

Gallie, M. 'Quietly following the Don', *The Cambridge Review* (24 May 1968).

Gamornikov, E. (ed.) (1983) *The Public and the Private*, Oxford, Heinemann.

Geertz, C. (1973) *The Interpretation of Cultures*, New York, Basic Books.

Gernet, L. (1968) *Anthropologie de la Grèce Antique*, Paris, Librairie François Maspero.

Gifford, D. and P. Hoggarth (1976) *Carnival and Coca Leaf, Some Traditions of the Peruvian Quechua Ayllu*, Edinburgh, Scottish Academic Press.

Gilder, R. (1931) *Enter the Actress*, London, Harrap.

Goffman, E. (1979) *Gender Advertisements*, London, Macmillan. First published in America, 1976.

Golde, P. (1970) *Women in the Field*, Chicago, Aldine Publishing Company.

Goody, J. (ed.). (1958) *The Development Cycle in Domestic Groups,* Cambridge University Press.

Gould, J. (1980) 'Law, Custom and Myth: Aspects of the Social Position of Women in Classical Athens', *Journal of Hellenic Studies.*

Gray, L. H. (1931) *Encyclopaedia of Ethics and Religion,* ed. J. Hastings. T. Edinburgh and T. Clark.

Greenland, C. (1980) 'The Entropy Exhibition', unpublished Oxford DPhil Thesis.

Guardia, M. C. (1971) *Diccionario Kechwa-Castellano, Castellano-Kechwa,* Lima, Editora Los Andes.

Haeri, S. (1990) *Law of Desire: Temporary Marriage in Iran,* Taurus Publishers. 'From Space to Place and Back Again: Reflections on the condition of postmodernity', 'Futures' Symposium, Tate Gallery, November.

Hall, E. T. (1959) *The Silent Language,* New York, Doubleday.

Hampshire, S. (ed.) (1978) *Public and Private Morality,* Cambridge University Press.

*Hansard,* London, HMSO.

Harper, P. (1970) 'The Role of Dance in the Gelede Ceremonies of the Village of Ijio', *Odu,* N. S. Vol. 4, pp. 67–74.

Harris, O. (1976) 'Kinship and the vertical economy of the Laymi Ayllu, Norte de Potosi'. Paper presented at the symposium on 'Organizacion social y complementaridad economica', the XLlle Congrès, International des Americanistas, Paris, 2–9 September.

Harvey, D. (1990a) 'Between Space and Time: Reflections on the Geographical Imagination', *Annals* of the Association of American Geographers, Vol. 3, September.

—— (1990b) 'From Space to Place and Back Again; Reflections on the condition of Postmodernity', 'Futures' Symposium, Tate Gallery, November.

Hastrup, K. (1978) 'The Semantics of Biology: Virginity', in S. Ardener 1978, pp. 49–65; 1993 ed., pp. 34–50.

Hertz, R. (1973) 'The Pre-eminence of the Right Hand'. Originally in French, 1909; transl. in R. Needham (ed.) *Death and the Right Hand.* Cohen and West.

Herzfeld, E. E. (1947) *Zoroaster and His World.* Princeton, Princeton University Press.

Herzfeld, M. (1987a) '"As in Your Own House": Hospitality, Ethnography, and the Stereotype of Mediterranean Society', *Honour and Shame and the Unity of the Mediterranean,* American Anthropology Association, Special Publication No. 22, pp. 75–89.

—— (1987b) *Anthropology Through the Looking Glass. Critical Ethnography in the Margins of Europe,* Cambridge University Press.

Hinderer, A. (1873) *Seventeen Years in the Yoruba Country,* London, Seeley, Jackson and Halliday.

Hirschon, R. (1976) 'The Social Institutions of an Urban Locality of Asia Minor Refugee Origin in Piraeus', DPhil Thesis, Oxford.

—— (1978) 'Open Body/Closed Space: the Transformation of Female Sexuality' in S. Ardener 1978, pp. 66–88; 1993 ed., pp. 51–72.

—— 'The Oppositions and Complementarity of Religious Life', paper presented to the Modern Greek Studies Association Symposium, University of Philadelphia, USA Nov. 1980.

—— (1983) 'Under One Roof: Marriage, Dowry and Family Relations in Piraeus' in *Urban Life in Mediterranean Europe.* M. Kenny and D. Kertzer (eds.), pp. 299–323. Urbana, Chicago, London, University of Illinois Press.

—— (1989) *Heirs of the Greek Catastrophe. The Social Life of Asia Minor Refugees in Piraeus,* Oxford, Clarendon Press.

Hirschon, R. and S. Thakurdesai (1970) 'Society, Culture and Spatial Organization: an Athens Example', *Ekistics,* Vol. 30, No. 178, pp. 187–96.

Hirson, B. (1979) *Year of Fire, Year of Ash,* London, Zed Press.

Hocart, A. M. (1969) 'The Divinity of the Guest, *The Living-Giving Myth* (2nd imp.) London, Tavistock & Methuen.

Hoch-Smith, J. (1978) 'Radical Yoruba Female Sexuality: the Witch and the Prostitute' in J. Hoch-Smith and A. Spring (eds.),*Women in Ritual and Symbolic Roles,* New York and London, Plenum Press.

226 | Bibliography

Hollister, J. N. (1953) *The Shi'a of India*, London, Luzac.
Hughes, T. P. (1885) *A Dictionary of Islam*, London, W. E. Allen.
Humphrey, C. (1974) 'Inside a Mongolian Tent', *New Society*, October.
Husain, S. A. (1976) *Marriage Customs Among Muslims in India,* New Delhi, Sterling Publishers.
Idowu, E. B. (1962) *Olodumare, God in Yoruba Belief*, London, Longmans.
Isbell, B. J. (1973) 'Andean Structures and Activities: Towards a Study of Traditional Concepts in a Central Highland Peasant Community', PhD Thesis, University of Illinois.
—— (1976) 'La Otra Mitad Esencial: Un Estudio de Complementariedad Sexual Andina', *Estudios Andinos*, Vol. 5, pp. 37–56.
James, W. (1978) 'Matrifocus on African Women' in S. Ardener 1978, pp. 140–62; 1993 ed., pp. 123–45.
Jimenez de Espada, M. (1965) 1881–97 *Relaciones geograficas de Indias - Peru*, Vol. 2 (Bibli de autores españoles, 3 vols.), U. Martinez Carreras (ed.), Madrid, Ediciones Atlas.
Johnson, S. (1921) *The History of the Yorubas from the Earliest Times to the Beginning of the British Protectorate*, London, Routledge.
Just, F. P. R. (1976) 'Ideas About Women in Classical Athens', B. Litt. Thesis, Oxford.
Kamau, L. J. (1976) 'Conceptual Patterns in Yoruba Culture' in A. Rapaport (ed.).
Karanja-Diejomaoh, W. (1979) 'Lagos Market Women'. Paper presented to the Oxford Women's Social Anthropology Seminar. Oxford, Michaelmas.
Khomeini, R. (1979) *Principes politiques, philosophiques, sociaux at religieux*, trans. J. M. Xavière, Paris, Editions Libres Mallier.
—— (undated). *Resale touzih al-masael.* Qom, Hozeii elmiye-Qom.
Kirkpatrick, J. J. (1976) *The New Presidential Elite*, New York, Russell Sage Foundation, The Twentieth Century Fund.
Knepler, H. (1968) *The Gilded Stage, The Lives and Careers of Rachel, Histori, Bernhardt and Duse*, London, Constable.
Krapf-Askari, E. (1969) *Yoruba Towns and Cities. An Enquiry into the Nature of Urban Social Phenomena*, Oxford, Clarendon Press.
Kristeva, J. (1977) *About Chinese Women*, London, Marian Boyers; paperback 1978; originally published in France in *Des Chinoises*, 1976.
Lacan, J. (1977) *Ecrits*, London, Tavistock, first published in Paris 1966.
Lane Fox, R. (1975) *Alexander the Great*, London, Futura Publications.
Leach, E. (1961) 'Two Essays Concerning the Representation of Time', in *Rethinking Anthropology*, London, Athlone Press.
Lefanu, S. (1988) *In the Chinks of the World Machine: Feminism and Science Fiction*, London, The Women's Press.
Le Guin, U. (1969) *The Left Hand of Darkness*, USA, Walker.
Leis, N. B. (1976) 'West African Women and the Colonial Experience', *The Western Canadian Journal of Anthropology*, Vol. VI, No. 3, pp. 123–32.
Lévi-Strauss, C. (1961) *World on the Wane*. London, Hutchinson. First published in France as *Triste Tropique*.
—— (1968) *Structural Anthropology*, London edition, Penguin.
Levy, P. (1969) *G. E. Moore and the Cambridge Apostles*, London, Weidenfeld & Nicholson.
Levy, R. (1931) *Sociology of Islam*, Vols I, II, London, William and Norgate.
Lloyd, P. C. (1965) 'The Yoruba in Nigeria' in J. L. Gibbs, Jr. (ed.), *Peoples of Africa*, New York, Rinehart and Winston.
—— (1966) 'Agnatic and Cognatic Descent among the Yoruba', *Man* , N. S. Vol. I, No. 4, pp. 484–500.
—— (1968) 'Divorce among the Yoruba', *American Anthropologist*, 70, pp. 67–81.
—— (1974) *Power and Independence: Urban Africans' Perception of Social Inequality*, London and Boston, Routledge & Kegan Paul.
Loizos, P. (1975) 'Changes in Property Transfer among Greek Cypriot Villagers', *Man* N. S. Vol. 10, No. 4, pp. 503–23.

Lukes, S. (1973) *Individualism*, Oxford, Blackwell.

Mabogunje, A. (1958) 'The Yoruba Home', *Odu. Journal of Yoruba and Related Studies*, 5, pp. 28–35.

—— (1959) 'Yoruba Market Women', *Ibadan*, 9.

—— (1962) *Yoruba Towns*, Ibadan, University Press.

Maher, V. (1992) *The Anthropology of Breastfeeding*, Oxford, Berg.

Mann, J. (1962) *Woman in Parliament*, London, Odham Press.

Marais, J. S. (1939) *The Cape Coloured People 1652–1937*, London, Longmans, Green and Co.

Matthews, J. A. 'Environment Change and Community Identity', paper delivered at Conference on Threatened Identities, under the auspices of the British Psychological Society, Oxford, April 1980. Forthcoming in a volume to be edited by Glynnis Breakwell for John Wiley.

Mauss, M. (1979) 'A Category of the Human Mind: The Notion of Person, the Notion of Self' in *Sociology and Psychology*, trans. Ben Brewster, London, Routledge and Kegan Paul.

May, E. (1971) *Parliamentary Practice*, 18th edition, ed. Sir Barnett Cocks, London, Butterworth.

Maybury-Lewis, D. *Akwe-Shavante Society*, Oxford, Clarendon Press.

McDowell, L. (1983) 'Towards an understanding of the gender division of urban space'.

Mead, M. (1976) *Males and Females*, Harmondsworth, Pelican. First published in 1950.

Meer Hassan Ali (Mrs) (1917) *Observations on the Mussulmauns of India*, England, Oxford University Press.

Mellen, J. (1974) *Women and Their Sexuality in the New Film*, London, Davis Poynter.

Middleton, R. 'Brother-Sister, Father-Daughter Marriage in Ancient Egypt', *American Sociological Review*, Vol. 27 (5 Oct. 1962).

Mitchell, J. (1971) *Woman's Estate*, Harmondsworth, Penguin.

—— (1976) *Psychoanalysis and Feminism*, Harmondsworth, Penguin.

Moghadam, V. M. (1991a) 'The Reproduction of Gender Inequality in Muslim Societies: A Case Study of Iran in the 1980s', *World Development*, Vol. 19, No. 10.

—— (1991b) Islamist Movements and Women's Responses in the Middle East, *Gender & History*, Vol. 3, Number 3.

—— (1992) Patriarchy and the Politics of Gender in Modernising Societies: Iran, Pakistan and Afghanistan, *International Sociology* Vol. 7, No. 1.

Moore, H. (1986) *Space, Text and Gender*, Cambridge University Press.

Morgan, N. (1977) 'Shadow Woman', *Spare Rib* (December).

Morton-Williams, P. (1956) 'The Atinga Cult among the Southwest Yoruba', *Bulletin de l'IFAN*, 18, pp. 315–34.

—— (1960) 'The Yoruba Ogboni Cult in Oyo', *Africa*, Vol. XXX, pp. 362–74.

—— (1964) 'An Outline of the Cosmology and Cult Organization of Oyo Yoruba', *Africa*, Vol. XXXIV, No. 3, pp. 243–60.

Murra, J. V. (1972) 'El control vertical de un maximo de pisos ecologicos en la economia de las sociedades andinas', in Ortiz de Zuniga (ed.), *Visites de la provincia de Léon de Huanuco*, Vol. 2.

Needham, R. (1969) *Structure and Sentiment*, Chicago, University of Chicago Press.

—— (ed.) (1973) *Introduction to Right and Left, Essays on Dual Symbolic Classification*, Chicago, University of Chicago Press.

—— (1979) *Symbolic Classification*, Santa Monica, California, Goodyear Publishing Company.

Nelson, C. (1973) 'Women and Power in Nomadic Societies of the Middle East' in C. Nelson (ed.), *The Desert and the Sown*. California, University of California Press.

—— (1974) 'Public and Private Politics: Women in the Middle Eastern World', *American Ethnologist*, 3, pp. 551–63.

Nichol, A. (1961) *The Development of the Theatre*, London, Harrap, 4th revised edition.

Oduyoye, M. (1972) *Yoruba Names, Their Structure and Their Meanings*, Ibadan, Daystar Press.

Ojo, G. J. (1966) *Yoruba Culture. A Geographical Analysis*, London, University of Ife and University of London Press.

Okediji, O. O. and Okediji, F. O. (1966) 'Marital Stability and Social Structure in an African City', *The Nigerian Journal of Economic and Social Studies*, Vol. VIII, No. 1 (March), pp. 151–63.

Okely, J. (1975) 'Gypsy Women: Models in Conflict' in S. Ardener 1975, pp. 55–86.

—— (1978) 'Privileged, Schooled and Finished: Boarding Education for Girls', in S. Ardener 1978, pp. 109–39; 1993 ed., pp. 93–122.

Ortner, S. (1974) 'Is Female to Male as Nature is to Culture?' in M. Rosaldo and L. Lamphere (eds.).

Paine, R. (1947) 'Ethnicity of Place and Time among Zionists'. Paper given to History and Ethnicity Conference of the ASA, Spring 1947.

Papanek, H. (1973) 'Purdah: Separate Worlds and Symbolic Shelter', *Comparative Stud. Soc. Hist.*, 15, pp. 289–325.

Parker, G. (1964) *English-Quechua, Quechua-English Dictionary – Cuzco, Ayacucho, Cochabamba*, Cornell University, Ithaca, N.Y.

Parrinder, E. G. (1956) *The Story of Ketu. An Ancient Yoruba Kingdom*. Ibadan, University Press.

Parsons, T. (1951) *The Social System*, Glencoe, Illinois, The Free Press.

Peristiany, J. G. (ed.) (1965) *Honour and Shame. The Values of Mediterranean Society*, London, Weidenfeld and Nicolson.

Pitt--Rivers, J. (1954) *The People of the Sierra*, London, Weidenfeld and Nicolson.

—— (1977) *The Fate of Shechem*, Cambridge, Cambridge University Press.

Port, M. H. (1976) *The Houses of Parliament*, New Haven and London, Yale University Press.

Pratt, F. (1979) *Privacy in Britain*, London, Associated University Presses.

Prideaux, T. (1976) *Love or Nothing, The Life and Times of Ellen Terry*, London, Millington.

Prince, R. (1961) 'The Yoruba Image of the Witch', *Journal of Mental Science*, 107, pp. 795–805.

Querry, A. (1871, 1872) *Droit Musulman*, Vol. I, II. Paris, L'Imprimerie Nationale.

Raglan, Lord. (1964) *The Temple and the House*. London, Routledge and Kegan Paul.

Rainwater, P. L. (1966) 'Crucible of Identity: the Negro Lower Class' in *Daedalus*, Vol. 95, No. 1.

—— (1971) *Behind Ghetto Walls*, Chicago, Aldine Publishing Co. 1970; London, Allen Lane, Penguin Press, 1971.

Rapoport, A. (1969) *House Form and Culture*, Englewood Cliffs, N. J., Prentice-Hall.

—— (ed.) (1976) *The Mutual Interaction of People and their Built Environment*, The Hague, Mouton.

Raverat, G. (1962) *Period Piece*, London, Faber and Faber.

Reiter, R. R. (ed.). (1975) *Toward an Anthropology of Women*. New York and London, Monthly Review Press.

Richardson, J. (1957) *Rachel*. New York, Putnam.

Ridd, R. E. (1980a) 'What's in a name?' *New Society*, Vol. 53, No. 920 (3 July).

—— (1980b) 'The Game Must Go On', *Spectator*, Vol. 245, No. 7931 (12 July).

—— (1980c) 'The Children and the Tortoise', *Spectator*, Vol. 245, No. 7935 (9 August).

Rivière, P. G. (1974) 'The Couvade: A Problem Reborn', *Man*, N. S. 9, pp. 423–35.

Robertson, C. (1976) 'Ga Women and Socioeconomic Change in Accra, Ghana' in N. Hafkin and E. Bay (eds.), *Women in Africa*, California, Stanford University Press.

Rosaldo, M. A. and Lamphere, L. (eds.) (1974) *Woman, Culture and Society*, Stanford, Stanford University Press.

Rosen, M. (1975) *Popcorn Venus: Women in the Movies and the American Dream*, London, Peter Owen.

Rosten, N. (1974) *Marilyn*, London, Millington.

Russ, Joanna (1971) 'The Image of Women in Science Fiction', *Red Clay Reader* (USA).

Sacks, K. (1975) 'Engels Revisited: Women, the Organization of Production and Private

Property' in R. R. Reiter (ed.), *Toward an Anthropology of Women*. New York and London, Monthly Review Press.

Safa, H. I. (1971) 'The Matrifocal Family in the Black Ghetto: Sign of Pathology or Pattern of Survival?' in C. O. Crawford *Health and the Family. New York and London, Monthly Review Press*.

Safilios-Rothschild, C. (1969) 'Socio-psychological Factors Influencing Fertility', *Journal of Marriage and the Family*, Vol. 31, pp. 595–606.

Sargent, P. (1978) *Women of Wonder*, Harmondsworth, Penguin. First published in America, 1974.

Saussure, F. de (1916) *Cours de linguistigne générale*; English trans., reprinted London, Owen, 1964.

Scanzoni, L. and J. H. Scanzoni (1976) *Men, Women and Change*, New York, McGraw.

Schildkrout, E. (1978) 'Age and Gender in Hausa Society: Socio-Economic Roles of Children in Urban Kano' in *Sex and Age as Principles of Social Differentiation* (ed. J. LaFontaine). London, Tavistock.

Schulz, D. A. (1969) *Coming up Black*, New Jersey, Prentice-Hall Inc.

Sciama, L. (1984) 'Ambivalence and Dedication: Academic Wives in Cambridge University, 1870–1970' in Callan, H. and S. Ardener, London, Croom Helm.

Scotellaro, R. (1972) *L'Uva Puttanella. Contadini del Sud*, Bari, Laterra.

Simmel, A. (1968) 'Privacy' in D. L. Sills (ed.), *International Encyclopaedia of the Social Sciences*, Cromwell Collier and Macmillan.

Sitwell, O. (1949) *Laughter in the Next Room*, London, Macmillan.

Skar, H. (1979) 'Duality and Land Reform Among the Quechua Indians of Highland Peru'. D. Phil Thesis, University of Oxford.

Skar, S. (1978) 'Men and Women in Matapuquio', *Journal of the Anthropological Society of Oxford*, Vol. 9, No. 1, pp. 53–60.

―――― (1980) Mag. Art. thesis, Institute of Social Anthropology, Oslo University.

Smock, A. (1977) 'Bangladesh: A Struggle with Tradition and Poverty' in A. Smock (ed.), *Women, Roles and Status in Eight Countries*. New York, Wiley.

Soto R. (1976) *Diccionario Quechua: Ayacucho-Chanca*. Lima, Instituto de Estudios Peruanos.

Spender, D. (1980) *Man Made Language*, London, Routledge and Kegan Paul.

Stahl, A. and P. Stahl (1976) 'Peasant House-building and its Relation to Church building: the Rumanian Case', in A. Rapoport (ed.).

Steiner, F. (1967) *Taboo*, Harmondsworth, Pelican Books.

Strathern, M. (1988) *The Gender of the Gift*, Berkeley, University of California Press.

Sudarkasa, N. (1973) *Where Women Work: A Study of Yoruba Women in the Market-place and in the Home*, Ann Arbor, The University of Michigan.

Sykes, C. H. (1972) *Nancy: The Life of Lady Astor*, London, Collins.

Tapper, N. (1968) 'The Role of Women in Selected Pastoral Islamic Societies', unpublished MPhil Thesis, SOAS, University of London.

―――― (1979) 'Mysteries of the Harem? An Anthropological Perspective on Recent Studies of Women of the Muslim Middle East', *Women's Studies International Quarterly*, 2, pp. 481–7.

Thakurdesai, S. (1974) '"Sense of Place" in Greek Anonymous Architecture' in *The Inner City*, D. and M. Kennedy (eds.), Architects' Yearbook 14. London, Paul Elek.

Tiger, L. (1969) *Men in Groups*, New York, Random House.

Tremayne, S. (1980) 'Haji Baba's Children in Limbo', paper delivered to the Women's Social Anthropology Seminar, Oxford.

Tynan, K. (1979) *Observer Magazine*, p. 46, 11 November.

Ullman, L. (1977) *Changing*, London, Weidenfeld & Nicholson.

Vallance, E. M. (1978) 'Women Members of Parliament: Background Roles and Prospects', PhD Thesis, London. See below, 1979, for published version.

―――― (1979) *Women in the House, A Study of Women Members of Parliament*, London, Athlone Press.

Vallée, L. (1972) 'Cycle ecologique et cycle ritual: le cas d'un village andin', *Canadian*

*Review of Sociology and Anthropology*, Vol. 9, No. 3, pp. 238–54.

Vico, G. B. (1968) *The New Science*, 1725; trans. T. G. Bergin and M. H. Fish, New York, Cornell University Press.

Watson-Franke, M. (1982) 'Seclusion Huts and Social Balance in Guajiro Society', *Anthropos 77*.

Watson, G. (1970) *Passing for White*, London, Tavistock.

Westermarck, E. (1921) *The History of Human Marriage*, Vol. III. London, Macmillan.

Williams, D. (1975) 'The Brides of Christ', in S. Ardener (ed.), 1975.

Wright, S. (1978) 'Prattle and Politics: the Position of Women in Doshman Ziāri', *Journal of the Anthropological Society of Oxford*, Vol. IX, No. 2, pp. 98–112.

——(1985) 'Identities and Influence: Political Organization in Doshman Ziāri, Iran', unpublished PhD Thesis, Oxford.

*Younger Report, Hansard*, London, HMSO, 1972/73.

# Index

## Name Index

## Subject Index

## Books about Women by members of the Centre for Cross-Cultural Research on Women

Queen Elizabeth House, University of Oxford

*Narrowing the Gender Gap*
G. Somjee

*Gender, Culture and Empire*
H. Callaway

*Images of Women in Peace and War*
Edited by Sharon Macdonald, P. Holden and Shirley Ardener

*Anthropology and Nursing*
Edited by P. Holden and J. Littlewood

*Roles and Rituals for Hindu Women*
Edited by J. Leslie

*Rules and Remedies in Classical Indian Law*
J. Leslie

*Visibility and Power*
Edited by L. Dube, E. Leacock and S. Ardener

*Wise Daughters from Foreign Lands*
E. Croll

*Arab Women in the Field*
Edited by S. Altorki and C. Fawzi El-Solh

*Growing Up in a Divided Society*
Edited by S. Burman and P. Reynolds

*The Perfect Wife*
J. Leslie

*Women's Religious Experience*
Edited by P. Holden

*Food Insecurity and the Social Division of Labour in Tanzania*
D. Bryceson

*Caught up in Conflict*
Edited by R. Ridd and H. Callaway